THE HORROR PEOPLE

By the same author
Movie Magic: The Story of Special Effects in the Cinema

THE HORROR PEOPLE

John Brosnan

ST MARTIN'S PRESS-NEW YORK

Contents

Acknowledgments   vi

Introduction   1

1   The Chaneys   9

2   Lugosi and Karloff   27

3   The Men Behind the Early Monsters: Karl Freund, Tod
    Browning and James Whale   59

4   Lewton and Company   73

5   Jack Arnold   87

6   Hammer   100

7   American International Productions
    and Roger Corman   125

8   William Castle   137

9   Vincent Price   147

10 Christopher Lee   159

11 Peter Cushing   181

12 Writing Horror: Richard Matheson
    and Robert Bloch   195

13 Directing Horror: Freddie Francis
    and Roy Baker   212

14 Producing Horror: Milton Subotsky
    and Kevin Francis   233

15 The Horror Fans   253

Epilogue   261

Appendix: More Horror People   265

References   290

Index   292

Acknowledgments

I would like to thank the following people for giving so freely of their time: Forrest J. Ackerman, Robert Bloch, William Castle, Michael Carreras, Jack Arnold, Freddie Francis, Kevin Francis, Terence Fisher, Milton Subotsky, Christopher Lee, DeWitt Bodeen, Richard Matheson, Peter Cushing, Roy Ward Baker – and a special thanks to Peter Saunders. In addition, I would once again like to thank the staff of the British Film Institute's reference library for their invaluable help.

Introduction

The horror film business is a strange cinematic phenomenon. By many in the film industry it is regarded as a sort of Sargasso Sea where the wrecks of second-rate actors and directors collect when they are no longer able to keep afloat in the more turbulent waters of the mainstream cinema, and many critics continue to dismiss horror films as mere fodder for the mentally under-developed. But in recent years a new generation of critics and film historians has come into being, and their assessment has moved to the opposite extreme – accompanied by a great deal of intellectual pretentiousness. Horror films have come to be regarded by this critical 'new wave' as important works that more accurately reflect the obsessions and tensions of society than their more serious, and respectable, counterparts. In some cases such claims are justifiable, but too often it becomes ludicrous when all manner of complicated symbolism

Boris Karloff, Peter Lorre and Vincent Price together on the set of **The Raven**

is read into a film that has obviously been designed as pure exploitation.

Nevertheless, I do support the new and rather audacious theory that the Hammer films of the 1950s, with their vitality, their colour and their sensuality, served to help revolutionize the then staid and frigid British cinema. An American parallel is the theory that the artistic liberation of the current Hollywood product grew not from the influence of the underground/*avant-garde* film-makers but from the cheapest roots of the commercial cinema itself – American International Pictures, who, in the 1950s and 1960s, adapted their films, often horror ones, to the changing tastes of the teenagers while adult America dozed in front of its collective television set.

Horror films have also gained a certain amount of respect within the industry simply because, since the mid-1950s, they have consistently made money. In Chapter 6, I quote Michael Carreras of Hammer Films, who points out that it wasn't until 1968, when the company received the Queen's Award for Industry, that many of his fellow British film-makers began to take Hammer seriously. Before the 1950s the popularity of horror films moved in cycles – the first major one occurring in the first half of the 1930s following the release of *Dracula* and *Frankenstein* (I am mainly concerned, in this book, with the people connected with the 'Hollywood' horror film and the later British product that grew from it), and it was during this period that a number of films were produced that are now regarded as horror classics, such as *Dr Jekyll and Mr Hyde*, *The Island of Lost Souls, Freaks, The Hands of Orlac, The Mummy*, and *The Bride of Frankenstein*. It was also during the 1930s that these films came to be considered as part of a separate *genre* – and thus the 'horror film' as such was born. (There *were* American horror films prior to 1930, of course, such as the work of Tod Browning and Lon Chaney, but at that time the category didn't exist. Their films can also be better described as *cinema of the grotesque* rather than Gothic horror – it took the influx of European talent, particularly German, to create the Hollywood horror film as we know it.)

By the mid-1930s the first horror cycle was practically finished, and though a few notable horror films, such as *Dracula's Daughter* and *The Son of Frankenstein*, were made during the second half of the decade (after the successful re-release of *Frankenstein* and *Dracula* together) it wasn't until the early 1940s that another real horror boom began. As before it was Universal Studios who led the way, but their horror films were no longer major productions – instead they had been relegated to the 'B' picture class. It was the period of Lon Chaney Jnr's second-rate reign as King of Horror in such films as *The Wolfman* (in which he did rather well), *Son of Dracula* and *The Ghost of Frankenstein*. Once again the cycle came to an end by the middle of the decade.

The next cycle occurred at the beginning of the 1950s, but the Gothic settings and supernatural forces had been replaced by pseudo-science and atomic radiation – it was officially called a science fiction film boom, but the monsters in *The Thing from Another World* and *The Creature from the Black Lagoon* had more in common with Dracula and the Wolf Man than with science fiction. The traditional horror film, however, seemed to have vanished from the screen (with the exception of the occasional film like *House of Wax*) but then, in the mid-1950s, it made an unexpected come-back, partly because of the popularity of the old horror classics when shown on television and also because of the timely decision by Hammer Films in Britain to remake *Frankenstein* in colour. At the same time American International Pictures also began their long line of horror films with such epics as *I Was a Teenage Frankenstein* and *Bucket of Blood* which later culminated in the more impressive Roger Corman/Poe series of the early 1960s. Since the 1950s the demand for horror films has remained undiminished and they are looked upon as a surefire way of making a profit – their big advantage being that they can be made for a relatively small sum of money, even today.

Another interesting aspect of horror films is that they seem to grow in stature as the years go by. Of the countless number of films made since the beginning of the film industry it's often the horror ones that manage to keep their heads above the waters of oblivion. Mention the early German cinema to anyone, for instance, and among the titles that readily spring to mind are usually *The Cabinet of Dr Caligari*, *Nosferatu*, *The Student of Prague*, *The Hands of Orlac* and *The Golem*. Commenting on this tendency, Robert Bloch, who has many horror screenplays to his credit, said: 'In 1933 when *King Kong* was released the Academy Awards went to a picture called *Cavalcade*, which was a classic film of its time. It had been a classic play, Noel Coward had done an excellent job on it, and the Titanic sequence was a very moving one, but who goes to see *Cavalcade* today? How many people would even recognize the name if they weren't students of the theatre? And how many film buffs have even seen it or care about it? But *King Kong*, which was just regarded as fun and games – though it did receive excellent reviews – is more alive today than it was forty years ago, and little kids in the street can tell you about Kong. They can also tell you about Dracula and Frankenstein, for the same reason.' One wonders which will be regarded in forty years' time as *the* film of 1974 – *The Sting*, which reaped so many Academy Awards, or *The Exorcist*?

In this book I use the term 'horror film' in its broadest sense – and if there is one thing that the people featured in the following pages all agree upon, it is their dislike of the word *horror* to describe their films. Personal definitions of horror films vary greatly – some feel that a true horror film must include a supernatural element or have a Gothic setting. William Friedkin, for instance, doesn't consider *The Exorcist* to be a horror film, while *I* couldn't describe it as anything else. To me a horror film is one that is basically involved with the bizarre; and so I include non-supernatural films such as *Freaks*, *Psycho* and so on, as well as the traditional ones like *Dracula*. I don't believe a film actually has to *horrify* to be called a horror film. For example, I have never found *Frankenstein* or *The Bride of Frankenstein* to be horrifying – I regard them instead as films of great beauty, as do many others, but for the sake of convenience one might as well continue to classify them as horror films rather than to try and invent some new term.

Valerie Hobson is menaced by Karloff as the Monster in The Bride of Frankenstein

The longevity of horror films also applies to their makers and their stars. Lon Chaney, Bela Lugosi and Boris Karloff are still remembered today while many of their contemporaries have drifted into obscurity. Yet horror actors rarely enjoy being typecast in such roles, quite understandably. No creative actor likes to be typecast in any role; and to be typecast as a horror actor is to experience the handicap in its most limiting and frustrating form, for satisfying horror roles are few and far between. There have been a few actors who have made a name for themselves in the horror field, then used it as a springboard to better things – actors such as Oliver Reed, Jack Nicholson and, it now appears, Christopher

Lee. The unfortunate ones are those such as Bela Lugosi, Lionel Atwill, Ray Milland, Peter Cushing and Vincent Price, who found themselves reduced to horror roles after more varied and impressive careers. Lugosi was an actor who at first tried to resist the horror tag, though he soon succumbed, whereas others like Cushing and Price have accepted it philosophically and exploited it for their own ends. Directors, even producers, can also be typecast and, like the actors, they have the choice of accepting and making the most of the situation or trying to break out. But the special ambience of the horror film has, in many cases, provided the opportunity for certain directors to display aspects of their talents that haven't been evident in their more conventional films. James Whale, always a stylish and impressive director no matter what his subject-matter, definitely produced his best work within the horror genre – though he himself probably wouldn't have agreed with that. The same applies to directors like Terence Fisher, Roger Corman, Val Guest and several others. Of course the sensationalist nature of many horror films is a major factor in their success, and even a mediocre director can't fail to attract attention when he's provided with the right ingredients. Tod Browning's *Dracula*, for instance, isn't a very good film, even in the context of its time, yet it's regarded as a classic – mainly because it was the first of its kind (and also because of Lugosi's performance). Hammer's *Curse of Frankenstein* is another example – a mediocre film, yet a break-through of a kind that would have caused a stir no matter who directed it. But it is still justifiable to claim that the making of a horror film can have a liberating effect on the creativity of its production team. Would Val Lewton be remembered today, one wonders, if he had, as he so dearly wished, managed to avoid becoming involved with horror films and had instead become a producer of 'prestige' films?

This book, as the title implies, is mainly concerned with the *people* who have been – or are – involved with horror films. It is not another survey of the horror field itself – that ground has already been ex-haustively covered – but, of course, many horror films are discussed in relation to the actor, director, writer or producer concerned. The first section of the book deals with the careers of those actors whose names have become synonymous with the early horror films and of those directors who were most influential in the creation of the *genre*. The first three chapters, covering the careers of the Chaneys, Bela Lugosi, Boris Karloff, Tod Browning, Karl Freund and James Whale, also span the development of the horror film from the 1920s to the 1940s. Chapter 4 is concerned with Val Lewton and his talented unit who, for a period during the 1940s, took the horror film in an entirely new direction by introducing such qualities as subtlety and intelligence – assets that were soon discarded by other horror film-makers. The next section of the book deals with four divergent developments in the horror film that took place in the 1950s and the people mainly responsible for them – Jack Arnold, whose films personify the science fiction/monster boom of the period; James and Michael Carreras of Hammer Films who, with directors and producers like Terence Fisher and Anthony Hinds, began their own horror boom in 1956; Samuel Z. Arkoff and James H. Nicholson who formed American International Pictures and financed Roger Corman in most of his productions; and William Castle, the flamboyant director/producer who made his horror films succeed by the use of audacious gimmicks rather than good scripts (though he later went on to make the classic *Rosemary's Baby*).

The book then deals with the careers of the three current reigning Kings of Horror – Vincent Price, Christopher Lee (who is attempting to

The Creature from the Black Lagoon, looking rather self-satisfied, carries off his unwilling victim (Julie Adams)

abdicate) and Peter Cushing (an interesting piece of trivia is the fact that all three were born on 27 May, though in different years). Chapters 12, 13 and 14 feature interviews with a cross-section of the people behind the scenes in horror films today – writers Robert Bloch and Richard Matheson talk about the problems involved in writing horror screenplays; Roy Ward Baker and Freddie Francis, both directors who have had varied careers in the film industry before they suddenly discovered that they had become typed as 'horror directors', discuss the effect this has had on them; and then two members of that much-maligned species – producers – are given the opportunity to talk about their profession – Milton Subotsky of Amicus Films and Kevin Francis of the newly-formed Tyburn Film Company discuss their careers and explain why they have chosen to make horror films. The book concludes with a brief look at the most enthusiastic supporters of horror films – the horror fans.

The format I have chosen for this book has meant the unavoidable omission of certain actors, actresses and directors (and their films) who have been involved, in varying degrees, with the horror film in America and Britain. There is also the possibility that some people may query my choice of those directors featured in the first half of the volume whom I consider to be the most important influences on the *genre*. With these points in mind I have included a comprehensive Appendix which contains information about the careers of many of the other people who have been, or still are, associated with the field.

The lives of many of the horror people have a bizarre streak running through them, but this has usually been imposed by the medium in which they work rather than having grown out of any innate quality of their own personalities, though in the case of people like Lon Chaney Snr and Roman Polanski there is room for speculation. But the very making of a horror film is a bizarre act in itself, and it's sometimes difficult for the people who work in the field, no matter how hard they may try, to remain totally unaffected.

1 The Chaneys

The story of Lon Chaney, the first real horror star, has all the elements of a classic tragedy; a humble beginning as the son of deaf mutes, years of hard struggle followed by fame and success, and then, at the peak of it all – illness and death. To many people Chaney was as bizarre a figure as any of the grotesque characters he portrayed on the screen. Studio publicity was partly to blame but he was, and remains to this day, something of a mystery man.

He was born on April Fool's Day, 1886, in Colorado Springs, the second of four children. According to the publicity stories he refused, out of sympathy with his deaf and dumb parents, to utter a word until he was eight years old – which sounds unlikely. But he *was* taken out of school, when he was in the fourth grade, to care for his mother who had become bedridden with inflammatory rheumatism. In his efforts to communicate with her more effectively during this period he became skilled in the use of pantomime, a talent which was to prove useful in later years. By the time Chaney had reached his teens his elder brother, John, had formed a small travelling theatre company. Chaney wanted to join him – he had already received a taste of theatre life while working briefly as a stage hand and scene painter – but his father disapproved and sent him away to learn a safe trade: carpet laying and paper hanging. Chaney endured it for a short time but when he turned seventeen he abandoned his apprenticeship and joined his brother's company.

When his brother's show folded he continued on the road with the Columbia Musical Comedy Repertory Company. He was nineteen years old when the next major event in his life occurred – his marriage to a young singer called Cleva Creighton whom he met in Oklahoma City. This was in 1905 and in the following year a son was born. He was christened Creighton but he was later to become known as Lon Chaney Jnr. According to his own account he almost died at birth. He often told the story of how his father was forced to plunge him into the icy waters of the lake outside the cabin in which he was born in an attempt to shock him into breathing; and he was then kept in a primitive incubator that his father had made himself.

The Chaneys then went to Chicago where an actor friend, Lee Moran,

Chaney in his bizarre make-up for the role of Erik in The Phantom of the Opera

found Chaney a job in a show called 'The Red Kimono'. Even so, times were hard for them. Chaney Jnr later recalled a Christmas Eve in Chicago when they were running out of money. 'Dad put most of it in the gas meter. Then he started out with me. When he came to the first saloon he sat me on the bar close to the free lunch. Then he did his dance and picked up the small change. Meanwhile I filled my overcoat pockets with pretzels and sandwiches.'[1]

From Chicago the Chaneys moved to Los Angeles, fulfilling their long-held ambition to live on the West Coast. John Chaney was already there and had become stage manager of a Los Angeles theatre. Through his brother, Lon got a job as a song-and-dance comedian and then later joined a couple of German comedians, playing a season with them in San Francisco. His marriage had been steadily deteriorating for some time and in San Francisco the situation became intolerable. There Cleva enjoyed great success as a singer and was much in demand, completely eclipsing her husband's minor fame. Apparently Chaney's masculine pride was hurt by this and they quarrelled frequently. She began to drink too much and he accused her not only of neglecting their son but also of being unfaithful to him. Events reached a climax on the night when she attempted suicide by swallowing poison in the theatre where Chaney was performing. She survived, but the poison ruined her vocal cords and finished her career as a singer. She was then committed as an alcoholic and Chaney gained custody of the boy. Demonstrating the hard, ruthless streak he possessed, Chaney refused to let his wife see her son again and ignored her letters. He finally divorced her in 1914. In the meantime he had fallen in love with a chorus girl named Hazel who worked at San Francisco's Princess Theatre. It is one of the many ironies that permeate the story of the Chaneys that she was married to a legless man who ran the theatre's cigar counter. She divorced him and later married Chaney, a man who was to specialize in portraying cripples.

Out of a job in 1912, Chaney went to Universal Studios where he was once again helped by his friend Lee Moran who got him some film work. He appeared mostly in slapstick comedies and in 1915 became a regular member of Universal's stock company. In a television interview in 1969 Chaney Jnr described his father's working life in those early days: 'He used to sit in the bullpen at Universal, which was a room about the size of this TV studio. He'd sit there and an assistant director would come out and say, "Anybody here that can play a college boy?" Dad would say, "Yeah, I can play a college boy." Then he'd come back and they'd come out and say, "Anybody here who can play a Chinaman?" Well this went on a few times and there wasn't anybody who could. So my Dad, being a natural artist from the word go, got his make-up kit and his own stuff together and took it to Universal. And when they asked, "Anybody play

Chaney prepares his make-up for Blind Bargain

a Chinaman?" he'd say, "Yeah, I can play a Chinaman." He'd make himself up as a Chinaman, go and work for ten minutes, come back, then go out and play a Greek. And this way make three or four pictures a day.'[2]

For six months he took a break from acting to direct an actor called J. Warren Kerrigan in a series of films. He was a competent director apparently, but he decided that he enjoyed acting most of all and returned to it, concentrating on his make-up techniques. He had already formed the opinion that his best chance of success lay in character acting, lacking, as he did, the good looks necessary for a leading man.

In 1918 he was still earning only $5 a day at Universal. So he sought out the studio manager, William Sistrom, and asked for more money – $125 a week and a five-year contract. It was a reasonable request as Chaney had become a relatively valuable member of the studio's stock company, but Sistrom turned him down. According to Chaney, Sistrom told him that he knew a good actor when he saw one but that looking directly at Chaney he saw only a wash-out. So Chaney walked off the lot. He was thirty-two years old at that stage. He had saved money during the years he had been working at Universal so he wasn't worried at first when he began looking for another job, but he soon discovered that outside of Universal he was unknown. As the weeks of job-hunting became months he was beginning to think Sistrom wasn't such an idiot, but before things really became desperate he was saved by the Western star William S. Hart. Hart had seen Chaney in some of his earlier Universal films, and offered him a part as a villain in one of his Westerns called *Riddle Gwane*. Chaney enjoyed working with Hart who, unlike many other stars of the period, expected his co-actors to *act* instead of holding back and letting him reap all the glory. After that, things improved for Chaney. More parts followed and he even started working for Universal again. Then came the assignment that changed his whole career, and it is to Chaney's credit that he was fully aware of its potential. Director George Leone Tucker had asked him to play in a film called *The Miracle Man* (1919). Tucker described to Chaney the various roles in the film, including that of the cripple who played such an important part in the story. Chaney immediately decided that his whole future rested on getting it.

'Tucker didn't really want me for the role of the cripple in *The Miracle Man*,' said Chaney in an interview with Ruth Waterbury for *Photo* Magazine in 1928. 'He wanted a professional contortionist but the five he had tried out couldn't act it. Tucker explained to me that the first scene he would shoot would be the one where the fake cripple unwound himself in front of his pals. If I could do that I got the job. I went home to try it out. I'm not a contortionist, of course. It would have been a lot easier in my subsequent work if I had been. While I was sitting pondering over the part I unconsciously did a trick I've done since childhood. I crossed my legs, then double-crossed them, wrapping my left foot around my right ankle. When I came to the studio on the test day Tucker was already behind the camera. He gave me one glance and called "Camera!" I flopped down, dragging myself forward along the floor, my eyes rolling, my face twitching and my legs wrapped tighter and tighter around each other. Tucker didn't speak and the sweat rolled off me. Finally I heard a single whispered word from him. "God," Tucker said. I wanted to say that too, but not for the same reason.'

The Miracle Man proved a success and Chaney and Tucker became close friends. They planned many projects together (Chaney had even intended to direct one of Tucker's productions) and Tucker's sudden death was an event that greatly upset Chaney. Chaney's next film was *The Penalty* (1920) in which he was cast as a legless criminal. The director, Wallace Worsley, wanted to use trick camera angles; but Chaney designed a leather harness which bound the calves of his legs against his thighs and he walked on his knees. This was the first of the many roles for which he underwent excruciating self-torture in order to achieve a desired effect, and which resulted in his reputation as something of a masochist. For his role in *The Hunchback of Notre Dame* (Wallace Worsley, 1923) he followed Victor Hugo's description of the creature very closely – and was later

Chaney as Quasimodo in The Hunchback of Notre Dame

accused of overdoing the make-up. It entailed wearing a rubber hump, weighing 70 lbs, attached to a leather harness which connected a large breastplate and pads similar to those worn by football players in such a way that he was unable to stand erect. Over all this he wore a skin-tight, flesh-coloured rubber suit covered with animal hair. The heat inside the costume was almost unbearable and he was perpetually drenched with perspiration. To add to his discomfort his face make-up included a device that prevented him from closing his mouth. He wore this cruel rig almost every day for three months. And as an example of his obsession with detail, he sought out the actor playing the executioner in the flogging scene (a giant Mexican called Nick De Ruiz) and said to him, 'Don't be afraid to lay that whip on. If you try to pull the blows it'll look just like that on the screen.'[3]

The following review, which appeared in the 29 November 1923 issue of *Bioscope*, was typical of the reception that Chaney's performance received.

Of the acting, Lon Chaney's remarkable performance as Quasimodo, the grateful hunchback, is, as it should be, easily the outstanding feature. His extraordinary make-up as a veritable living gargoyle reaches the limit of grotesquery (and at moments seems to go a shade beyond it) but his sprawling movements and frantic gestures are brilliantly conceived, and his final dance of frenzy at the defeat of Clopin's rabble is a scene of delirious passion which has seldom been equalled on the screen.

His make-up in *The Phantom of the Opera* (Rupert Julian, 1925) was another exercise in self-torture. For the scene where the girl (Mary Philbin) creeps up behind the phantom and removes his mask – one of the great moments in horror films – Chaney inserted a device in his nose that spread the nostrils and lifted the tip to produce the appearance of a naked skull. He emphasized this effect with protruding false teeth to which were attached small prongs that drew back the corners of his lips. Celluloid discs in his mouth were used to distort his cheekbones most effectively. Ruth Waterbury gave a first hand description of Chaney's suffering after she visited the set of *The Hypnotist* (1928).

For nearly an hour it seemed impossible for a human body to suffer severer torture than that Lon Chaney subjected himself to in order to gain that effect with his eyes. [Chaney was playing a man with distended eyes] I promised him not to reveal the make-up trick yet it would make little difference to the profession if I did, for few men could have endured it. Yet in this visible suffering Lon was plainly an artist in the exquisite travail of creation. To endure pain for his work brought him a strange joy.[4]

Chaney as the fake vampire in London After Midnight

Was there something unhealthy behind his apparent need to cause himself pain while performing? It seems doubtful. After all, he wasn't obliged to suffer every time he played a character in make-up, it's just that the publicists of the time tended to emphasize that aspect of his work. And as far as he was concerned, the *real* Chaney appeared in *Tell It to the Marines* (George W. Hill, 1927) in which he played a tough sergeant – without make-up. His unusual childhood, his unhappy first marriage and other personal tragedies must have contributed to his melancholy outlook on life and his choice of roles. (For instance, during the making of *The Phantom of the Opera* his father fell ill and began to lose his sight – a terrible fate for somebody already deaf and dumb. It was a time of great strain for Chaney until his father died a few days after the picture was completed.) But it's more likely that the pain he inflicted upon himself was merely a combination of professional pride and the results of a strong puritan upbringing. Associates described him as being someone who despised all forms of weakness (demonstrated by his attitude to his first wife after her breakdown) and it's possible that deep down he considered acting a rather easy, unmanly way of earning a living unless it involved a certain amount of pain and discomfort. He certainly liked to think of himself as one of the workers rather than as a film star. Clarence A. Locan, writing in *Photoplay* after Chaney's death said:

On his days off he would be around the studios talking to the workers. He knew all their troubles and the first name of every worker in the studio. At Christmas there was a present for every worker from Lon. Every girl in the offices got a glove order, the office boys, the electricians, and the rest all had presents. It was genuine.[5]

Even director Tod Browning referred to Chaney as: 'The star who lived like a clerk.'[6]

Actually Chaney insisted that he didn't go out of his way to play grotesque characters. 'People seem to think I study scripts all the time,' he said in 1928.

I don't. I don't even try to find stories for myself like some stars. I wouldn't know where to look for them. I trust my producers to look out for my own good. All I want to know is what the character is like and what rules him. It takes me two to four weeks to work out a make-up for a new picture. That set I don't worry.[7]

There is no doubt that Chaney's more gruelling performances affected his health. The primitive contact lenses he used to simulate blindness (believed to be the white of an egg but according to Chaney Jnr his father devised, with the help of his doctor, a special lens) resulted in his having to wear glasses, and the various rigs he wore to contort his body affected his spine. He kept this a secret until after appearing in *The Unknown* (Tod Browning, 1927) in which he played an armless wonder who could throw knives with his toes. For this Chaney wore a straitjacket which bound his arms to his sides so tightly that the illusion was effective even when he appeared dressed in silk tights. He said later, 'I can't play these crippled roles any more. That trouble with my spine is worse every time I do one, and it's beginning to worry me.'[8]

Chaney restrains his hairy companion in this scene from The Unholy Three

Apart from that his last few years seemed to be happy ones. He was successful and famous – he had become a household name and a common saying of the time was 'Don't step on it . . . it may be Lon Chaney!' His marriage to his second wife, Hazel, was, by all accounts, a happy one. They lived quietly, avoiding the usual Hollywood social life, preferring a close circle of friends. His two main interests, outside of acting, were visiting his private camp high in the mountains and filming with his own 16mm movie camera. He avoided publicity as much as possible and rarely gave interviews. His dislike of journalists apparently dated back to the time of his first wife's suicide attempt which had resulted in a lot of bad publicity.

In 1928 he seemed almost complacent about his career, an unusual state of mind for any actor, particularly one who had had such a hard struggle to get to the top. Talking about directors he said : 'I don't worry over who they hand me. The chief thing for an actor to remember is that it wasn't his brains that got him to stardom. It was only his acting. He isn't paid to think about production plans and when he starts he usually sinks his whole career.'[9]

In 1929 Chaney began to have trouble with his throat. While filming *Thunder* (William Nigh), a railroad story set in the snowbound Northwest of America, a piece of artificial snow lodged in his throat and worsened the condition. Chaney went into hospital and his tonsils were removed, but his throat continued to trouble him. Nevertheless in 1930 he filmed his first talkie *The Unholy Three* (Tod Browning) which was a remake of the 1925 silent version. Chaney feared the talkies, not only because they had ended the careers of other silent stars whose voices had disappointed the public, but also because they meant the end of his speciality – pantomime. As it turned out, audiences and critics were just as impressed by Chaney's versatility with his voice as they had been with that of his body. During the film Chaney imitated the voice of an old

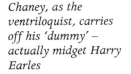

Chaney, as the ventriloquist, carries off his 'dummy' – actually midget Harry Earles

lady, a ventriloquist and his dummy, a girl, and even a parrot. To prove it he had to sign an affidavit which was reproduced in the publicity material sent out with the film. A reviewer in *Bioscope* said, in the August 1930 issue:

Lon Chaney's first talking appearance is an event in film history. It is pleasing to state that he speaks with remarkable distinction. This is as much the case when he impersonates the old woman as when he plays the virile Echo.

When the film was completed Chaney journeyed east to New York where he consulted throat specialists. They discovered that he had bronchial cancer, though they didn't tell him this. Chaney returned to his mountain cabin in California where he hoped that a long rest would improve his health but was then struck down with pneumonia. He rapidly deteriorated after that and died in hospital on 6 August 1930, as the result of a throat haemorrhage. A grim, ironic touch was added to his final hours – he lost his voice and was forced to revert to the sign language that he had used as a child to communicate with his parents. Clarence A. Locan described his death scene to the readers of *Photoplay* in the November 1930 issue:

He had had a good day at the hospital. Messages from his friends had cheered him. They played the radio. He felt so much better that he asked for a smoke. 'Of course,' the nurse answered, 'You'll have to wait to see what the doctor says about that.' He had told the nurse that, if he found he could not speak, he would raise one finger. If he feared serious trouble he would raise two. During the night the nurse saw that he had raised one finger. She leaned over him. 'Speak, speak!' she urged him. Chaney smiled and raised two fingers. Then died.

Chaney had not wanted his son to follow him into the film business. When asked about it in 1928, when Creighton was twenty-two years old, he said, 'He's six feet two inches tall. That's too tall. He would always have had to have parts built around him. He couldn't build himself for the part. Besides, he's happy in business and he's got a great wife.'[10] Chaney Jnr himself later verified this: 'Dad never wanted me to be an actor so he never made it attractive. I watched Dad work out his disguises at home, so it was pretty much a business with me.'[11] Chaney Jnr rarely saw his father at work before the cameras. 'In the early days of motion pictures it was not considered a good thing for a star even to be married, much less have a son of my age. Therefore I saw very few of his performances.'[12] Chaney Jnr had once told his father, 'I wouldn't want to go into pictures on your name. If I could use another name – and top you – I'd give it a fling, but nobody's ever going to top you.' Prophetic words which he would be forced to ignore within a few short years.

At the time of his father's death Chaney Jnr was enjoying moderate success in the plumbing trade, but the Depression soon changed all that. He went against his better judgment and tried to get film work. His first film was a 1932 comedy called *Girl Crazy* in which he played a chorus dancer. From 1932 to 1935 he appeared as an extra or a stuntman in scores of thrillers, Westerns and serials. 'I worked under five names,' said Chaney, 'I did extras under one name, stunts under another name, bits under another and leads under my own name [Creighton Chaney]. I'd get a call to do a fight, so I'd get on the set and I'd go quick to the assistant director and I'd say, "How long's the fight going to take? And how long am I going to be here?" And he'd say about twenty minutes. "And when are you going to do it?" He'd say about an hour from now. "Okay, I'll see you." I'd run to the next set and work under a different name. And between the three or four sets I'd come off smelling like a rose.'[13]

Chaney had had a stock-acting contract with RKO, but after it expired in 1935 he went through a difficult period when he found it almost impossible to get work. It was during this time that his first marriage also came to an end. He decided to do what he had told his father would never happen – he changed his name to Lon Chaney Jnr. 'I am most proud

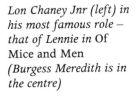

Lon Chaney Jnr (left) in his most famous role – that of Lennie in Of Mice and Men *(Burgess Meredith is in the centre)*

of the name Lon Chaney,' he said later. 'I am *not* proud of Lon Chaney Jnr, because they had to starve me to make me take this name.'[14] Even that drastic step didn't help his career at first. He married for a second time in 1937; his new wife was a former model called Patsy Beck, and by 1939 they were so broke their car and furniture had been repossessed.

Then his luck changed when he landed a role in the West Coast production of *Of Mice and Men*. He played the part of the shambling, moronic Lennie and was so impressive he was cast in the film version made the following year (directed by Lewis Milestone). RKO had planned to star him in a remake of *The Hunchback of Notre Dame* in 1939 but that fell through (Charles Laughton got the part). His next film part after *Of Mice and Men* was Hal Roach's production *One Million Years BC* (1940) in which he played the disfigured and crippled tribal patriach. Then Universal – his father's old studio – offered him a long-term contract. They had decided that the time was right for a new cycle of horror films, and who better to star in them than the son of the great Lon Chaney. With that Chaney's fate was sealed.

He was originally promised *Phantom of the Opera* by Universal but Claude Rains got that role. Chaney had to settle for *Man Made Monster* (George Waggner, 1941) which was about a circus performer who is turned into an electrical freak. It wasn't a hit with audiences but another

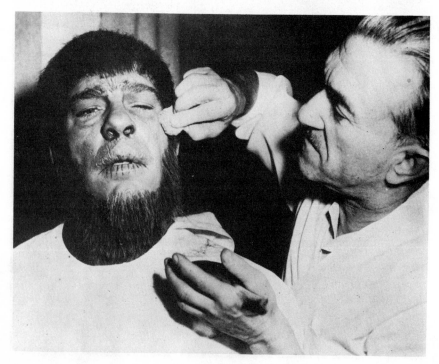

Chaney Jnr being made up by expert Jack Pierce

*The one horror
character that Chaney
Jnr considered to be
solely his own – the
Wolf Man*

film he made soon afterwards was – *The Wolf Man* (George Waggner, 1941). Apart from Lennie this was to be the role that Chaney Jnr became most associated with, and one which suited him better than the other traditional horror characters he was later to portray. 'Of course I believe that *The Wolf Man* is the best of my horror films – because he is *mine*!'[15] said Chaney in 1971. (Henry Hull had played a wolf man in the 1935 film *Werewolf of London*, directed by Stuart Walker, but Chaney's *was* the definitive version). During the making of the film Chaney had to endure discomfort similar to that suffered by his father, especially during the complicated transformation sequence from man to monster. According to Chaney it took over twenty hours to film and for a lot of the time his head was held still by means of a brace. 'They pinned my fingers down with pins, through the *skin*, so I couldn't move them,'[16] said Chaney years later, though that was probably an exaggeration.

Chaney Jnr as a somewhat overweight Dracula in Son of Dracula

Son of Dracula (Robert Siodmak) followed in 1942 with Dracula turning up in Louisiana before the turn of the last century. The film wasn't as bad as some have made it out to be, but Chaney, with his heavy build, wasn't physically suited for the role. He gave a good performance despite his handicap and the film contained a number of fine atmospheric moments – one such being when Dracula's coffin, bearing the vampire, emerged from the middle of a mist-shrouded swamp and glided silently across it to the water's edge.

In the same year he played the Frankenstein monster in *Ghost of Frankenstein* (Erle C. Kenton) and again his physique worked against him. Not having Karloff's lean, expressive face his monster was the inferior of the two, though Chaney obviously tried hard and managed to invest the role with a few of his 'Lennie' characteristics (actually Lennie and the monster have much in common — both are child-like creatures possessed of great, and often uncontrollable, strength). In *The Mummy's Ghost* (Reginald le Borg, 1944) Chaney again followed in Karloff's footsteps, but while Karloff, in *The Mummy* (Karl Freund, 1932), only appeared in his bandages briefly, Chaney was obliged to shuffle fully wrapped through the whole film.

His relations with Universal rapidly soured. Despite his relative popularity in the horror roles the studio insisted that he should perform routine parts in their most dismal productions. In between playing Dracula and the wolf man, Chaney was appearing in such films as *Crazy House, Badlands of Dakota, Cobra Woman, Weird Woman, Follow the Boys* and *Ghost Catchers* (in the last he had to dress up as a bear). His contract expired in 1946 and was not renewed. (When Chaney bought a new house overlooking the San Fernando Valley in 1957 he was quoted in a newspaper as saying: 'All my life I've wanted to look down on Universal Studios and now at last I can.')

After that Chaney battled on with various stage and film parts with other studios. He found that he had not only become typecast as a horror actor but also as the Lennie character. 'It haunts me,' he said, 'I get a call to play a dumb guy and the director tells me not to be Lennie but he's never happy until I play the part like Lennie. Then he doesn't know why he likes it.'[17] A typical example of this is his role in the 1947 Bob Hope comedy *My Favourite Brunette* (Elliot Nugent).

Things didn't improve in the early 1950s. Good roles such as that in *High Noon* (Fred Zinneman, 1952) where he played the elderly ex-marshall who rejects Gary Cooper's plea for help were rare. More typical were films like *Bride of the Gorilla* (Curt Siodmak, 1951) in which he played a native policeman, and *The Black Castle* (Nathan Juran, 1952) which had him doing his Lennie role again. In the mid-1950s he appeared in a series of television films (some of which were theatrically released) based on the novel *Last of the Mohicans* in which he played the Indian with the jaw-breaking name of Chingachgook.

In 1955 Chaney sold his father's life story to none other than Universal Studios. It should not have surprised him that there were problems, but apparently it did. He claimed later, with bitterness, that the day after he sold the story the studio put five writers on to the job rewriting it. The result was *Man of a Thousand Faces* (1956) starring James Cagney. Chaney didn't consider the film to be an accurate account of his father's life and career but he was pleased with Cagney's portrayal of Chaney Snr (handsome Roger Smith, who later starred in the *77 Sunset Strip* TV series, played Chaney Jnr in an odd piece of miscasting).

Chaney worked more frequently in the second half of the decade when a new cycle of horror films began (a whole new generation had discovered Dracula, Frankenstein and friends when the old films were shown on late-night television). A number of producers quickly jumped on the bandwagon by turning out cheap new variations of the old themes. The first of these that Chaney appeared in was *The Indestructible Man* (Jack Pollexfen, 1956). He played an executed killer brought back to life by a mad scientist to commit more murders, a story similar to that of an old Boris Karloff film *The Walking Dead* (Michael Curtiz, 1936). One bright spot was his appearance in Stanley Kramer's *The Defiant Ones* (1958) when he gave a fine performance as Old Sam, a former convict met by escapees Tony Curtis and Sydney Poitier during their run for freedom.

Television was Chaney's mainstay during the 1960s though he still made films. Most of them, apart from exceptions like Roger Corman's *The Haunted Palace* (1963), were rather terrible. A few of them, such as *House of the Black Death* (1965) and *Night of the Beast* (1966), never even got a theatrical screening. As the years went by the films grew progressively worse, and so did their titles. Two of the films he made in 1967 were *Hillbillys in a Haunted House* and *Dr Terror's Gallery of Horror* (described by *Films in Review* as the *worst* film of Chaney's career – a damning observation considering the quality of some of his previous films). In 1968 he made *Cannibal Orgy or The Maddest Story Ever Told*, and in 1969 made one of his last films *A Time to Run* (Al Adamson – released as *The Female Bunch* in 1971) in which he was cruelly billed as Lon Chaney *Jnr* – for the first time in twenty-five years.

It wouldn't be surprising to learn that Chaney, especially in his later years, held a great bitterness towards the acting profession and Hollywood in particular. But Forrest J. Ackerman, editor of a magazine devoted to horror films and their stars, who knew Chaney slightly, doesn't think he did. He was even planning to make a big come-back in a new horror film. 'He had personally written a script,' said Ackerman, 'called *Gila Man* which was somewhat like another film he was in once called *The Alligator People* (1959). He had written in roles for two of his sons.' This was a curious change of heart for someone who had said in 1957: 'My sons in show business? Heck no! They're both solid citizens in good substantial businesses.'[18] These words unwittingly echo those of his father thirty years previously.

'I don't think he was particularly bitter about the way his life had turned out,' said Ackerman, 'but the one meeting I had with him in his own home was extremely disappointing. I never reported anything of it in my magazine because frankly there wasn't much to report. At any time I attempted to talk about his own career or his father's he would become very vague and uninterested. I asked where his father was buried and he said – "Oh, over there, somewhere." He didn't even know where he was pointing. He did tell me that he had assisted his father in many of his make-ups and took pride in the fact that he could make himself up very well too. I would say, judging from the one or two stills that survive, he'd done a very original job on himself for *One Million Years BC* [1940]. But he wasn't allowed to use it for the film because by then the unions had come into Hollywood and they required a make-up man to do all the make-up rather than the actor himself. Actually I thought Chaney had done a better job on himself than the make-up man subsequently did on *One Million* but he wasn't permitted to use that talent. It was a handicap that his father never had to face.

'But frankly, he just wasted my time that afternoon. He just wanted to talk about fishing and other subjects that were not in the least bit rewarding in trying to find out anything about his career. He had started work on a book called "A Century of Chaneys", which was going to go back earlier than his father and tell something about his grandfather. He asked me to participate in some way. I was going to supply some of the stills and write the captions for them. After his death there was talk of one of his relatives continuing the project but I'm rather sceptical that it will ever come off. Chaney *Snr*'s brother, who must be quite old now, is also planning to write a biography of his brother.

'I observed a real magic moment with Chaney once when the Count Dracula Society had him as the guest of honour at their annual banquet. I was sitting opposite him and I saw he didn't eat a morsel of food at the banquet, he just sat there drinking. It worried me because I knew from experience that he was only good until afternoon and from then on he was blotto. I had been slightly involved with a minor movie he had been making a year or two earlier and he had frankly warned the director and producer about his drinking. He told them, "Get everything you can out of me before 1 p.m. because after that I can't guarantee anything." He carried a hip flask that supposedly contained iced tea but was actually liberally laced with alcohol.

'When his name was announced at the banquet I made the introductory speech about him. He then appeared on the stage and he got a standing ovation and that really turned him on. He said, "Would you like to see me do Lennie?" Everyone said yes and he did Lennie. And he really had it down pat. He stood up there and he became that powerful figure from *Of Mice and Men* and it brought tears to everybody's eyes to see how great he could be when he tried.

'Ironically, just like his father, he died of cancer of the throat. I had known about it for some time but it was a closely guarded secret and I wasn't going to put it into print even when it looked like he might die. It was his own wife who chose to reveal it to our readers and I ran the letter she sent.

'He had absolutely clung to at least half a voice. He should have had all his vocal cords removed, but they just went halfway. I was told privately that the cobalt treatments were killing him faster than the cancer. I guardedly called it to the attention of his fans that he was in serious shape, and that it might be wise to let him know right away if they cared for him. I asked them to please not pester him for pictures or ask him to tell stories of how it was in the old days and that sort of thing; but if they wanted to send get well cards or expressions of appreciation, now was the time. I was quite surprised and flattered when one day I picked up the telephone and heard a very rough, gruff voice say: "Say, young fellow, you sure been doing a great job for me. Want to thank you for all them letters I been getting. Really makes me feel good."

'I don't know whether it was just bravado or whether he didn't know he had terminal cancer but he was preparing to go 3,000 miles back east to appear live on the stage in a revival of *Arsenic and Old Lace*. I couldn't believe it when I received a phone call from someone in New York, very excited, who had heard the announcement on the radio. So I called his wife and she said yes, he's learning his lines and will be using a throat mike. And two weeks later he was dead [13 July 1973].'

2   Lugosi and Karloff

The two names most synonymous with horror films in the 1930s were those of Bela Lugosi and Boris Karloff. Lugosi achieved fame as Count Dracula in 1930; and the following year Karloff made his mark as the Frankenstein monster. But though they shared the glory and even starred together in a number of films they had very little in common. In fact they were totally different in most ways – in terms of personality, in their acting styles and especially in the way they reacted to the horror stardom that had suddenly been thrust upon them. By 1940, due to a certain amount of carelessness on his part, Lugosi's career was floundering; whereas Karloff was still relatively successful and remained so for the rest of his life. Relations between the two of them were not particularly warm. Lugosi actually resented Karloff's success, particularly since

Bela Lugosi as Ygor and Boris Karloff as the Monster in Son of Frankenstein

it started with a role that was originally to have been Lugosi's. Karloff later said of him: 'We didn't really socialize. Ours was simply a professional relationship. But I have warm recollections of him as a fine actor and a great technician.'[19]

Two things they *did* have in common were that they were both born outside America and both became famous fairly late in life. Lugosi was born in a small Hungarian town in 1882 (though he later claimed he was born in 1888). His real name was Béla Blaskó but after becoming an actor he changed it to Lugosi, after his home town of Lugos. He was attracted to the theatre at an early age and began acting professionally when in his twenty-first year. His subsequent career in the Hungarian theatre was a moderately successful one, but certainly not as spectacular as later publicity hand-outs were to claim. For instance, one studio press release said that Lugosi became known as 'the idol of the Royal National Theatre in Budapest'. Robert Bloch commented, 'Several people I know have tried to verify that. They've tried to find out to just what degree he was famous in Hungary and how much of it was a product of his press agent. It's undoubtedly true that he played some of those classic roles he later talked about, but he was not, so far as those cast and credit listings that have been unearthed show, a great matinée idol of the stage prior to World War One.' Lugosi's biographer, Arthur Lennig, who researched Lugosi's early life quite extensively, has said: 'Lugosi was never a "great" actor in Hungary, nor was he ever a "leading" one at the National Theatre, although his very presence there showed that he was among the best.'[20]

During the First World War Lugosi served in the Hungarian army as a lieutenant, but he returned to the National Theatre in 1916 after being badly wounded. In 1917 he became involved with the Hungarian film industry and made a number of films, none of which has survived. Also in that year he married for the first time. His wife was Ilona Szmik, the daughter of a Budapest banker. Those were good times for Lugosi and in later years he would look back on that period of his life with a great deal of nostalgia. When, in 1919, Béla Kun led a successful Communist revolution in Hungary, Lugosi was one of his ardent supporters – mainly because, it seems, he thought that actors would get a better deal under the new regime. But the Kun government was soon overthrown and in that same year Lugosi was obliged to flee the country. He first went to Vienna, then moved on to Germany where he appeared in several films. His wife had accompanied him to Vienna but had then returned home where, on her family's insistence, she divorced Lugosi.

Work was hard to find in Germany, so in 1921 Lugosi made his way to New York where he formed a small theatre company consisting of other out-of-work Hungarian actors. With this he toured various American cities, putting on plays for the Hungarian communities (at this point he still couldn't speak English). The venture wasn't a very successful one but it was during this period that he married for the second time – his new wife being Ilona Montagh de Nagybányhegyes. In 1922 things improved when an American producer saw one of his plays and offered him a major part in a New York production of *The Red Poppy*. Since he was unable to speak English, legend has it that Lugosi learned his part entirely by rote. But however he managed it, his performance earned him praise from the critics. One, Alan Dale, said: 'Lugosi is the greatest actor to come to America!' The following year he appeared in his first American film – *The Silent Command* (J. Gordon Edwards), and a sign of things to come in his film career he was cast as the villain (whereas in his Hungarian films he had usually played the romantic lead). The years between 1922 and 1927 were relatively successful ones for Lugosi – he made a number of films and appeared in several plays, but without having much impact on either public or critics, though the latter took note of his distinctive acting style. Then, in 1927, came the role that changed his life – Count Dracula. Lugosi got the part mainly because of his thick Hungarian accent, something that worked in his favour at times, as on this occasion, but was often to prove a handicap.

The play opened in New York in September 1927 and soon became a great success with audiences, though most of the critics were condescending about it. Lugosi went on tour with the play when it had finished its

Lugosi in his most famous role – Dracula

profitable New York run in 1928, and the following year, while touring California, he met and later married Beatrice Woodruff, his third wife. That same year he appeared in a film called *The Thirteenth Chair*, playing a strange detective who solved his crimes with the assistance of the spirit world. The director was, significantly enough, Tod Browning.

Lugosi appeared in five other Hollywood films before being offered the lead in *Dracula*, a property that Universal had considered for several years but were dubious about buying because of its unusual, and possibly controversial, nature – until the success of the play convinced them otherwise. Filming began in September 1930 and covered a period of about seven weeks, actually running over schedule by a week (later scenes were apparently shot rather hastily, which accounts for some of the film's shoddiness in the second half). It was released in New York on 14 February 1931 and was an immediate box-office success, though the critics weren't very impressed. The main fault with the film lies in the fact that it was mainly adapted from the play and not from the novel. As a result it was a very static and talkative film, apart from the early scenes set in Transylvania. Lugosi's performance attracted the praise of many of the critics, but seen today it seems too theatrical and even a little ludicrous. At that time his acting methods were heavily stylized – something he inherited from his Hungarian film days – and he spoke with very slow and precise enunciation. But one must admit that his portrayal of the vampire was certainly a distinctive one; and for many people, even since the arrival of Christopher Lee, he remains *the* Count Dracula.

After *Dracula* had been completed Lugosi appeared in four non-horror films made by other studios, but by April 1931, with the success of *Dracula* assured, Universal decided that Lugosi was going to be their replacement for the late Lon Chaney Snr and went ahead with plans to film *Frankenstein*. Originally Frenchman Robert Florey (see Appendix) was assigned to direct, and Lugosi was to play the monster. Some test reels were shot, but Carl Laemmle Jnr, son of Universal's founder, didn't like what he saw and temporarily cancelled the picture (the assignment was then given to James Whale, much to Florey's disgust). Lugosi later claimed that he had turned down the role because it lacked dialogue and would have meant wearing too much make-up. It's possible there is some truth in the story because at that time Lugosi obviously believed that his overnight fame in Hollywood had come about because of his acting ability and personal charisma – he didn't realize it was due to the bizarre nature of his Count Dracula role. He certainly did not think of himself as the successor to Lon Chaney.

The part of the Frankenstein monster went, of course, to Karloff and before long Lugosi was regretting his reluctance to don the make-up, for Karloff rapidly became the major horror star at Universal. By then Lugosi

Edward Van Sloan and Bela Lugosi in a publicity shot for Dracula

Lugosi having pet trouble in a scene from Murders in the Rue Morgue

had realized that his future lay in the horror field, whether he liked it or not. For a time Universal planned to star him in a remake of *The Hunchback of Notre Dame*, but this didn't come to anything. Instead they starred him in *The Murders in the Rue Morgue*, which was directed by Robert Florey (as a consolation prize for missing out on *Frankenstein*). Lugosi played Dr Mirakle, a mad scientist who wanted to mix the blood of his pet gorilla with that of a girl in order to prove some peculiar evolutionary theory. This strange film, with its hints of bestiality, wasn't particularly successful when it was released though Lugosi gave his usual bravura performance.

His next film was *White Zombie* (Victor Halperin, 1932), a supernatural melodrama set on the island of Haiti. Lugosi played Legendre, a totally villainous villain with the power to create zombies (he uses them to work in his sugar mill). As usual, he pulled out all the acting stops, but in this particular film, with its fairy-tale atmosphere, his unique style fitted in quite well. After that came a role in *Chandu the Magician* (Marcel Varnel and William Cameron Menzies, 1932), which was based on a popular radio serial of the time, and was a film so bad it was funny. (Lugosi was to be involved with many like that during the rest of his career.)

By this time Lugosi was grabbing whatever parts came along; he had stopped being choosy – he couldn't afford to be. After his sudden elevation to Hollywood stardom he had given full rein to his expensive tastes, and to maintain this high standard of living he needed to keep working. Also, in 1933, he married again. His fourth wife was Lillian Arch, his former secretary (this was to be the longest of Lugosi's five marriages – lasting twenty years – despite the thirty-year difference in their ages). After *Chandu*, Lugosi accepted a relatively small part in *The Island of Lost Souls* (Erle C. Kenton, 1933), one of the best horror films of the period. Not only was it a small part, he also agreed to appear under a mountain of hairy make-up that made him completely unrecognizable (he looked even hairier than Chaney Jnr's wolf man of the 1940s) – but no amount of make-up could obscure his distinctive voice, and as the leader of the Beast Men, Lugosi used it to full advantage when chanting the disturbing 'Are we not men?' litany.

The next few films that Lugosi appeared in after *Moreau* weren't horror films but they didn't advance his career in any way or help him to escape the horror star tag. *The Death Kiss* (Edward L. Marin, 1933) was a routine murder mystery; *International House* (Edward Sutherland, 1933) had Lugosi acting as a foil for W. C. Fields; *Night of Terror* (Benjamin Stoloff, 1933) was another murder mystery (in the so-bad-it's-funny class); *The Whispering Shadow* (Albert Herman and Colbert Clark, 1933) was a far-fetched serial; and *The Devil's in Love* (William Dieterle, 1933) was not, as the title suggests, an early version of *Rosemary's Baby* but a film about the Foreign Legion.

In 1934 Lugosi returned to the horror field with *The Black Cat* (Edward G. Ulmer), the first film in which he co-starred with Boris Karloff (they appeared in seven films together). 'Poor old Bela,' said Karloff many years later. 'It was a strange thing. He really was a shy, sensitive and talented man. But he made a fatal mistake. He never took the trouble to learn our language. Consequently, he was very suspicious on the set, suspicious of tricks, fearful of what he regarded as scene stealing. Later, when he realized I didn't go in for such nonsense we became friends. He had real problems with his speech and difficulty interpreting lines. I remember he once asked a director what a line of dialogue meant. He spent a great deal of time with the Hungarian colony in Los Angeles and this isolated him.'[21]

Someone else who worked with Lugosi in the 1920s was William Castle, who directed him in a revival of the Dracula play. He, too, commented on Lugosi's shyness. 'At the time I knew him, in the early thirties, he was a very delightful man. He seemed strange and moody at first – very quiet, very morose, but when you got to know him he opened up and became

*Before and after the
operation – Lugosi's
surgical handiwork in
The Raven doesn't
exactly impress Karloff*

warm and gracious. Many people thought he was a snob because he kept very much to himself, but he was actually a very shy and introverted man. He always seemed ill at ease but when you pierced that armour he surrounded himself with you found a very likeable human being.'

Actress Carol Borland, who co-starred with Lugosi in the revival of the play and also in the film *Mark of the Vampire* (Tod Browning's 1935 remake of his 1927 silent production of *London After Midnight*) had a similar impression of him. 'She toured with Lugosi in *Dracula* when she was quite young,' said Robert Bloch, 'and has many times discussed the fact that the off-screen character of the 1930s was not at all like the screen character. He was an easy-going, genial man who took a very paternal attitude towards her and was very prim and proper. In the very final sequence in *Mark of the Vampire* when he's exposed as an actor – that's the real Lugosi, just as, to a certain extent, Peter Bogdanovich captured a portion of the real Karloff in his film *Targets*.'

Lugosi apparently succumbed to his Dracula image very quickly. William Castle remembers him as enjoying the role in the mid-1930s, and Forrest J. Ackerman, who knew him towards the end of his life, agreed. 'During the years that I knew Lugosi he never said anything to me that suggested he resented Dracula. His classical acting career was long in the past. I imagine there was a time when he felt he was being wasted and felt that he should have been a romantic or Shakespearean figure, but I have the feeling that in the end he took a great deal of pride in having added this indelible impersonation to the lore of the world. He was Count Dracula right up to the end.'

However in 1933 Lugosi was saying: 'I can blame it all on Dracula. Since then Hollywood has scribbled a little card of classification for me and it looks as if I'll never be able to prove my mettle in any other kind of role. Not only have I a pathological leaning towards *Pollyanna* roles, my one real ambition in life is to retire from the screen and settle down in peace and solitude on a little farm far away from Draculas and other of my monsters.' The latter was an ambition Lugosi never realized.[22]

Another time he complained to an interviewer about the letters people sent him: 'The writers ask if my parents were hypnotists; if I commune with ghosts, and whether or not I practise the supernatural in my private life. They say my eyes have an expression unlike the eyes of any human being! As a matter of fact, my childhood in the Black Mountains was the usual husky, healthy, everyday life of any country boy. My father – Baron Lugosi – was a banker and there was nothing weird or extraordinary in my family background.'[23] A childhood spent in the Black Mountains, a Baron for a father – it sounds more like a scenario for one of Universal's films than an illustration of normality. Actually it was more likely a product of the studio's publicity department. Lugosi's father, surnamed

Blaskó, wasn't a Baron and neither was he a banker when Lugosi was born – his profession at that time was listed as baker, though he later became one of the directors of the small-town bank.

As the 1930s wore on, Lugosi's career began the downward plunge from which it would never recover. By mid-decade horror films were already out of fashion and the demand for Lugosi's services was diminishing. Strangely enough, Universal never followed up their success with *Dracula* by making a proper sequel as they did with *Frankenstein*. They did make *Dracula's Daughter* (Lambert Hillyer) in 1936, an interesting film, with its hints of lesbianism, but Lugosi was conspicuous by his absence (he was represented by a dummy in a coffin). Despite being forever associated with the role of Dracula he played the Count even fewer times on the screen than Karloff played the monster, though he did play numerous other vampires.

Probably Lugosi's best role in the late thirties was in the excellent *Son of Frankenstein* (Rowland V. Lee, 1939), the third in the Frankenstein series. Lugosi played Ygor, the evil, misshapen shepherd – he had once been hung for his crimes but survived, despite a broken neck – who uses the monster as an instrument for revenge. Lugosi later repeated the role in *Ghost of Frankenstein* (Erle C. Kenton, 1942).

Also in 1939 he made a temporary escape from his monsters and mad scientists by appearing in the classic Greta Garbo vehicle *Ninotchka* (Ernst Lubitsch). Lugosi played a Russian official but it was only a small role and his hopes that it would lead to better things came to nothing. By the beginning of the 1940s his career was in very bad shape and both the quality and the size of his roles continued to lessen. In 1941 he had a small part in *The Wolfman* (George Waggner) and in 1943 he played the role that he once claimed he had rejected – that of the Frankenstein monster in *Frankenstein Meets the Wolfman* (Roy W. Neill). Apart from those, the previously mentioned *Ghost of Frankenstein*, and *The Body Snatcher* (Robert Wise, 1945), which teamed him up with Karloff again, most of the films he appeared in during this period were forgettable. Unwisely he chose to become involved with producer Sam Katzman – king of the hopelessly mean 'Z' films – and made a whole series of cheap, terrible movies with titles like *The Corpse Vanishes* (Wallace Fox, 1942), *Bowery at Midnight* (Wallace Fox, 1942) and *Ghosts on the Loose* (William Beaudine, 1943).

In the second half of the decade, with the horror film once again out of fashion, most of Lugosi's income came from live performances. At first he did a revival of the Dracula play, but later went on tour doing a special act he had contrived that involved a comedy routine as well as a few scenes from the play. His manager, and loyal supporter, Don Marlowe, described an amusing incident that occurred during one of these tours:

To get the show off to a good start we flooded the town with publicity. Lugosi's picture could be seen on almost every fence and telephone pole in town. At ten o'clock the night before the opening, as Bela and I were walking briskly along the street we noticed a young boy about ten years old coming towards us. Lugosi, usually a modest man but now in an elated mood, turned to me with a twinkle in his eye and said, 'He'll spot me any minute. Watch.' As the boy approached us we could see his expression of disbelief. Bela was smiling and as we got near to the boy he said in a gentle voice, 'Good evening, my young man.' The astonished boy timidly returned the smile and managed to blurt out, 'Could I have your autograph please?' 'Certainly,' said Lugosi, turning to me with a triumphant grin. As he was about to sign, Bela Lugosi paused momentarily and said to his young fan – 'And, young man, what is my name?' Without hesitation the boy said, 'Boris Karloff.'[24]

Marlowe didn't say what Lugosi's reaction to that was, but another of his stories about the star belies the claim often made that Lugosi lacked a sense of humour. This time they were touring with a special adaptation of Poe's *The Tell-Tale Heart* which Marlowe produced. He also had the task, during each performance, of simulating the beating of a heart by hitting a large drum off-stage. As the performance progressed the drumming was supposed to get louder and louder. But on one occasion, near the end of the play, the drum-stick broke in Marlowe's hand, he over-balanced and fell out on to the stage at Lugosi's feet. Lugosi just looked down at him and then said, 'Ladies and Gentlemen, my manager Mr Don Marlowe.' Marlowe made a hasty exit and Lugosi continued with the performance as if nothing had happened.

In the course of his lifetime, [said Marlowe] Lugosi earned hundreds of thousands of dollars. He was, however, always in one of two extreme predicaments – either incalculably wealthy or completely broke. He never worried about money. He spent it faster than anyone I have ever known. He lived luxuriously in a stately mansion with lavish furnishings – wore elegant clothes and entertained in superlative taste. He owned a priceless stamp collection and his only other hobby, to which he devoted his leisure time, was reading books mainly dealing with scientific subjects and world history.[25]

But by the 1950s Lugosi was in a bad situation, both professionally and personally. He didn't make any films in 1950 or 1951, though he did make one in 1952, a British production called *Old Mother Riley Meets the Vampire* (John Gilling). In 1953 he made *King Robot* but it was never released. 'During the last three years of his life,' said Forrest J. Ackerman, 'he was desperately trying to get a little work and to hang on to his fame. And one whole year went out of his life when he had to have an operation. He'd taken drugs for many years to kill the sciatic pains that he had, but finally his doctor felt it was no longer safe to give him such quantities of pain-killers and that he would have to have an operation. But though the operation killed the pain, to his dismay he found that his system still required the drugs. So, quite courageously I would say, he dared public disapproval and revealed to the newspapers that he was a drug user. It took him a year in hospital to get his system cleared up and during that time he became involved with a woman who was to become his fifth and final wife. She was a strange person called Hope Lininger and she had decided, many years before, that one day she would marry Bela Lugosi. She was three thousand miles away from him at that time and he was already married, of course, but she drew her plans up. Every move she made after that was to get physically close to him. First she moved to Chicago, then to Hollywood and then into the movie industry as a studio clerk. Finally, when he was old and ailing, and being cured of his drug addiction, she wrote to him at the hospital – she wrote him daily. She said in her letters that it was ironic that her name was Hope and that she, in effect, gave him hope, and that she was someone who cared about him. So when he was released in 1955 he naturally wanted to meet this woman. And he married her that same year (she was thirty-nine, Lugosi was in his seventies). He lived just short of one year after that. He quietly died in bed. I think his heart just simply stopped from old age.

'Strangely enough, Hope Lugosi ultimately became weary of being Mrs Dracula. I'm afraid the world used her rather badly. People constantly came and took up her time asking about Bela and she told her stories but she never got anything out of it. Finally she got tired of it all. And here was a woman who, for maybe twenty years before she ever laid eyes on him in the flesh, had decided she was going to marry him. She kept scrapbooks on him and had seen his pictures many times. But a year or so after his death I was in her apartment and was looking at a scrapbook that she had there – it had her wedding photos, all the congratulations that famous people had sent them at the time, Lugosi's work permit, his birth and death certificates and other collector's items. My mouth was watering at the sight of it, but I thought it would be disgraceful to even dare suggest to someone who had admired him so much that I would like to own it. And all of a sudden my eyeballs popped out of my head when she said: "Forry, would you want this? I was going to throw it away but you can have it if you want." She really seemed to be quite sincere about no longer caring. She was sick and tired of the fact that nobody regarded her as a human being but only as the wife of the late Bela Lugosi.'

One of the last films that Lugosi appeared in was *The Black Sleep* (Reginald Le Borg), a mediocre production about a mad scientist whose experiments in new surgical techniques had resulted in the inevitable

Lugosi, flanked by Basil Rathbone, Akim Tamiroff, John Carradine and Lon Chaney Jnr, in one of his last films – The Black Sleep

collection of misshapen monsters. Apart from Lugosi the cast included Basil Rathbone, John Carradine and Lon Chaney Jnr. 'I play the role of a mute,' he said at the time, 'but even with no lines to speak it's tiring just getting to the set each day. But everyone is kind and it's good to be working with old friends.'[26] (Old age had apparently mellowed him, for though he merely resented Karloff, Chaney Jnr was one person he actively disliked.)

His last film was *Plan 9 from Outer Space* (Edward D. Wood Jnr, 1955), the final in a long series of cinematic humiliations. *Plan 9* is so *very* bad that it exerts a strange fascination. The budget was apparently non-existent and the sets so small it appears to have been made in somebody's garage. Once again Lugosi didn't have a speaking part and close-ups were avoided. A few shots, supposedly of Lugosi in his cape prowling through some woods, were obviously of someone else. Lugosi died, in fact, half-way through the film's shooting schedule.

Shortly before Lugosi's death, Ackerman had accompanied him to the premiere of *The Black Sleep* and had observed an incident similar to the one he later observed with Chaney Jnr. 'He was an inveterate cigar smoker and in that particular theatre you couldn't smoke downstairs. So I went upstairs with him, along with this devoted young fan he had. For the last three years of his life this young man was at his every beck and call. So the two of us sat on either side of him while he smoked and watched the movie and afterwards, as we were coming down the stairs, he was spotted by a TV crew. They motioned that they would like him to come over. Well, he was too proud to wear glasses in public so he whispered to us: "Boys, point me in the right direction." So we just kind of squared him around and said: "Now Bela, you just take about eight paces forward and stop and you'll be right in front of the camera." Well, at that point it was a minor miracle. Here was this broken, decrepit old man, admitting to seventy-three years of age but probably older, but the world wanted him, the eye of Hollywood was upon him and the limelight was shining – so right before my eyes he changed! It was like Mr Hyde changing back into Dr Jekyll – it just seemed like he filled out and rose three or four inches taller. He was proud and strong as he strode towards the waiting television camera, and once again the magic and charisma of the great Count Dracula was pouring out for the public.

'Officially he was seventy-three when he died but I would not have been surprised if he was more like seventy-eight. [He was.] Personalities in the motion picture business like to revise history à la 1984 every once in a while. I've always felt that Lugosi fudged a bit on his age. Now I found that Karloff and Lugosi were exact opposites in that respect. Karloff was always very proud of his advancing years and the fact that even though he was seventy-eight or seventy-nine he had just been signed on to do another film. He was proud to announce it to the press. In any event, it was pitiful to see pictures of Lugosi in the last year of his life. He really looked like someone who had been in a concentration camp – just skin and bones. And although he had been cured of the drug habit he was also an alcoholic. He used to go to Alcoholics Anonymous and he couldn't say enough in praise of them. He even wanted *me* to go to their meetings with him – and I don't drink.

'There were a hundred and one people at his funeral. For some reason or other I just happened to count them as they passed by his coffin. Earlier in the day, if they had known it, anyone who wished to could have walked in off the street and stood there as I did – alone with Lugosi for several minutes. I looked at him in his coffin and it passed my mind that if there was such a thing as survival of the personality after death, and Lugosi was there in spirit form looking at himself, I thought he would have been very pleased with his final appearance. You almost expected him to open his eyes and rise once again from the grave. At his request, he had been buried in one of his Dracula capes. And his young acolyte, knowing Lugosi's attachment to cigars, told me that when no one was around he had sneaked a last one into Lugosi's coat pocket. So he took a cigar to the grave with him.'

Bela Lugosi is buried in the Holy Cross Cemetery in the Southern part of Los Angeles, an ironic resting place for the king of the vampires.

'Lugosi was completely different from Karloff,' said Ackerman. 'Lugosi with his huge ego and Karloff with virtually none at all. When I was in Karloff's home I was disappointed, as a collector and admirer, that he didn't have all kinds of scrapbooks and everything on display. But no, if he had any such thing he kept them hidden. Whereas Lugosi had an infinity of scrapbooks on every movie he ever made. He got every shot that he was in. He must have subscribed to collectors who sent him clippings from all over the world. But I've never met a person who knew Boris Karloff who had anything but praise for him. I never found a chink in his armour, no flaw of any kind. He was just what he seemed to be – a very gentle, unpretentious person. He just felt that he was like a surgeon or lawyer; he did his job and then he went and played cricket, tended his garden and minded his business.'

Karloff was born as William Henry Pratt on 23 November 1887, in Camberwell in south London. He was born into a large family – he had seven brothers and one step-sister – and had a moderately happy childhood though his father and mother died when he was quite young. After their deaths William was raised by his step-sister Emma and by whichever brother happened to be around at the time (William was the youngest of the family). Most of his brothers held important positions in the diplomatic corps and spent a good part of each year in foreign countries.

The one brother who was at home more than the others was George; and George was an actor. He was obviously the major influence on young William though his career on the stage wasn't very successful and George eventually gave in and got a job in the City. William's other brothers weren't happy about his own theatrical leanings and constantly tried to talk him out of it. But despite their best effort to get him into the consular service William remained adamant and deliberately failed his exams. This plunged him into family disgrace and in those days the black sheep of British families were obliged to emigrate, usually either to Australia or Canada. William flipped a coin and Canada won. It's interesting to speculate on what would have happened to him if he had gone to Australia. Probably very little.

Curiously, William Pratt arrived in Canada, in 1909, with the idea of becoming a farmer. But after six months of back-breaking work on a farm in Caledonia – seven days a week for only food and lodging and a few extra cents – he moved to Banff where he tried to get stage work. But there was none available and he found himself helping to dig a racetrack instead. After that he worked for a railroad company laying tracks for 28 cents an hour. Things improved in late 1910 when by chance he met one of his brothers in a Vancouver hotel. The brother, on his way from China to London, loaned William enough money to support him while he tried again to get theatrical work. For months he kept trying but without success. One night he decided that Pratt wasn't the best of names for an actor and that he should change it to something else. He chose Karloff because it was an old family name on his mother's side; and the name Boris was just an invention. Thus Boris Karloff was born.

While in Vancouver Karloff visited an agent and told him that he was an experienced actor who had worked successfully in London's West End. He didn't expect the agent, whose name was Kelly, to believe him; but several months later, while Karloff was working with a survey team 160 miles northeast of Vancouver, he received a telegram from Kelly informing him that he had a job with the Jean Russell Stock Company in Nelson. Karloff immediately caught a train to Nelson. He was hired by the company as 'an experienced character actor' at $30 a week. 'I went to the theatre,' said Karloff later, 'feeling no slight trepidation at the prospect of my first professional stage work. I hadn't the foggiest idea of how to take stage direction. Rehearsal routine and make-up were completely foreign to me. I mumbled, bumbled, missed cues, rammed into furniture, and sent the director's blood pressure soaring. When the curtain went up I was getting $30 a week. When it descended I was down to $15!'[27]

Despite this disastrous beginning Karloff stayed with the company for almost two years, during which time he toured through Western Canada. As a sign of things to come, Karloff became popular as a villain.

He then worked for a haulage company before joining another theatre company – The Harry St. Clair Players. During the years that Karloff spent touring he later said that he '. . . learned the acting trade, playing vintage pieces all over Western Canada and the United States, living on eggs fried on inverted pressing irons in "no cooking" boarding houses.'[28]

In 1917 Karloff joined the cast of the popular Western play *The Virginian*, playing the part of Trampas. In December of that year the company arrived in Los Angeles. Karloff had no intention of becoming a movie actor, for all his ambitions lay in the theatre (besides, movie work was looked down upon by 'legitimate actors' in those days), but the great influenza epidemic of 1918 ruined theatrical business in the West. He was forced to return to heavy labour to avoid starving and for two months he earned a living piling sacks of flour on to lorries. The only outlet remaining now for an out-of-work actor was the rapidly growing film industry and Karloff finally succumbed. He appeared before the camera for the first time in a film shot, significantly, at Universal City. Not that things improved for him after that. The one day's work was all he was able to obtain and so he went to San Francisco where he was able to get a job with a theatre company for a three-month season. A friend, Alfred Aldrich, persuaded him to return to Los Angeles and introduced him to an agent. Thanks to the efforts of the latter, Karloff found work as an extra in the Douglas Fairbanks film *His Majesty, the American*. More small parts followed and over the years they grew bigger. Not surprisingly, with his deep-set eyes and gaunt features, Karloff once again became typecast as a villain. But for some reason casting directors regarded him as a French-Canadian type so in a number of films made in this period he played a French-Canadian villain.

By 1922 Karloff was earning $150 a week and was feeling reasonably secure – but a sudden slump in production knocked the bottom out of the French-Canadian villain market. It was back to the hard labour again, this time as the driver of a 17-ton truck (as well as having to load and unload it). Now thirty-six years old, it seemed to Karloff that he hadn't really progressed very far since leaving England. He also had a wife to support – he had married Helene Vivian Soule, a dancer, in the spring of 1923. But during his time as a truck driver he was still able, thanks to a kindly boss, to get the occasional job as an extra, and in 1925 the parts began to grow bigger again.

One of the people Karloff met while working at Universal City was Lon Chaney Snr. They were both fans of boxing and whenever they met at a match Chaney always had time for a few pleasant words. 'One day,' said Karloff, 'after work as I walked through the studio gate and set off home, I heard a big car honking behind me. I thought the driver wanted me to get out of the way. I had only 15 cents in my pocket, but I had plenty of pride and I resented the honking. I slowed down and walked calmly ahead; the car slowed down too and a voice said, "Don't you recognize old friends, Boris?" I looked inside the car and saw Lon Chaney smiling at me. He invited me to ride with him and for more than an hour he talked to me of the picture industry and asked me my ambitions. That talk with Lon gave me the courage to keep trying in later years when the going was far from easy. One of the things that Lon said was: "If you're going to act – you're going to act. Even if you have to starve, never give up. It's the only way." He also said that "The secret of success in Hollywood lies in being different from anyone else. Find something no one else can or will do – and they'll begin to take notice of you. Hollywood is full of competent actors. What the screen needs is individuality!" '[29]

In 1926, when Karloff was nearing forty, he appeared in *The Bells* (James Young), a foretaste of the type of films he would be making in later years. In it Karloff played a hypnotist in make-up based on the appearance of Werner Krauss in *The Cabinet of Dr Caligari* (Robert Wiene, 1919). It was a major part and Karloff hoped that it would prove to be the breakthrough he desperately needed, but the film flopped and he returned to his former small roles. In 1929 he divorced his wife. Strangely enough, the usually genial Karloff went out of his way to avoid ever mentioning his first wife's name after they parted. In later years he always referred to his third wife as his second.

The next major event in Karloff's career was when he got a part in the successful play *The Criminal Code* which had run for six months in New York. Harry Cohn of Columbia Pictures visited the West Coast version and decided to buy it for filming. Howard Hawks was the director, and it was Karloff's good fortune to be asked to repeat his stage role, that of the convict trusty who is actually a killer, in front of the cameras. The film resulted in more work for Karloff – he made three pictures in a row at RKO and then four for Warner Brothers. In 1931 Karloff went back to Universal Studios for a relatively small part in a film called *Graft* (Christy Cabanne) and while working on it was noticed by director James Whale in the studio commissary. 'I was having lunch, and James Whale sent either the first assistant or maybe it was his secretary over to me, and asked me to join him in a cup of coffee after lunch, which I did. He asked me if I would make a test for him tomorrow. "What for?" I asked. "For a damned awful monster!" he said. Of course I was delighted, because it meant another job if I was able to land it. Actually that's all it meant to me. At the same time I felt rather hurt, because at the time I had on very good straight make-up and my best suit – and he wanted to test me for a monster!'[30]

Whale had been fascinated by the shape of Karloff's head and face. Karloff's physique wasn't really suitable for the Monster but Whale de-

Karloff as the Monster in a famous scene from Frankenstein

Mae Clark, as Dr Frankenstein's bride, receives an unwelcome visitor on her wedding night (from Frankenstein)

cided that it could be easily altered with padding. The man responsible for turning Karloff into the Monster was make-up expert Jack Pierce. Together they spent three weeks preparing for the screen test. The most distinctive aspect of the make-up was the high, built-up forehead that Pierce gave Karloff. 'I discovered there are six ways a surgeon can cut the skull,' said Pierce, 'and I figured Dr Frankenstein, who was not a practising surgeon, would take the easiest. That is, he would cut the top of the skull straight across like a pot lid, hinge it, pop the brain in, and clamp it tight. That's the reason I decided to make the Monster's head square and flat like a box.'[31]

But the best thing about the facial make-up was that it didn't conceal Karloff's expressive features and allowed him to give full rein to his talents as a mime. Almost the only changes Pierce made below Karloff's forehead, apart from the texture of his skin, were to the eyes which he half-concealed with strips of rubber to give a sleepy, unintelligent look. Apart from padding, Karloff's physique was changed by the use of steel struts to stiffen his legs, huge boots to add to his height, and the sleeves of the coat were shortened to make his arms look longer.

When Pierce was satisfied they made the screen test. James Whale was delighted and the production of *Frankenstein* went ahead as planned. To Karloff it was just another acting assignment, even though Pierce had told him, 'This is going to be a big thing.'[32] But none of Karloff's previous roles had involved so much sheer suffering before. He was following in Chaney's footsteps in more ways than one. Apart from the heavy suit and the steel leg braces, he had to drag those heavy boots – the same type that asphalt spreaders wore, each of which weighed 18 lbs. After a day's work was completed on the set Karloff required a massage and infra-red treatment to help him recover. It must be remembered that by this time Karloff was in his mid-forties and the strain obviously affected his health. 'To fill out the Monster costume,' said Karloff, 'I had to wear a doubly quilted suit beneath it. We shot *Frankenstein* in midsummer. After an hour's work I'd be sopping wet. I'd have to change into a spare undersuit, often still damp from the previous round. So I felt, most of the time, as if I were wearing a clammy shroud. No doubt it added to the realism.'[33]

The make-up took three and a half hours to apply each day – a long and tedious process. Removing it took less time but involved a great deal of pain. 'It required an hour and a half of prying, pulling and coaxing,' said a journalist who had visited the set, 'plus special oils and acids. First the eyelids came off – most painful, to say the least; and enough to inspire any quantity of questionable language! The deep scar on the Monster's forehead was then pried into as a good starting point, and from then on it was just one pry and push and acid soaking after another until Boris was himself again.'[34]

Karloff takes a meal break during the making of The Bride of Frankenstein

After a preview at a cinema in Santa Barbara, to which Karloff was not even invited (the studio regarded Colin Clive, who played Frankenstein, as the star of the production) Universal decided to alter the film before putting it on general release. The changes included a happy ending (originally Frankenstein was killed), as well as the cutting of the famous sequence where the Monster accidentally drowns a little girl, but the film still shocked people when it was released. Some of the reviewers' reactions sound similar to those that recently followed the release of *The Exorcist. Film Weekly* said of Frankenstein that:

It has no theme and points no moral, but is simply a shocker beside which the Grand Guignol was a kindergarten. It is the kind of film which could only induce nightmares.

Nevertheless it was what the movie audiences wanted and proved to be very successful for Universal. It cost just over a quarter of a million dollars to make but has made many millions of dollars for the studio over the years.

Unlike *Dracula, Frankenstein* stands up very well when seen today. James Whale's directing style, which hasn't become as dated as that of some of his contemporaries, is responsible to a large extent; but it is still

Karloff's portrayal of the Monster that remains the film's strongest asset (Colin Clive, as the neurotic, guilt-ridden Frankenstein, tended to go over the top). It was a truly classic performance – the Monster was no monster, but a pathetic, confused creature caught in a situation it couldn't comprehend. Karloff portrayed all this with marvellous pantomime, restricted as he was to a series of grunts and despite the handicaps of his heavy costume. 'Whale and I both saw the character as an innocent one,' he later said, 'and I tried to play it that way. The most heart-rending aspect of the creature's life, for us, was his ultimate desertion by his creator. It was as though man, in his blundering, searching attempts to improve himself, was to find himself deserted by his God.'[35]

Frankenstein had many repercussions – its success prompted Universal, and the other studios, to try and repeat it, and so the first big horror film cycle was begun (*Dracula* had been a success too but it took *Frankenstein* to set the seal) – and of course it changed Karloff's life completely. He was put under contract to Universal, which was a dream come true for him. At last, after years of a struggling actor's insecurity he would know where

Karloff poses for a gag shot with his 'double'

his next meal was coming from – for a while, at least. Old habits of thought were hard to change and Karloff didn't really think that his new success would last. Neither, for that matter, did his brothers. 'I hope you are saving every farthing you can lay your hands on, my boy, because obviously this can't go on for much longer,' wrote one of them.[36]

Universal had soon realized that Karloff was the star of *Frankenstein*. The studio knew they had a good thing on their hands with the actor but they weren't sure what to do with him. While various horror projects were discussed, such as remakes of *The Hunchback of Notre Dame* and *The Phantom of the Opera*, Karloff was back playing supporting roles. In *Behind the Mask* (John Francis Dillon, 1931), Karloff's next film after *Frankenstein*, he played one of the villain's henchmen. He also played another criminal henchman in *Scarface* (Howard Hawks) made the same year. Significantly enough, in his first film for Universal after *Franken-stein, The Cohens and Kellys in Hollywood* (John Francis Dillon) Karloff played himself, a role he was to repeat many times on cinema and TV screens during the remainder of his career. On the strength of really just one film he had become more than just a star: his name had come to represent something unique. He had accidentally achieved what Lon Chaney had advised him to do.

But Karloff took this sudden and unexpected metamorphosis in his stride. He was married again, this time to a former librarian called Dorothy Stine, and lived a quiet life with his new wife in a house in Coldwater Canyon. Like Chaney, he avoided the Hollywood social life, preferring to work in his fruit and vegetable garden. Always with his eye on an uncertain future, he told a reporter at the time that they could probably live on the produce from their garden if things went bad for him. Apart from gardening his other main indulgence was cricket, which he played with the rest of the English exiles living in Hollywood.

Karloff's next horror role was in *The Old Dark House* (James Whale, 1932), a black comedy, in which he played the grotesque butler Morgan. This was followed by *The Mask of Fu Manchu* (Charles Brabin) at MGM, a lavish far-fetched spectacle in which Karloff played Fu with obvious relish. Back at Universal at the end of the same year Karloff appeared in another classic horror role – that of the Mummy. Actually *The Mummy* (Karl Freund) wasn't really a horror film, it was more of a fantasy thriller. Except for a sequence near the beginning when the Mummy wakes and walks out of its tomb, trailing bandages behind it, Karloff spent most of the film unwrapped and relatively normal though somewhat aged (thanks again to the make-up skills of Jack Pierce).

In 1934 Karloff was teamed with Lugosi for the first time in *The Black Cat* (Edward G. Ulmer), a film more ludicrous than horrifying and which had very little to do with Edgar Allen Poe, despite the title. In 1935

Karloff made the long-awaited sequel to *Frankenstein* with *The Bride of Frankenstein*, again directed by James Whale. He was forty-eight years old then and playing the Monster was even more of a trial than it had been originally. He was already suffering from arthritis that was to plague him for the rest of his life, and on the first day of shooting he broke a hip. The film itself is probably the best of the Karloff/Frankensteins but Karloff wasn't happy with it. 'They made a great mistake,' he said, 'about which I complained, but, you know, you don't have much say in it. Speech! Stupid! My argument was that if the Monster had any impact or charm, it was because he was inarticulate – this great, lumbering, inarticulate creature. The moment he spoke you might as well take the mick or play it straight.' (It would be interesting to know what Karloff thought of a TV series made in the mid-1960s called *The Munsters* which featured Fred Gwynne as a clownish monster in make-up similar to Karloff's.)

Karloff played the Monster in only one more feature film (though many years later he appeared as the Monster in an episode of a TV series called *Route 66*), and that was *Son of Frankenstein* (Rowland V. Lee, 1939). Though Karloff again had misgivings about the treatment of the Monster – this time its costume had been altered – the film itself was an impressive one, with its Expressionistic sets, superb photography by George Robinson, a fairly good script, and memorable performances from Basil Rathbone as Frankenstein (though somewhat hammy), Bela Lugosi as Ygor and Lionel Atwill as the police inspector with the artificial arm. It certainly succeeded in maintaining the high standard set by James Whale in the previous two *Frankenstein* films (Mel Brooks's affectionate spoof *Young Frankenstein*, incidentally, is a virtual remake of *Son of Frankenstein*). Karloff's performance was, of course, as good as ever and despite his advancing years he still managed to endow the Monster with an aura of vitality and great strength. He also succeeded in retaining the Monster's basic poignancy and there was a marvellous scene where the creature compared its own grotesque reflection in a mirror with that of the handsome Frankenstein.

Karloff was much more fortunate than Lugosi during the 1930s (as he was to be during the 1940s and 1950s too) and his roles tended to be of a higher standard, though he also did his fair share of bad movies. In the latter category is one he did with Lugosi in 1935 called *The Raven* (Louis Friedlander). As usual the title was the only thing that the film had in common with Poe, though the character that Lugosi played, Dr Vollin, was a man obsessed with the dead author and his work. Karloff played a criminal who came to the mad doctor seeking plastic surgery and ended up looking almost as ugly as the Frankenstein monster. Vollin also had a basement full of Poe-like torture instruments and the film ended with him attempting to bisect a judge with a device out of *The Pit and the Pendulum*.

*Karloff stoically endures
the tedium and
discomfort of being
transformed yet again
into the Monster for*
Son of Frankenstein

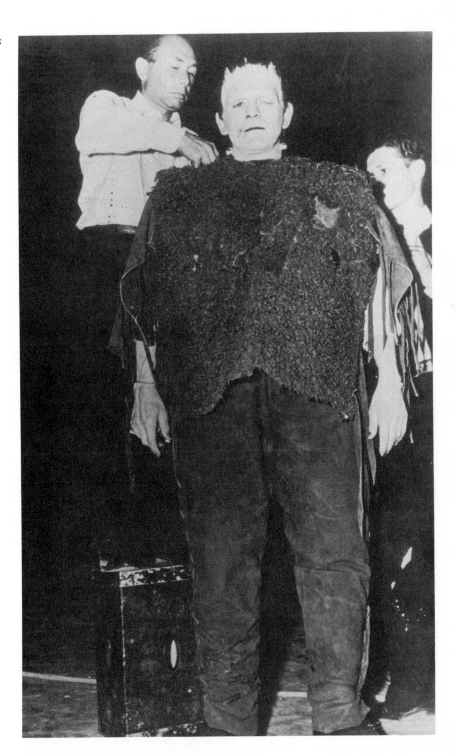

A better film that the two of them starred in together was *The Invisible Ray* (Lambert Hillyer 1936), more science fiction than horror, in which a scientist, Karloff, discovered a mysterious radioactive meteorite. Infected by the radiation, Karloff is turned into a walking death ray who sets out to destroy those he feels have betrayed him in the past. The special effects were particularly good and there was an impressive sequence where Karloff melted six statues, simply by *glaring* at them (Lugosi, for a change, had the sympathetic role).

The first horror cycle came to an almost complete end during the years of 1937 and 1938. Hollywood's apathetic attitude towards horror films had been greatly influenced by the decision of the British film censor (who had already banned films like *The Island of Lost Souls* and *Freaks*) that they had absolutely no redeeming feature and were not to be permitted into the country, which meant the disappearance of a valuable market. But the successful re-release, in the late 1930s, of *Frankenstein* and *Dracula* together proved to the studios that there was still money to be made out of the *genre* and the horror stars suddenly found themselves back in demand. The films, though, they soon discovered, were not the major productions that they had been back in the golden days of 1931–36.

In 1939, however, Karloff did appear in at least two films that possessed some of the grandeur of the earlier productions – the previously mentioned *Son of Frankenstein*, and *Tower of London*, which was also directed by Rowland V. Lee. In the latter film Karloff played Mord the Executioner (wearing a bald cap) and the cast also included Basil Rathbone, as Richard III, and Vincent Price. But in 1940 Karloff's film career began another decline and he was obliged to sign a contract with Harry Cohn of Columbia Pictures to make five cheap horror films in a row. They turned out to be of a low quality and kept to a strict formula with Karloff invariably playing the part of a mad scientist. Where this downward slide would have ended it's hard to say but his luck, unlike Lugosi's, turned. In the same year he was offered a part in a Broadway farce called *Arsenic and Old Lace*. The play was a huge success and Karloff benefited from it in more ways than one because the character he portrayed, a psychopath named Jonathon Brewster, was based on his screen image. He even had a line: 'I killed him because he said I looked like Boris Karloff!'

When Karloff returned to Hollywood to fulfil his contract with Columbia he found that his salary had risen, and also that the last film in the mad doctor series had been swiftly rewritten so that it resembled an inferior version of the play. Ironically, he didn't appear in the film version of *Arsenic and Old Lace* (directed by Frank Capra in 1941, though its release was held up until the play had finished its New York run in 1944); instead his part was filled by veteran character actor Raymond Massey. Actually Massey's interpretation of Karloff was very impressive as well as being rather disturbing – it's surprising that Massey was not deluged with other horror roles. Also in the cast was Peter Lorre, who was very good as Jonathon's reluctant assistant. (Ironically, Lugosi later went on tour with the play in the Jonathon role.) There are conflicting stories as to why Karloff wasn't in the film version: one is that Massey was under contract to Warner Brothers, who were obliged to use him; and the other is that Karloff was committed to the play and couldn't spare the time.

Just one look from Karloff, even when his hair is in curls, is enough to chill the blood (from Isle of the Dead*)*

When he returned to Hollywood in 1944 one of the films he appeared in was *The House of Frankenstein* (Erle C. Kenton), which had Dracula, the Wolfman and Frankenstein's monster almost rubbing shoulders. The Monster this time was played by stunt man Glenn Strange while Karloff played a mad doctor. In 1945 he made the first of three excellent films for producer Val Lewton (see Chapter 4) at RKO. They were *The Body Snatcher, Isle of the Dead* (also 1945) and *Bedlam* (1946). These were the best films that Karloff would appear in for many years. He spent the remainder of the 1940s more often on the stage than on the screen, in such plays as *On Borrowed Time* and *The Linden Tree*, though he did have minor roles in two successful but overrated films in 1947, in *The Secret Life of Walter Mitty* (Norman Z. McLeod) as a villain, and in *Unconquered* (Cecil B. De Mille) as an Indian chief.

In 1945 he divorced Dorothy Stine and the following year married Evelyn Helmore, an Englishwoman who had worked as an assistant story editor to Darryl F. Zanuck, and whom Karloff had known for some years. In 1951 the Karloffs moved from Hollywood to New York and when they discovered that they could be in England within a few hours they began to make frequent trips back to their home country. In 1959 they moved back to England permanently. 'It's good to be living at home in England,' he said. 'I've lived abroad for most of my life but when you get older you feel the roots of home very deeply.'[37] Another move he made in the early 1950s was into television, and it was a wise one. He appeared as a guest in numerous shows, playing against his horror persona as he had done in earlier movie spoofs such as *You'll Find Out* (David Butler, 1940) and *The Boogie Man Will Get You* (Lew Landers, 1942). In 1954 he appeared in the British made TV series *Colonel March of Scotland Yard*, and in later years hosted TV shows such as *Thriller*, a suspense series which included many supernatural episodes (Karloff himself acted in five of them) and *Out of This World*, a British science fiction series.

Nineteen fifty-seven saw the start of the third big horror film cycle (which is still continuing), mainly as a result of the old horror classics being shown on late-night television and the timely arrival of Hammer Films' new versions in shocking colour. Karloff, like Chaney and others, suddenly found himself back in demand as a horror star, but the quality of his new films left much to be desired. *Voodoo Island* (Reginald Le Borg, 1957) was one of the first and one of the worst – Karloff played one of a group of people investigating an island populated with man-eating plants. This was followed by *Frankenstein 1970* (Howard W. Koch) made in 1958. Another inferior film, it was only interesting for the fact that Karloff played Baron Frankenstein. He made a few relatively good horror films in the early 1960s, notably the Roger Corman production *The Raven, Comedy of Terrors* (Jacques Tourneur), and Mario Bava's *Black Sabbath*. The first two were black comedies and the latter consisted of three separate stories for which Karloff provided the link as well as giving a fine, menacing performance in the final one as a vampire. After that the only other film of importance that he made was *Targets*, the first film directed by Roger Corman's now famous protégé Peter Bogdanovich. Karloff played a character obviously partly based on himself – an ageing horror star called Byron Orlock who is tired of appearing in cheap, quickie films that are made merely to cash in on his name. Bogdanovich played the young director who was trying to persuade the actor to make just one more film for him. Tied into this story was the contemporary theme of a young man who starts to kill people for no apparent reason. The climax of the film comes with a skilfully arranged confrontation between the killer and the horror star.

Unfortunately Karloff seemed to lack the integrity of Byron Orlock, and he continued to make cheap, exploitation films – all of them for-

Director Peter Bogdanovich and Karloff discuss a scene during the making of Targets

gettable. Incredibly, in the final year of his life, when he was eighty-one years old and in bad health, he signed a contract to make *four* films in as many weeks. They were co-productions between the U.S.A. and Mexico and originally it was planned to shoot them all in Mexico, but Karloff's rapidly failing health forced the producers to make the films in Hollywood. But perhaps it's not really fair to blame Karloff for the quality of the films he made in his later years – he obviously had a great need to keep on working and, outside of television, those films were all that was available to him. When asked why he kept on working at the age of eighty-one he replied: 'My leg in a steel brace – operating with only half a lung – why it's a public scandal that I'm still around! But as long as people want me, I feel an obligation to keep on performing. After all, every time I act I provide employment for a fleet of doubles!'[38] On another occasion during the same period he said: 'I am never really alive unless I am at work, merely recharging for the next spell. To know that I was never to work again would be something akin to the death sentence for me.'[39]

Forrest J. Ackerman saw at first-hand the suffering that Karloff went through to continue working: 'That dear man – it would break your heart. I remember visiting the set of *The Raven* which he was making with Vincent Price and Peter Lorre, and when I saw Karloff he only looked about five feet tall. He was just like a crustacean, he was so bent over and bandy-legged because of the arthritis. But he would do anything and go anywhere. I saw him making those four final films and I also saw him make his final public appearance which was on a Hallowe'en TV special. By this time he practically lived in a wheel chair because he was so badly arthritic and had to have an oxygen tank nearby at all times, but he wanted to keep that knowledge away from the public. He would politely request when you took pictures of him to try and cheat around the wheel chair. For this TV special they had it all worked out so that he could do it seated but at the penultimate moment, so I was told by the make-up man, Vern Langdon, Karloff said: "No, no, I think my public will be disappointed. They will sense it." So, by God, he got up on his feet – I watched it with my jaw hanging open. He came bounding out like a fifty-year-old man. He must have been in great pain but he did everything on his feet.

'A lady called Terri Pinckard, who wrote an article for my magazine called *Monsters Are Good for My Children*, took one of her four children to meet Karloff while he was working on those final four films. She chose a little Korean war orphan whom she had adopted called Ricky, and he was about eight years old at the time. Now when Karloff finished a scene he practically collapsed in upon himself and you felt almost criminal to approach him to ask questions, that he had probably heard a hundred thousand times, or to ask him for his signature. I finally took mercy on him and said I'd be very satisfied if he would just put his initials instead of writing his whole name. So there he was, sitting kind of collapsed in a chair, when Mrs Pinckard brought Ricky forward. You would have thought he was being escorted to meet Santa Claus, he was just trembling with excitement. He held out his hand and said: "Oh, Mr Karloff, I've waited for this moment all my life." And Karloff was so great. He put his arm around the boy and said: "Get a photographer. I want a picture taken with this boy." '

Terri Pinckard herself later described another incident that took place that day:

Later the group gathered in the dressing room of the actor. The questions thrown at him were the ones he'd heard countless times before. 'What was your favourite film? Why did you go into horror films? What does your wife think of your acting? What was the sequence of events in film X? Karloff's voice grew weary and the hand passed over the brows and eyes in what was already now a familiar gesture. He reacted less and less to the queries. There was a lull in the conversation and, gathering my nerve, I broached a question that had been gathering on my mind all morning. 'Mr Karloff, my twelve-year-old daughter is handicapped. She sometimes feels self-conscious of her braces. If I told her you wore braces on your legs exactly as she does it would make her feel so much better. But are you in pain?' Karloff's face lit as he turned to me. His voice became animated at the personal question and interest. He went into a discussion of the pain, the diffi-culty in movement that arthritis had brought to him. And the questions I threw back at him prompted more remarks. He seemed to enjoy going into his personal life. The horror of a back operation and the bill sent to him for it took all signs of tiredness from his face. The discussion quickly led to the benefits of socialized medicine and England's contribution to the Utopian need for free medical care. He led the discussion into politics and his feeling that the USA, beloved as it was to him, was sometimes betraying its own people by not providing for them out of fear of Socialism, the dirty word – the word so many interpreted as Communism.[40]

The above provides an interesting insight into Karloff's political beliefs – a subject that rarely came up during the many interviews he gave over the years. It's also worth noting that in 1933 he was one of the founders of the powerful Screen Actors Guild and was a Director of the Guild for over thirty years. But Terri Pinckard also shows how wearying it must have been for Karloff, sick and in pain, to be constantly plagued at the end of his life by those people who claimed to be his admirers. Of further evidence is publisher Bill Warren's account of his visit to the same set:

When I arrived Karloff was seated to one side, out of the way, holding an oxygen mask to his face and studying his lines. Fellow fan Jon Berg and I hovered around him, not talking but merely pleased to be in his presence. We also half-heartedly tried to keep visitors to the set from bothering him. For example, one mother dragged her son up to the tired old actor and said – 'See, he played Frankenstein.' The child said – 'You mean Herman Munster?'[41]

Karloff had caught bronchitis during February 1968 while in California. When he completed the four Mexican/American films he flew back to England where he was admitted to hospital. Three months later he died, on 2 February 1969.

The last words on Karloff come from his good friend Robert Bloch: 'Boris Karloff was an exemplar of the actor of the earlier generation who came up the hard way. I once asked him, "Boris, what do you consider to be the climax of your career – what was the greatest moment?" And he said, "I'll tell you. It was in 1925 when I was getting five dollars a day and they raised me to seven and a half." He was sincere about that. But the point I'm making is that he was in his mid-forties when he got the role in Frankenstein and by that time he had been in the business over twenty years. He wasn't someone who was taken off the streets because he was eighteen years old and looked right for the part of a young assistant to the lead in a TV series and who in one year becomes a star. Boris had a lot of perspective and that was why he remained simple, unaffected, and felt largely that his background was that of the theatre. His only regret, he told me, was that he had never played the West End in London. He had played Broadway, and very successfully, and he was proud of working with Julie Harris in *The Lark* and that sort of thing, but by the time the West End offers came he said he was just too old for the nightly trooping. That was his only regret.

'But he was a lovely and charming man. Everyone in the business really loved, respected and admired him and we miss him greatly still.'

Both Lugosi and Karloff were the first real victims of the horror film. They were typecast in a much more restricting way than Lon Chaney had ever been – at least he had the choice of a variety of roles right up until his death. Lugosi and Karloff became completely associated, in the mind of the public, with their screen images. Their very names were enough to produce delighted shudders – it didn't matter what their roles were. This meant, however, that the film-makers soon began to opt out of trying to make horror movies of the standard of, say, *Frankenstein* or *The Island of Dr Moreau*. They reasoned that all they really needed to do was to include one, or both, of the horror stars in the cast and the audiences would be satisfied, no matter what the film itself was like. The audiences, of course, *didn't* accept that for very long, and this is probably the main reason why the first horror cycle came to an end so quickly. Hollywood then discarded the two monsters it had built, believing them to have out-lived their usefulness, until it was discovered that there was still more money to be made out of them. But neither Karloff nor Lugosi ever made it back to the top again, though Karloff was much more fortunate than Lugosi. It's hard to say why Karloff survived so well compared to Lugosi. Karloff was definitely the shrewder of the two but probably his main advantage was that he never took himself very seriously, while poor Lugosi never got the joke. And a rather cruel one it was.

3 The Men Behind the Early Monsters: Karl Freund, Tod Browning and James Whale

To the film audiences of the 1930s Karloff and Lugosi were *the* horror people. The public rarely, if ever, gave any thought to the producers, writers and directors responsible for the horror films. In the last category the three men who made the biggest contribution to the shape and style of the Hollywood horror film were Karl Freund, Tod Browning and James Whale.

Freund, like Carl Laemmle, the head of Universal Studios, was German, and it was the German influence that was pre-eminent in the horror film *genre* as a whole. The traditional German love of horror stories was soon reflected in the cinema – with such classics as *The Student of Prague* (D. Stellan Rye, 1913 and Henrik Galeen, 1926), *The Golem* (Paul Wegener, Henrik Galeen, 1914, and Paul Wegener, Carl Boese, 1920), *The Cabinet of Dr Caligari* (Robert Wiene, 1919), *Nosferatu* (F. W. Murnau, 1922) and *The Hands of Orlac* (Robert Wiene, 1924). But in America, during the same period, very few horror films were made. Fantasy films had never been popular there, and there was a saying that to make one was the fastest way possible of losing money. (Douglas Fairbanks' *Thief of Baghdad* epic, made in 1924 and inspired by the films of Fritz Lang, was a financial failure, despite the star's popularity.) American audiences at that time were too pragmatic and sceptical to accept stories based on the supernatural. Discussing special effects techniques in a Los Angeles newspaper in 1930 one writer noted:

Although UFA and other foreign film companies revel in weird camera work, such as we saw in *The Cabinet of Dr Caligari* and *Variety*, American audiences demand realism in their stories, and in their photography at least apparent realism. Therefore while European special effects men go in for bizarre shots, their American counterparts have only one endeavour: to make every trick shot look as realistic as possible.

Even when apparently supernatural pictures were made in America, the pill was sugared. For example, the 1920 version of *Dr Jekyll and Mr Hyde* (John S. Robertson) ended with Jekyll waking up to discover that it had all been a dream; and in *London After Midnight* (Tod Browning, 1927)

Lon Chaney's vampire was revealed to be a hoax. But all this changed as Hollywood began to import more and more of the best European film talent, particularly German (it seems that practically the whole of the German film industry ended up in Hollywood). The German influence soon became noticeable across the whole spectrum of the Hollywood product.

Karl Freund was part of this mass migration of talent. Born on 16 January 1890, in Koenigshof, Bohemia, he arrived in Hollywood in 1929. His film career had begun at the age of seventeen when he was hired as a cameraman on two small features. When he was eighteen he became a cameraman for Pathé newsreels, and this was followed by a job in Vienna filming a two-reel feature called *The Ladies' Man*. After that he was offered the position of chief cameraman at Union Projection KG's new studios at Templehof (they later formed the basis for UFA). When the First World War began Freund joined the Austrian army and was released after serving for only three months due to being overweight, a problem that was to remain with him all of his life (at times he weighed almost 300 lbs). During the war he again worked as a newsreel cameraman and then went back to feature films. The first important director he worked with was Robert Wiene, who later directed *The Cabinet of Dr Caligari*, the classic Expressionist film about a sinister doctor (Werner Krauss) who is in control of a zombie-like creature (Conrad Veidt). In 1919 Freund began working for F. W. Murnau, who had then directed only one film, and photographed *Satanas* for him, and, in the following year, *The Hunchback and the Dancer*, both of which starred Conrad Veidt (Murnau later directed *Nosferatu*, an impressive, if unauthorized, adaptation of Bram Stoker's *Dracula*). Also in 1919 Freund worked on his first picture with the great German director Fritz Lang, *The Golden Sea*; and in 1920 he filmed, with Guido Seeger, Paul Wegener's *The Golem*, a remake of Wegener's 1914 production based on the old Jewish legend about a huge man of clay animated by supernatural forces.

In 1924 Freund reached the peak of his career in Germany when he photographed *The Last Laugh* for Murnau at UFA. His camerawork for the film, which starred Emil Jannings, contained many stylistic innovations, such as very fluid camera movements and low-key lighting, it established his reputation as a major talent. Then, in 1925, he worked on another important production – Fritz Lang's *Metropolis*, which he photographed with Gunther Rittau. He subsequently became involved with the development of a new colour process and was persuaded by his associates in the industry that Hollywood was the place where this process could best be marketed. When he arrived in Hollywood he was put under contract almost immediately by Universal, and in 1930 he photographed six films for the studio, among them *Dracula*.

Dracula didn't really make full use of Freund's talents. The fluid, atmospheric camerawork that he was famous for was only utilized in the early sequences in Dracula's castle (apparently Browning ignored many of Freund's suggestions). After that the picture became very much a 'talkie' and rather static, but much of the credit for whatever eerie qualities it still possessed must go to Freund. It is regrettable that Freund wasn't allowed a freer hand as *Dracula* would have been the perfect subject for his unique form of visual poetry. But another horror film he worked on the following year, *The Murders in the Rue Morgue*, provided him with a better opportunity to display his skills – there are some marvellous shots of misty Paris streets – but Freund was once again hindered by uninspired directing (by Robert Florey) and a rushed shooting schedule. The Universal executives, however, were pleased enough with his work to give him his first directing assignment. This was *The Mummy* in 1933, and actually something of a disappointment considering that it was Freund's directing debut. Seen today it seems much too restrained and talkative, though it is far superior to *Dracula* in the way that it succeeds in creating its mood out of the carefully photographed settings. Of course, as noted in Chapter 2, it isn't so much a horror film as a romantic fantasy.

Freund was then to have directed a Universal remake of *The Golem* but that project was abandoned, as was a proposed film entitled *Bluebeard*

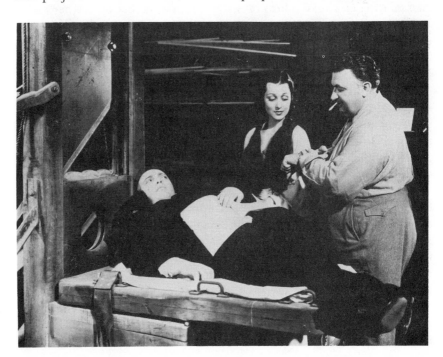

Freund (right) poses for a publicity shot on the set of Mad Love

which would have starred Karloff. He directed a number of non-horror films such as John Ford's *Air Mail* before his contract with Universal expired in 1934; one of his last for that studio was *The Gift of Gab*, a musical in which both Karloff and Lugosi had cameo roles.

The last film he ever directed was also his best. This was *Mad Love* for MGM in 1935 – a remake of the German classic *The Hands of Orlac* – and starred Peter Lorre (it was his first appearance in an American film). The story concerned Dr Gogol (Lorre) who transplanted the hands of an executed murderer on to the arms of a pianist (Colin Clive). Assisted by a typically fine performance from Lorre, Freund succeeded in making a memorable film that was the exact opposite of *The Mummy*. Extravagant, bizarre and very fast-paced, *Mad Love* is almost a parody of the typical horror film of the period. It also gave Freund the opportunity to indulge in his speciality – marvellously fluid camerawork.

Still in great demand as a cameraman, Freund decided to forsake directing and return full-time to his old profession, which was apparently more secure financially. He photographed numerous feature films until the early 1950s when he entered television and began a new and success-ful career as a television cameraman. He seemed content in his new role and won several awards for his work on such long-running and popular shows as *Our Miss Brooks* and *I Love Lucy*, but one cannot help but regard it as something of a comedown for one of the German cinema's greatest talents. Of course, like others of his generation, he became rather bitter about the state of the film industry in his later years and considered the Hollywood product to be nothing more than 'legalized pornography'. He retired from television in 1959 and died in 1970 at the age of eighty.

Tod Browning, unlike the other two subjects of this chapter, was American-born (12 July 1880). At the age of sixteen he ran away from home and joined a circus where he worked for several years as a clown, acrobat, contortionist and ringmaster. His experiences in the circus greatly influenced his later career in Hollywood and echoes of those years can be found in many of his films. After the circus Browning went into vaudeville as a comedian and toured the world with various companies. He arrived in Hollywood in 1914 and appeared in many short films as a comedy lead. During this period he became friendly with D. W. Griffith and was one of that great director's assistants on *Intolerance* (1916). By this time Browning had also started to write scripts, having realized that his future lay behind the camera rather than in front of it. He learned a lot from working with Griffith and in 1917 he directed his first full-length film, *Jim Bludso* but it wasn't until 1920 that he established a reputation within the industry. That was when he directed, for Carl Laemmle at Universal, a melodrama set in Turkey called *The Virgin of*

Stamboul. His next film for Laemmle, *Outside the Law* (1921), starred Lon Chaney but Browning then left Universal for two years. During that period he worked only sporadically, spending most of his time trying to cope with a drinking problem. But in 1925, at the age of forty-five, he made a fresh start and had soon re-established himself as a major director. With the assistance of Laemmle's legendary young protégé, Irving Thalberg, he convinced Universal to film *The Unholy Three*, a story that contained many ingredients close to his heart, concerning, as it did, the activities of three ex-circus performers who, in varied disguises, run a pet store as a front for their criminal activities. It was a big success for Universal and Laemmle decided that the teaming of Browning with Chaney was a guaranteed formula for making money.

A scene from Tod Browning's The Unholy Three *(with midget Harry Earles as the baby and Chaney as the old lady)*

During the remaining five years of Chaney's life they made several more films together, including *The Road to Mandalay* (1926), *The Unknown* (1927) and *London After Midnight* (1927). In an interview in 1928 Browning said: 'When I am working on a story for Chaney I never think of the plot. That follows by itself after the characterization. *The Unknown* began merely with an armless man. I asked myself what would be the most startling situation in which a man so deformed could be involved. The plot about a circus performer who uses his feet as he would his hands, who loves and loses the girl, and eventually attempts a terrible crime with his toes, grew out of my speculations. The same applies to *The Road to Mandalay*. The nucleus idea was merely that of a man of such revolting hideousness that he was ashamed to reveal himself to his daughter. You can get any number of plots from that.'[42] He used, with a certain amount of pride, *London After Midnight* as an example of how to get audiences to accept supernatural events. 'The audience was not asked to believe the horrible impossible, only the horrible possible. The plausibility increased rather than lessened the chills and thrills.' Yet within two years of that interview he directed *Dracula*, and a more implausible story it would be hard to find. It demonstrates the speed with which American audiences adjusted themselves to the 'horrible impossible'.

Of Chaney, Browning said: 'I'm especially lucky to have an artist like Chaney who can take on guises and disguises of the more grotesque nature. He will do anything, and permit almost anything to be done to him for the sake of his pictures.'[43] Strangely enough, the relationship between Chaney and Browning seems to have been a purely professional one despite their mutual fascination with the grotesque (perhaps they had too much in common). In one interview, Chaney actually sounded somewhat dismissive of Browning. 'I've had good directors,' he said, 'Tod Browning and I have worked so much together he's called the Chaney director. I like his work. I think Victor Sjöstrom and Benjamin Christonson are great directors. Their values are finer. But I don't really worry over who they hand me.'[44]

Browning was not really a horror director in the traditional sense and his version of *Dracula* is evidence of that. He had no real feel for the supernatural or the creation of a Gothic atmosphere, neither was he a very *visual* director (it's a film legend that Dracula was one of his pet projects, but there is no evidence to support that – he became involved in the picture at a late stage of its development). Whatever visual style *Dracula* possesses is due to Freund's influence. His main attribute as a director was his effective handling of actors: Lugosi, during the making of *Dracula*, found Browning to be extremely helpful. Despite the success of *Dracula*, and the boost it gave his career, Browning's chief interest continued to lie not with films dealing with the supernatural but with films that dealt with the *naturally* grotesque and bizarre. So, after *Dracula*, he returned to his beloved circus setting with a rather controversial idea – a film about a group of circus freaks, using *real* freaks – and it was this that proved the cause of his professional undoing. Not surprisingly, the executives at Universal were not very enthusiastic about the project, but once again Thalberg, then at MGM, came to Browning's assistance and persuaded a doubtful Louis B. Mayer to accept the idea.

A furious Harry Earles (centre) reacts to the taunts from his full-size companions in this scene from Freaks

Freaks was about a beautiful but evil trapeze artist called Cleopatra (played by the Russian-born Olga Baclanova) who marries one of the circus midgets when she discovers that he will inherit a large amount of money. (The midget, called Hans, was played by an old friend of Browning's, Harry Earles, who had also appeared in both versions of *The Unholy Three*.) After they marry she plots with the circus strongman, her lover, to poison Hans slowly. The midget is part of the circus freak show and when the others learn of the plot they take drastic action. In a sequence full of menace they attack Cleopatra and the strongman with knives at the height of a thunder storm. Just what they do to the two plotters isn't made clear but the final scene shows the once beautiful Cleopatra horribly disfigured and part of the freak show: she has been turned into a 'Chicken Woman'. The impression is given that the strongman is killed during the storm, though originally there was a scene in the film that had him singing in an unnaturally high voice (suggesting that he had been castrated), but it was edited out before the film went on release. But this retaliation by the freaks, though partly justified, is a major flaw in the picture. Up to then Browning had effectively presented them as basically 'normal' people, despite their physical handicaps (they were real freaks, gathered together by Browning from various shows all over America), and much more likeable than the two physically perfect people. But by resorting finally to the popular image of circus freaks as being strange and sinister creatures he destroyed all his previous good work, laying himself open, at the same time, to the charge of exploitation – though to be fair to Browning the idea for the story came from the midget, Harry Earles, himself.

It was Browning's insistence on using real freaks, which would have been justified if the film had been a serious attempt to examine the plight of such people rather than the melodrama it was, that proved to be the film's downfall. The trouble began when the picture was still in production. Though it was filmed 'undercover' the freaks were often in evidence around the MGM studios – the producers of so much wholesome, escapist material – to the increasing horror of the other studio workers. Mr Wholesome himself, L. B. Mayer, once he saw what the making of the picture entailed, was aghast and tried to have it halted. Thalberg, strangely enough, maintained his support of the project, one of the few times his famous instinct let him down. A sensitive area was the studio canteen – a group of MGM executives organized a petition to stop the production on the excuse that it would be unbearable to eat with the freaks in the same room. The production continued but the freaks were banned from the canteen. A film editor who worked on *Freaks* said: 'It was bad enough to see them during the day when you went down on the set, but when you had to look at it on the movieola for eighteen hours a day, it drove you up the walls.'[45]

Critical reception to *Freaks* was mixed but not entirely adverse. The real damage to the film was done both by the cinema managers and by cinema audiences themselves. Their horrified reaction ensured that the film was a financial flop (it had a good run in a couple of American cities but not enough to make any difference – and in Britain it was banned for over *thirty* years). People were willing to take the make-believe horror of Karloff lurching around as an animated corpse but they weren't willing to endure a close-up view of some of reality's more unpleasant aspects, especially in 1932 when they considered that their own lives were grim enough. The film has never been widely shown and the reaction from audiences even today would still probably be an adverse one.

Freaks became one of MGM's worst failures and a saddened, and surprised, Browning realized he had made a serious error of judgment. His next film for MGM (he was under contract to them) made the following year was about a very different subject – riveters working on skyscrapers – and was called *Fast Workers*. Surprisingly enough, MGM did give him further horror assignments (probably on the insistence of Thalberg). In 1935 it was *The Mark of the Vampire*, a rather flaccid remake of *London After Midnight* with Lugosi in the Chaney role. More interesting was *The Devil Doll* in 1936 which had Lionel Barrymore as a man wrongly convicted of a crime. He escapes from prison and encounters an old scientist who has invented a process by which he can shrink animals and people so that, while inanimate, they resemble dolls. When brought to life the tiny people have no will of their own and will follow any command. Barrymore steals several of the 'dolls' and returns to New York where he opens a doll's shop, then proceeds to send his tiny creatures on missions to kill the men who framed him. To avoid detection he dresses up as an old woman – a favourite Browning device – and much of the film's enjoyment comes from watching Barrymore's amusing portrayal of this unlikely character. Browning's last film for MGM was in 1939, a light-hearted mystery about stage magicians called *Miracles for Sale*. He retired from the industry then and spent the remainder of his life living on his ample savings and, according to Carlos Clarens in his book *Horror Movies*, 'gently deprecating the films that had made him rich and celebrated'. He died on 6 October 1962, while recovering from a cancer operation.

Whenever the name of James Whale is mentioned in film literature the word 'enigmatic' usually accompanies it. Whale remains something of a mystery man to this day and many of his films have become extremely rare (some seem to have disappeared completely). Today he is best remembered for his horror films – a less than adequate description of them – which is something that would probably amuse him if he were alive today, though his amusement would surely be tinged with a certain amount of regret.

Like Lugosi, Whale also rewrote history. Most records put his date of birth as 21 July 1896, but he was actually born in 1889. His birthplace was the town of Dudley in Worcestershire, England. He trained as an art student and was working as a cartoonist when the First World War began. He was commissioned as a Second Lieutenant in the Seventh Worcester Infantry Regiment and served in France, where he was captured by the Germans. It was during his incarceration in German prisoner-of-war camps that he became interested in the theatre, after appearing in some of the shows organized by the prisoners. Back in England he worked in various theatre repertory companies but without much success. R. C. Sherriff, in his autobiography *No Leading Lady*, described his first meeting with Whale in 1928.

He was a man-of-all-work in the theatre. He played many small parts, designed and painted scenery and occasionally got a job as a stage manager, but he had never been in charge of a play in a West End theatre. He told me later that he had never earned beyond £5 a week for anything he had done.

Sherriff had just written *Journey's End*, a play about the First World War

James Whale (seated to the left of the radio) on the set of the film version of Journey's End *(recently filmed again as* Aces High – *the setting having been changed from the trenches to the air). Colin Clive is seated to the right of Whale*

which is set entirely in a dug-out. But Sherriff found it impossible to interest established stage producers in the play, revolutionary for its time. Whale was someone who had nothing to lose.

I went to the stage door, and was taken to Whale's dressing room where he was making up for his part. He scarcely looked at me: he kept his eyes on the mirror as he rubbed on the greasepaint and talked to my reflection in the glass where I sat in a chair behind him. He didn't seem very enthusiastic about *Journey's End*.

The play was a huge success, of course, first in London, then in New York. Whale accompanied the play to New York and was then asked by the Tiffany-Stahl Studio to direct the film version. While negotiating with Tiffany in Hollywood Whale worked as a dialogue director at Paramount on a film called *The Love Doctor* and was then hired by Howard Hughes to work in a similar capacity on *Hell's Angels*. He apparently learned the rudiments of screen directing quite swiftly as the film of *Journey's End* is a competent cinematic interpretation of the play, though not outstanding. The play was opened out for certain sequences but most of the action still took place within the single dug-out set, which must have been restrictive for Whale.

After this success he was put under contract by Universal, always on the look-out for new foreign talent. They quickly searched for an English subject for him to direct and came up with *Waterloo Bridge*. Despite the English setting it was filmed entirely at Universal, London being represented mainly by a great deal of fog, courtesy of the special effects department. Among the properties they next offered him was *Frankenstein*. He chose it and, in a later interview, explained why:

Of the thirty or so stories available it was the strongest meat and gave me a chance to dabble in the macabre. I thought it would be amusing to try and make what everybody knows is a physical impossibility believable for sixty minutes. Also it offered fine pictorial chances, had two grand characterizations, and had a subject that might go anywhere.[46]

Frankenstein, as noted in Chapter 2, remains an impressive film even today. The years have been much kinder to it than to Browning's *Dracula*, on account of Whale's superior direction, which was visually stylish as well as fast-moving. With his atmospheric lighting, smooth tracking shots and numerous low-angle shots that were never obtrusive but made effective use of the high-ceiling sets – in particular Frankenstein's laboratory – Whale succeeded in making a horror film that possessed a real sense of grandeur. The dialogue is unfortunately risible in places, especially during the romantic scenes, but that fault lies with the script writers Garrett Fort, Francis Edward Faragoh and Robert Florey rather than with Whale. But *Frankenstein* does differ from his later horror films, and many of his conventional ones, in that he presents it in an almost entirely 'straight' fashion. Apart from Frankenstein's father there are none of those amusing eccentrics that Whale delighted in featuring. In fact there was very little humour at all in *Frankenstein* and even the happy ending that now accompanies the film was added later (originally Frankenstein was killed by the Monster).

The success of *Frankenstein* meant that Universal's executives immediately decided that horror films were Whale's *forte* – a typical example of Hollywood's strange sense of logic. Whale was not pleased by this unexpected categorization, but he decided to make the best of the situation by hiring a number of his old friends from the British stage. In his next film *The Old Dark House* (1932) Whale cast Charles Laughton, Ernest Thesiger, Una O'Connor and Raymond Massey, as well as Boris Karloff, and to write the dialogue he brought over R. C. Sherriff. Based on a J. B. Priestley play and novel called *Benighted*, *The Old Dark House* was a very *English* picture to be made in an American studio and gave Whale plenty of opportunity to indulge his quirky sense of humour.

Sherriff also wrote the script for Whale's *The Invisible Man* (1933), another very English film full of Whale's idiosyncratic humour. It was based on H. G. Wells's novel about a scientist who discovers the secret of invisibility but whose mind is affected as a result (as well it might be). Claude Rains gave a fine performance as the scientist, Griffin, who becomes a complete megalomaniac and sets out to conquer the world – 'We'll start with a few murders. Big men. Little men. Just to show we make no distinction.' Rains's success in the part (or rather the success of his voice, as he didn't appear visible until the very end of the film) led to a long Hollywood career, and Karloff, who was originally supposed to play Griffin, must have later regretted turning it down. The picture was full of black humour with some hilarious scenes near the end of the film when a horde of straight-faced policemen, dressed in traditional British bobby uniforms, go to extravagant lengths to capture the invisible man. Particularly funny was Una O'Connor as the scatter-brained inn-keeper's wife with a tendency towards hysteria (Miss O'Connor's speciality was an ear-splitting, high-pitched screech).

Whale's most eccentric film was *The Bride of Frankenstein* (1935), an artful combination of the bizarre and the humorous, though not many people thought so at the time of its release. Even Karloff, as noted previously, thought that Whale went too far, especially in the sequence where the Monster meets an old blind hermit and shares a meal with him – including a cigar! Yet that sequence is one of the most memorable in a film full of memorable moments (it was parodied most effectively in Mel

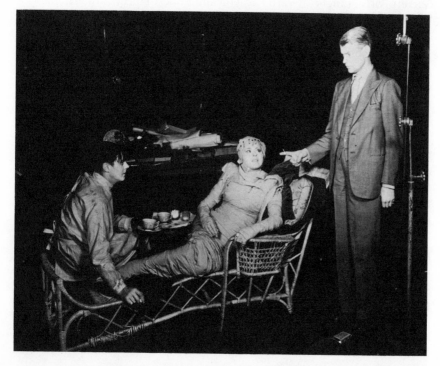

James Whale (standing) on the set of The Bride of Frankenstein. *With him are Colin Clive and Elsa Lanchester*

Brooks's *Young Frankenstein*). Karloff wasn't the only one who dis-approved – the studio executives also were unhappy and *The Bride of Frankenstein* was to be the last horror film that Whale directed. It is possible that this was precisely his intention when he set out to make *Bride* as off-beat as possible.

In a cast studded with talent at least two people managed to stand out – Ernest Thesiger as the fey Dr Praetorius and the charismatic Elsa Lanchester in the dual role of Mary Shelley (in a short prologue) and the female monster that is created as a mate for Karloff.

While it is possible that he may not have taken it very seriously when he was making it, Whale nonetheless ended up with a film to which the word 'classic' can be applied, for a change, with complete justification.

In 1935 Whale was one of Universal's top directors. Apart from the horror films he had also made several others on more conventional subjects – films such as *By Candlelight* (1933), *A Kiss Before the Mirror* (1933), *One More River* (1934), and *Remember Last Night* (1935), most of which contained strong elements of humour. In 1936 he directed Universal's big picture of the year, a film version of the musical *Showboat*, though the material apparently wasn't to his taste. He was at the peak of his career and in an interview for the *New York Post* he said:

That they [in Hollywood] should pay such fabulous salaries is beyond ordinary reasoning! Who's worth it? And the architecture! And the furnishings! I can have modernistic designs one day and an antiquated home overnight! All the world's made of plaster of paris![47]

But that year Universal City was sold and from then on Whale's career began to suffer. At first he and Carl Laemmle Jnr planned to set up an independent producing organization but the project fell through. His next big film was *The Road Back* (1937), a sequel to *All Quiet on the Western Front*, which was a failure. (Whale demonstrated an eccentric aspect of his own character during the making of this when he insisted on wearing the uniform of a German officer – and made his crew dress as his subordinates.) He never again had a major success but a couple of his other films did moderately well, in particular the 1939 production of *The Man in the Iron Mask* (which included, interestingly enough, the young Peter Cushing in its cast). But Whale, no longer enjoying the same sort of artistic freedom that he had had at Universal, became soured with Hollywood. During the making of *They Dare Not Love* in 1941, which was about war refugees, he walked off the set after an argument and never returned. The film was completed by Charles Vidor. Whale never directed another feature film though in 1949 he did direct a short, experimental film called *Hello Out There*, which was never released.

After directing a few plays in both America and England, Whale spent most of his retirement painting and set designing. He was financially well-off, having wisely invested his 'fabulous salaries' in real estate. He was worth over $600,000 when he died in 1957.

As noted earlier, Whale wasn't a gregarious person and he kept his private life separate from his professional one. 'I guess the best one-word description of Mr Whale was "aloof",' said David Horsley, who once assisted John P. Fulton, the special effects expert who worked on many of Whale's films (Horsley himself later became head of the Universal effects department). 'There was a sound mixer who used to work with Whale whose name was Bill Hitchcock. Someone once asked Bill what Whale was like and he said, "Well, I'll tell you. On the first picture that I ever worked on with the man, he didn't look at me and didn't speak to me. On the second picture he spoke to me but wouldn't look at me. After I had made four pictures he would look at me and talk to me and then I felt as though I had been accepted." '[48]

Since he was a known homosexual, Whale's rather unusual death – he was found drowned in his swimming pool on the night of 29 May 1957 – provoked several rumours of a sinister nature, the most popular being that he was beaten up and pushed into the pool by one of his homosexual acquaintances. A much more likely explanation was that his death was entirely accidental. He had suffered a mild stroke earlier that year and it is possible that, having fallen in the pool, he was too weak to climb out. Nevertheless the exact circumstances of his death remain a mystery.

4 Lewton and Company

By the beginning of the 1940s the horror film had reached a low level. The days when such illustrious film-makers as James Whale, Karl Freund, and even Tod Browning had been active in the *genre* were far in the past and the high standards they had established had long since languished. Erle C. Kenton was still involved with horror films but he never again reached the heights of his 1932 classic *Island of Lost Souls* (though *The Ghost of Frankenstein* wasn't the failure that some have made it out to be), and Rowland V. Lee, who directed two of the best horror films of 1939, *Son of Frankenstein* and *Tower of London*, had already moved on to other things. Universal still dominated the field, but their new cycle of films, such as *Son of Dracula, The Invisible Woman, The Mummy's Hand* and *Frankenstein Meets the Wolfman*, were but pale shadows of the original versions they had produced a decade earlier. Horror films had become the equivalent of the pulp magazines – popular but not considered worthy of serious attention. Then, in 1942, came a producer called Val Lewton who changed all that – for a brief time, at least.

The films of Val Lewton have a unique place in the history of the horror film. Despite titles like *I Walked With a Zombie* and *Curse of the Cat People* they were subtle in their style and presentation, depending upon the psychological aspects of horror, suggested by atmospheric photography and clever editing rather than the more blatant shocks of conventional horror films. Not only the public but also the critics responded to Lewton's new style of horror film, and he received a great deal of praise, one of his most vocal supporters being James Agee. Lewton, however, wasn't satisfied – his own attitude towards horror films approached that of contempt and he had pretensions towards higher things, despite his success in the *genre*.

The first in Lewton's series was *The Cat People*, made in 1942 and directed by Jacques Tourneur, which starred Simone Simon as a New York fashion designer who believes that she is descended from a race of Balkan women who possessed the power to transform themselves into large cats. Whether this is true or not is deliberately left unclear in the script – though the studio insisted that a shot of an actual panther be inserted into one scene – and the film ends on an ambiguous note. Despite being a

Simone Simon with Tom Conway in a scene from Cat People

variation on the werewolf theme it contains none of the usual clichés, such as a close-up of the victim getting progressively hairier under the light of a full moon. Instead the set-piece of the film is a sequence where a girl is menaced, while swimming alone at night in an indoor pool, by nothing more substantial than a fleeting shadow and a number of strange sounds (script-writer DeWitt Bodeen based the sequence on a real-life incident when he had almost drowned while swimming alone in similar conditions).

I Walked with a Zombie followed in 1943 and, though loosely based on *Jane Eyre* (a favourite novel of Lewton's), is a story about voodoo and zombies, set on the island of Haiti. Its highpoint is the nocturnal walk that the two leading ladies take through the cane fields, during which the tension mounts to an almost unbearable level. Of a similarly ambiguous nature to *The Cat People* was *The Leopard Man* (1943), whose action takes place in a New Mexico town and concerns a series of murders which might, or might not, have been caused by a runaway leopard. Though not as satisfying as most of Lewton's horror films it does contain a masterful shock sequence when a young Mexican girl is ordered, by her mother, to journey out into the night and buy some urgently needed provisions from a shop on the other side of town. Afraid of the dark, the girl is unwilling, but her mother locks her out and refuses to let her back in the house until she returns from the shop. Her journey through the shadowy streets is full of suggested menace, but her return trip, after she has been informed at the shop of the escaped leopard, is even more of a nightmare – until her fears are finally confirmed when she encounters, under a railway bridge, what she believes to be the leopard. Terrified, she runs the rest of the way home, only to find that the front door is still locked. Her frightened cries are ignored by her mother – until there is a loud animal snarl and the door shakes as if hit by something heavy. Before the mother can get the door open blood begins to seep in under it.

The Seventh Victim (1943), Lewton's blackest film, is about a group of devil-worshippers in Greenwich Village, New York, and ends with the suicide of the lead character (played by Jean Brooks). *The Ghost Ship* (1943) was a more conventional mystery-thriller involving a number of deaths on board a ship, but was produced with Lewton's customary attention to atmosphere. *Curse of the Cat People* (1944) wasn't really a sequel to *Cat People* – though that's what the studio expected to get from Lewton – but an unusual film about a lonely little girl (Ann Carter) who is visited by the ghost of her dead mother (Simone Simon). Whether the ghost is real or a fantasy manufactured by the child is never made certain.

Youth Runs Wild (1944), about wartime juvenile delinquency, was one of Lewton's attempts to make a non-horror film, but the studio didn't appreciate his efforts and insisted that parts of it be reshot. Similar studio pressure hampered him during the making of *Mademoiselle Fifi* (1944), based on two Guy de Maupassant stories. After that it was back to the horror, this time with Boris Karloff whom RKO had put under contract to make three films. Lewton wasn't happy about having the star foisted upon him, as he believed that Karloff was too closely associated with the more traditional type of horror film. The first of their films together was *The Body Snatcher* (made in 1943 but not released until 1945), a costume melodrama about grave-robbers which featured a truly terrifying climax in a runaway coach where a corpse apparently comes back to life (the sequence was so effective that it was cut out when the film was released in England). *Isle of the Dead* (1945) was the second Karloff/Lewton film and concerned a small group of people who are trapped on a Greek island during a plague. It demonstrated, once again, Lewton's obsession not only with death but also with the *process* of dying. The sequence where the British consul's wife wakes up in her coffin is one of Lewton's most horrifying. *Bedlam* (1946) was the last film he made for RKO and also his last horror film. Set in a London lunatic asylum of the eighteenth century, with Karloff as the sadistic supervisor, it continued Lewton's rather black view of life, though it at least had a happy ending (though Karloff's evil asylum keeper wouldn't agree – he was walled up alive by the understand-

A scene from **Bedlam**

ably aggrieved inmates at the close of the picture). It was, of course, banned in England for many years.

Lewton was born in Yalta on 7 May 1904 (his full name was Vladimir Ivan Lewton) but was educated in America. After graduating from university he worked as a journalist as well as writing poetry and short stories. A book he wrote on the history of the Russian Cossacks led to him being hired by Hollywood producer David O. Selznick who was, at that time, preparing a film of Taras Bulbas. He worked with Selznick for nine years before joining RKO as a producer. RKO had, in 1941, decided to make a series of low budget horror films and they chose Lewton to supervise them. The first, *Cat People*, was directed by Jacques Tourneur, who described how the film originated: 'One day he [Lewton] called and asked me over to his office. He told me that Charlie Koerner, the head of the studio, had been at a party the night before and somebody had suggested that he make a picture called *Cat People*. The next morning, Charlie asked Val to come up with a script to suit that title. Val said: "I don't know what to do." It was a stupid title and Val, with his good taste, said that the only way he would do it was not to make the blood and thunder cheap horror movie that the studio was expecting but something intelligent and in good taste. The first person to join us on that one was DeWitt Bodeen. We started reading and talking and then invented this story, out of whole cloth you know.'[49]

Bodeen himself continued: '*Cat People* was a group project. Val had the initial idea, then I did the story on it, and then the screenplay, co-operating entirely with Val and Tourneur, and then Mark Robson, who was going to be the editor, and later with Roy Webb, who wrote the musical background. Tourneur was entirely responsible for the style of *Cat People*, but if you read the screenplay you would find that everything in the film was in the original script – and that's simply because it was a group project. Val, Tourneur, myself, Robson – we all talked about it and I put it all down on paper.'

'If you made *Cat People* today, exactly as we did,' said Tourneur, 'they'd laugh you out of the theatre because it was naive – a kind of joke. But there were some very good things in it. The front office made me put a cat in the drafting room scene; I had only intended to suggest the cat's presence by shadows. Despite orders to reshoot the scene, I shot it so that you couldn't really be sure what you were seeing. That's the only way to do it. In the swimming pool sequence the cat was my fist. We had a diffused spotlight and I used my fist to make shadows on the wall. But to this day, people swear that there was a cat by that swimming pool.'[50]

Jacques Tourneur was born in the same year as Lewton (1904), a native of France. His father, Maurice Tourneur, directed a number of silent films in Hollywood and it was there that Jacques grew up and received his education. He returned to France with his father in 1926, and there worked with his father as a film editor before directing his first film in 1932. He returned to Hollywood in 1934, after having made four films in France, where he was hired by MGM to make shorts. He later became a second unit director and it was during this period that he first met Lewton. He directed three films for Lewton's unit at RKO: *Cat People*, *I Walked With a Zombie*, and *The Leopard Man*. In 1944 he made *Days of Glory* for RKO, a prestige film, but his later career was something of a disappointment, most of his work being in the 'B' film category. His later films included *Flame and the Arrow* (1950) with Burt Lancaster, the overrated *Curse of the Demon* (1958), and *Comedy of Terrors* (1963), an enjoyable spoof on horror films. He last worked in 1965, directing *War Gods of the Deep*, an inferior AIP production. He is now in retirement, though in an interview with Joel E. Siegel in 1969 he expressed the hope of making a film based on a supernatural story idea of his own. 'My only fun in life,' he said, 'is making films. Today is the day of the promoter. You have to find your own script and stars. I liked it better when the studio arranged these things.'[51]

DeWitt Bodeen was a reader in the RKO reading department when

Lewton, who was working as a story editor for Selznick at MGM, saw a play he had written on the Brontës. Selznick was planning to produce a film based on *Jane Eyre* and wanted the writer for it, Aldous Huxley, to have someone working with him as a research assistant. 'Val remembered me,' said Bodeen, 'and the fact that I had done what he thought was a good play on the Brontës. He found out where I was working at RKO and had Selznick borrow me. And then, when Val moved over to RKO as a producer, seeing as he and I got on very well together, he said he'd like me to write his first screenplay. At that time he had no idea what it was going to be. He said to me: "Maybe you won't want to work for me as I'm going to do horror stuff. I'm going to try and make it high-class horror but I don't know what luck I'll have." So I went over there to RKO and everything went well, on *Cat People* at least, because Val was very co-operative. The whole arrangement could have worked out fine because in the beginning Val was a marvellous producer, but then he attempted to do too much. He tried to move into every department, which was un-fortunate. Val was the only producer, in the American sense of the word, to whom the credit *producer* really applied. People give him credit for the whole thing and in a way they're right. It's just that it became impossible for Val to work with anybody, and he couldn't do it *all* by himself. It would have been marvellous if he had just stayed as producer and father to the whole project but he wanted his hands on everything. He became very difficult to work with, and very nervous, and a story session be-came a trial instead of the joy it once was. You had to be, eventually, a very patient person to work with him. And, of course, after he had a heart attack you had to be even more patient with him. He had it in mind that the front office was trying to kill him – and I think that Hollywood *really* did ruin him in the end.

'When *Cat People* was done I was getting only $75 a week, which was the minimum rate at RKO. And then Val said he thought they could afford to keep me on the payroll as dialogue director. He knew I had directed plays and so forth at Pasadena and was interested in direction. I was dialogue director all through *Cat People* and later on *The Curse of the Cat People*, so any changes in the dialogue that were necessitated on the set, *I* made. The next Lewton picture after *Cat People* I had nothing to do with because Val was staggering his productions at that time. It was *I Walked With a Zombie* and a very talented writer called Ardel Wray worked on that with Curt Siodmak. She was the daughter of John Wray, a director and actor, and her mother was an actress. She was the only girl whom Val ever employed. He had a thing about women writers. He just didn't like to work with women, one reason being that he liked the informality of working with men. But Ardel was marvellous, loads of fun and very talented. She worked on three or four of our pictures.

The bizarre walk through the cane fields – the highlight of I Walked With a Zombie

'There is a lot of Val in *The Seventh Victim* (1943) (the second of his films that I worked on) as it came out on the screen, because it's a reflection, really, of the happiest time of his life – when he was living in New York City and working on a newspaper and as a freelance writer. He was mad about Greenwich Village and a lot of the film takes place there. And it was his idea to change the whole outline of the story because the first draft that I had written was entirely different. It took place in an oil field in Southern California but while I was in New York researching *Curse of the Cat People* he wrote to me and said: "When you come back you're going right on to a new story for *The Seventh Victim* because we've discarded the story you originally wrote and I've already put Charles O'Neal on it and you'll be working with him." O'Neal was a writer working in Hollywood who later became the father of Ryan O'Neal. I had an inkling of what it was to be about because he also said in another letter to me: "See if it's possible for you to get to a devil-worshipping society meeting." So I got to one through RKO because they had a marvellous office there in New York. I went to them and said, is there any chance of me going to a devil-worshippers' meeting and they started laughing, but they called me back and said yes, it had been arranged. But I would have to go under a pseudonym. The society would be glad to have me but I wouldn't be able to say anything – just sit there and observe. And I must say that they were exactly like the devil-worshippers in *Rosemary's Baby*. It was even in the same neighbourhood on the West Side that they used in that film. It was during the war and I would have hated to be Hitler with all the spells they were working against him. They were mostly old people and they were casting these spells while they knitted and crocheted. A bunch of tea-drinking old ladies and gentlemen sitting there muttering imprecations against Hitler. I made use of the experience in that the devil-worshippers in *The Seventh Victim* were very ordinary people who had one basic flaw, an Achilles heel which has turned them against good and towards evil. This is the one thing that I got out of the meeting. Of all Val's pictures, that one is becomingly increasingly admired, and I think it would have been better if they had allowed it to be six or seven minutes longer. Certain things that should have been kept in the picture, and were shot, were edited out. And there are times, in my opinion, when the story that exists now, doesn't make sense. It was the front office who did that – interfering again. That was Mark Robson's first directorial job, he had been the editor for Val on *Cat People* and Val liked him very much and gave him this first directing chance.'

Robson was born in Montreal on 4 December 1913. He first studied law but decided on a career in the film industry instead. He got a job in RKO's film laboratory where he learned editing and later worked for Orson Welles's Mercury Group at RKO, but he was demoted to Lewton's unit after Welles fell into disfavour. Apart from *The Seventh Victim*, he directed *The Ghost Ship, Youth Runs Wild, Isle of the Dead* and *Bedlam* for Lewton. He was later fired from RKO by producer Dore Schary ('because I hadn't done any important films as far as he was concerned,' said Robson) and was out of work for two years before Stanley Kramer asked him to direct *The Champion* in 1948, Kirk Douglas's first big success. His later films include *Home of the Brave* (1949), *The Bridges at Toko-Ri* (1955), *Peyton Place* (1959), *Valley of the Dolls* (1967) and *Earthquake* (1974). Of his years with Lewton he said: 'We took those films very seriously. We worked long and hard on them and our standards were very, very high. My contribution to *Cat People* lay in editing techniques that were quite good. We developed a sharp cutting technique we later grew to call "the bus". We first used it in the *Cat People* when we cut from a close-up of the girl running along the street in terror to a bus coming to a stop with a loud hiss of air-brakes. The sharpness of the cutting would knock people out of their seats in a theatre. We tried to do it very often. The "bus" was done again in *Bedlam* with the hands shooting out of the cell. And we did it in *The Seventh Victim* when a frightened Jean Brooks crawls along the alley wall and suddenly there is the sound of someone laughing shrilly. I recall that after a horror sequence we always tried to give the audience relief by going to something very beautiful,

Julia Dean (left) in
Curse of the Cat People

lyrical if possible. We tried to make the films visually interesting. We didn't have anything else, you see.' (Lewton's films, made on small budgets, had to utilize existing sets at RKO.)

'*Curse of the Cat People*, the last of his films that I worked on,' continued Bodeen, 'was Val's conception entirely. When he was given the assignment to make the sequel to *Cat People* he groaned because he was told to call it *The Curse of the Cat People*. So he said: "What I'm going to do is make a very delicate story of a child who is on the verge of insanity because she lives in a fantasy world." I would say that my most important contribution to the story was the old lady, played by Julia Dean. Val was quite tenacious about nobody touching that character in the script because, he said, a little scornfully of me: "DeWitte likes old actresses." In a way I was responsible for Miss Dean getting the part because a number of character actresses were considered, but I suggested to the casting director that Val come and see Miss Dean at tea. There was an important sequence in the film concerning a tea party and I thought if Val could see the way she pours tea he would want her. And so Gunther von Fritsch [the director], Val and I went to tea with her and a few days later he came to me and said: "You'll be glad to know she's got the part." But the whole ending of the picture is not mine at all. Val, after the preview, thought that the ending did not come off. He came up to me on the lot one day and told me that he had a new ending for it and described it to me. I said I was not very moved by it and that I didn't see the ending that way. He said: 'Well, I'm not asking *you* to see it, *I'm* going to write the ending.' Which he did and that is the ending you see on the picture.

'We had another problem on that picture because the first director, Fritsch, was going too slowly and had to be replaced. A satisfactory explanation was made about his removal because he was going into the army anyway. Then the editor of that picture, Robert Wise, came on. It was Bob's first job as a director and he did a marvellous job. You can't tell what scenes he directed and what scenes Fritsch did.'

Wise, born in Indiana on 10 September 1914, started in the industry the same way that Robson did – carrying cans of film around RKO's film lab. Like Robson he became a film cutter, and by 1939 was a fully-fledged editor. He worked on *Citizen Kane* and also directed a few scenes in *The Magnificent Ambersons* while Welles was out of the country (the new scenes were shot on RKO's insistence and Welles wasn't exactly pleased when he saw the result). Again, as with Robson, his assignment to work with Lewton was a form of demotion by the studio. He directed three films for Lewton – *Curse of the Cat People, Mademoiselle Fifi* and *The Body Snatcher*, and stayed with RKO until 1949. His later successes include *The Day the Earth Stood Still* (1951), a superior science fiction film, *I Want to Live* (1958) with Susan Hayward, *West Side Story* (1961),

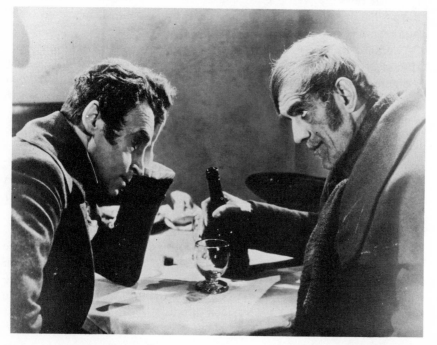

Henry Daniell and Boris Karloff in The Body Snatcher

The Haunting (1963) which was an effectively chilling ghost story in the Lewton style, and, of course, *The Sound of Music* (1963). He considers *The Body Snatcher* to be one of his favourites among the films he has made and said of Lewton: 'His philosophy, in addition to scaring the wits out of people, was that he had a responsibility to the millions who saw our pictures. He aimed at more than mere exploitable crook shows, and wanted their impact to result from legitimate psychological conflicts. Lewton's pictures were cheaply made, but not cheap.'[53]

'After *Curse*,' said Bodeen, 'Charles Koerner, who was still head of production at RKO, called me up on the phone one day and said, go see Herbert Wilcox. So I went and saw him and he was shopping for a writer for an espionage drama he was going to do with his wife, Anna Neagle, called *The Yellow Canary*. And so I read the story he had and gave him some of my ideas on it which he liked, so he put me on it. When I thanked Koerner for giving me, as it were, a promotion, he said: "Well, I think it's about time, after three box office hits, that you went up." I learned an awful lot about films working with Val and I would have liked to have had a longer and closer relationship in his unit but it did become impossible to work with him, and I was glad when I moved on.

'Tourneur got on famously with Val. They had worked together before at MGM when Val had been working for Selznick, before Selznick had formed his own company. They came together on *A Tale of Two Cities*, when they did the whole storming of the Bastille sequence. Jacques was the second unit director on the picture and Val assisted him. They had a great deal of mutual respect for each other. But Val had a falling out with Bob Wise and Mark Robson when they went into production together and after that they never really did anything together again, though Mark and Bob did. Val, more than anything else, wanted to move out of the horror film category but it was very difficult for him to do so, though he never had any objection when anyone else who had worked for him was able to move on. When Jacques moved out – Mr Koerner had promoted him to be the director of an 'A' budget film with Gregory Peck called *Days of Glory* (1944), the first important film that Peck did – Val was very pleased that a director from his unit had been promoted. He was delighted when I was promoted too – at least he said he was. He said: "They're taking away all my best people but you've earned it." And naturally he had earned it too. He had many fine ideas of what he wanted to do but the studio wouldn't give him permission. He was the first I know who wanted to make a film of *The African Queen*, and he did everything to try and persuade them to let him make it, but he failed.

'RKO was practically bankrupt because of Orson Welles when they brought Val in. Mr Koerner brought Val and several other people in to make pictures that he hoped would be box office successes, and *Cat*

People certainly was. The budget on it came to little over $134,000 and
it grossed $4,000,000. *Cat People* and another picture, not made by Val,
Hitler's Children, grossed so much money between them that they lifted
RKO out of the red and into the black for the first time.

'It was entirely Val's idea to make these horror films in a subtle way.
When I started working with him at RKO he said: ''Now there are two
kinds of horror films in my opinion. One is the monster type where they
shoot the works in the first reel and from then on it's all downhill. And
the other is a very carefully built up mood picture of terror where you
never see the monster the monster is all in the minds of the people.
They're all obsessed with fears and there are certain basic fears in everybody that can be dramatized.'' He didn't get much opposition from the
studio in the beginning really, because at first they let him alone. It was
only after *Cat People* was a big success that they began to interfere. Val
became rather paranoid later but he really did have opposition at the
studio, especially after Mr Koerner died suddenly of leukemia. The
people who came in then as heads of production were rather antagonistic
towards him. Val certainly *thought* they were. I remember after *Curse of
the Cat People* the front office thought Val had betrayed them because
they wanted more horror. It was put back into production in an attempt
to achieve more horror with retakes. The retakes were ridiculous but
they were used.

'There were certain people who had no regard for Val at all, but that
happens with everyone in a studio. You always have either one person
who is jealous of you or with whom you cannot work. This Val took,
being rather unsophisticated in this respect, as a personal attack. And
he did have a great problem working with women. I remember that
Phyllis Calvert, who was the leading lady on his picture at Paramount,
refused to talk to him. She didn't like him and there was a great lack of
empathy. I think his problem with women was caused by his mother who
was so terribly intelligent. She had gained some distinction as a writer
and was head of the foreign reading department at MGM, and she couldn't
understand why he was making what she thought were awful pictures.
She would never go to see them. And his aunt, Alla Nazimova, was a
very famous actress and she was rather scornful of his films as well. He
really had no one around him who was sympathetic, except for the men
he worked with, and Ardel Wray. He was married though, and had a
son and daughter. His wife, Ruth, was very charming but she was completely subjugated to him. Anything he wanted she did. He adored his
son but he had problems with his daughter and she made a very early
marriage, I think, to get away from him.

'He was a big man, sort of like a big Russian bear, and he hated
physical contact, he didn't even like to shake hands, but he was very

kind. When he had his first heart attack I was working with Harriet Parson's unit [Harriet was Louella Parson's daughter] on *The Enchanted Cottage*. Later I went to see him at his office, which they had moved to the ground floor so that he wouldn't have to climb any steps, and he was very sad looking. He grew worse and worse as time went by. His feeling of persecution increased, especially when he left RKO because, during everything else he did, at Paramount, at MGM and at Universal, he had the feeling that the studio was against him. He really began to be a psychological case and it was very sad – but in some respects his paranoia had a basis of truth.'

After the war Lewton told Bodeen that he believed that the popularity of his type of picture was over. It was his opinion that during the war audiences wanted to be frightened by something other than wholesale slaughter; they wanted danger to be particularized. With the war over they wanted more comedies and large-scale spectaculars. He tried once again to convince RKO to let him venture into new areas outside of horror, but the studio wasn't impressed by his plans and terminated his contract. In 1949 he made *My Own True Love* (Compton Bennett) for Paramount, which was a lightweight piece about a father and son in love with the same girl (Phyllis Calvert). In 1950 he made *Please Believe Me* (Norman Taurog) for MGM, with Deborah Kerr as a British girl who inherits a ranch. Neither film was particularly memorable. In 1951 he made his final film, an above-average Western called *Apache Drums* (Hugo Fregonese) for Universal. He died of a heart attack on 14 March 1951, aged forty-six.

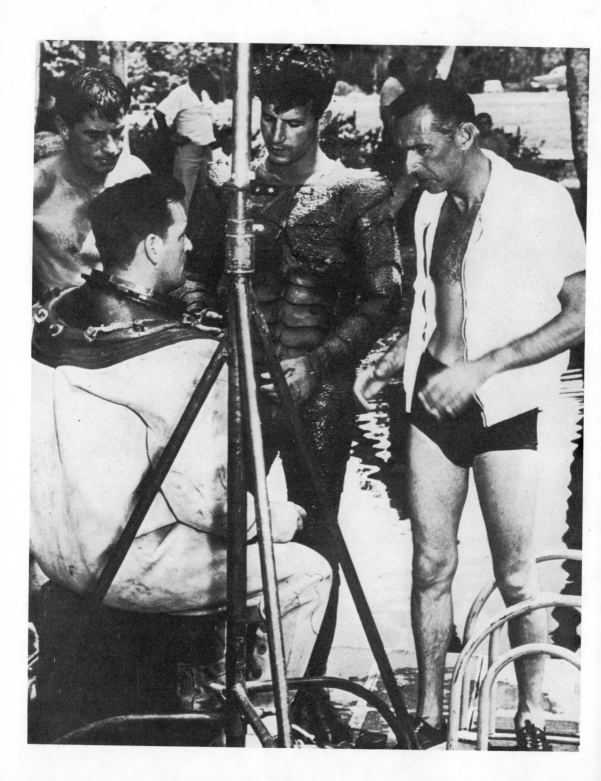

5   Jack Arnold

Despite the popularity in America of horror films based on the supernatural during the 1930s and 1940s there was still a tendency among
American audiences to prefer their horrific happenings to have some
sort of logical explanation. It didn't have to *be* logical, but merely to seem
logical; hence the existence of all those mad scientists among the vampires and werewolves. So when the science fiction movie boom began in
the 1950s it provided an ideal opportunity to release a whole new host of
monsters accompanied by plenty of pseudo-scientific trappings. The
sf/horror films of this period usually incorporated Cold War-induced
paranoia and fears about atomic weapons, with the result that the new
monsters either came from outer space (like *The Thing*) or were accidentally created by some misuse of atomic radiation (*Them!*).

The director most associated with this *genre* was Jack Arnold, but the
film that started it all was *The Thing*, released in 1951 and credited as
directed by Christian Nyby, though it was actually directed by Howard
Hawks (Nyby had been the editor on many of Hawks's pictures and as a
favour to him Hawks arranged for Nyby to get a directing credit), and is
full of Hawks's trademarks. It moves at a great pace, the cast mesh
together marvellously and the sharp, overlapping dialogue is delivered
with real expertise. 'We all kind of fell in love with his [Hawks's] style,'
said Kenneth Tobey, star of the picture, 'and, as it happens in dramas,
you get a camaraderie and essence of jollity and fun that comes across
very clearly. Of course we rehearsed a great deal on that picture. It takes
a lot of rehearsal to get that unrehearsed quality.'[54]

The 'Thing' itself was a humanoid vegetable (with a blood-lust) from
outer space that terrorizes an American military base in the Arctic. Played
by James Arness of Gunsmoke fame (apparently in a state of constant
embarrassment) it resembled a rather mediocre Frankenstein monster in
a track suit, but Hawks wisely kept if off-screen for most of the time,
except at the climax where the camera lingers upon it for far too long.
The creature's earlier appearances in the film had been masterful examples of cinematic shock techniques – in particular where Tobey and some
of his men open a door and come face to face with it. The build-up was
very clever – the preparations the men go through prior to opening the

Jack Arnold (right)
during the making of
The Creature from the
Black Lagoon

door lead one to expect that there will be nothing on the other side, as would be the case in most cinematic situations of this type, and so the shock of actually seeing the creature is doubly effective. According to Tobey, that scene was rehearsed privately. Those members of the crew not in on the secret received as big a shock when the door opened as did cinema audiences later when the picture was released. But the film as a whole is filled with an atmosphere of genuine suspense which at times builds to almost intolerable levels, proving that a good director can achieve memorable results with what might appear, at first glance, less than satisfactory material.

But Jack Arnold was the one director who consistently lifted this type of picture to new heights during the 1950s – and it was one of his creations, the Creature from the Black Lagoon, that has had the rare honour of being placed among the pantheon of classic monsters that includes Dracula and the Wolf Man. Most of Arnold's films managed to combine the blatant shock effects required in the horror films of that period with an atmosphere of unease worthy of Lewton. The first of these was *It Came from Outer Space* (1953), based on a story by Ray Bradbury. Set in the Californian desert, it concerned mysterious creatures from a crashed spaceship who could change their shape, enabling them to replace a number of the local inhabitants with their own kind. Many of the se-

An eerie moment from
It Came from Outer
Space

quences that take place in the desert are masterpieces of eeriness, and even the creatures themselves, when seen in their true forms, are bizarre enough, despite the limitations of the make-up department, to have a certain impact.

Creature from the Black Lagoon (1954) was a continuation of the high standards established in the previous film – the highpoint being a sequence where the girl (Julie Adams) goes for a swim in the lagoon and we see the creature looking up at her from below. Attracted by her graceful movements he doesn't reveal his presence (one presumes it is a 'he'), except briefly to touch her legs at the end of her swim. Before the relationship has time to develop further she is ordered from the water by one of the men on the boat (Richard Carlson). It is only when she is back on the boat that the water is suddenly churned up with great violence, revealing that something unbelievably powerful is lurking below the surface.

Revenge of the Creature followed in 1955 (with the Creature captured and taken to Marineland in Florida) and in the same year Arnold made one of that giant-monster-on-the-loose-and-stepping-on-buildings type of film which was so popular at the time, but his contribution to the *genre* was a cut above the others. *Tarantula* (1956), again set in the desert, relied on an atmosphere of menace as much as it did on the giant spider seen scuttling over hills (a disturbing enough image in itself). A spider also featured in what many people consider to be Arnold's masterpiece – *The Incredible Shrinking Man* (1957). Based on a novel by Richard Matheson (who also wrote the screenplay), it concerned the fate of Scott Carey (Grant Williams) who, due to the inevitable dose of atomic radiation that caused so many problems in the sci-fi films of the 1950s, found himself growing smaller and smaller until his familiar world took on nightmarish dimensions. At the end of the picture he faded away from sight completely, which was quite unusual (in more ways than one) as most films of that type and that era would have had the antidote to his condition being found at the last moment.

'My career in films started because I was an actor,' said Arnold. 'I was mainly a stage actor though I did act in films in England when I was there in 1937. I appeared in a couple of Edgar Wallace films and I stage-managed and also appeared in *Three Men on a Horse* in the West End. I was about eighteen years old at the time. When I came back from England I appeared in a number of plays on Broadway. I was working in *My Sister Eileen* when Pearl Harbor happened and I immediately enlisted in the Air Corps. Since I had done some private flying I thought that was where I could best serve. I gave my notice to the theatre, thinking I would be called right away, but a month went by and I still hadn't heard from anybody. I was out of work but as they'd given me a hero's farewell at the theatre I was a little embarrassed to show my face around Broadway. I went down to the Army Centre – the Air Corps was part of the army at that time – and told them my plight, but they said they couldn't help me as the flight schools just weren't organized yet. So one bleak day, when I was walking down Broadway not knowing what to do with myself, I bumped into a friend of mine and I complained bitterly about the damn army not calling me and he said, I've seen the films you make so why don't you go to Astoria, which was then a studio owned by Paramount that the Army Signal Corps had taken over. They were going to make training films of all kinds and were hiring civilian personnel. I had this hobby when I was a young actor of making films. I had built a blimp to quiet this old model 16mm Kodak camera, and in between jobs I would go to the theatre and surreptitiously photograph the actors in whatever play they were in at the time. Over a period of three performances I would cover long shots, go up into the boxes and get angle shots, put a telephoto lens on and get close-ups and then I would splice the reels together. I would screen the result for the actor concerned and there wasn't one alive who could resist buying a record of himself acting. I charged them a hell of a lot more than it cost me so it was quite a lucrative hobby of mine. But as I said to my friend, I didn't know anything about filming except for my 16mm stuff. So he said, come and meet a friend of mine, and he took me to a camera equipment company and introduced me to the son of the man who owned it. And he showed me how to set up a Mitchell camera, how to thread it and how to use the lenses. So I went over to the Astoria, and I was just full of piss and vinegar and nothing daunted me, and I told them I was a cameraman. They said, alright, there's a Mitchell. Put it up and thread it. Of course I'd just finished practising it so I did it quick flash! So they gave me a civil service rating as a cameraman – not an assistant cameraman, but a *cameraman*! I told them that I was waiting to be called-up; but they were so desperate for person-nel they gave me a civil service rating anyway.

'As luck would have it they sent me to join a unit that was making a film produced and directed by Robert Flaherty. Now Flaherty was a kind of idol of mine so I decided to tell him the truth. I went up to this giant of an Irishman and I said, look, I've got something to tell you – I'm an actor, not a cameraman. But I told him that I thought I would be able to handle the job. And I guessed he liked the fact that I had told him the truth instead of trying to fake my way through it and he kept me on. I had a crash course in cinematography under Flaherty; it was something I couldn't have bought anyplace. He liked me and we became fast friends. I was like a blotter, absorbing anything I could learn from him. I became so engrossed in film making Flaherty tried to get me transferred out of the Air Training Command that I was technically in, but they wouldn't release *anybody* because we were so short of pilots at the time. So I reluctantly left Flaherty's unit and went into the Air Corps where I eventually became a pilot. Strangely enough I found myself back in England in a D17 squadron.

'After I got out of the Air Force I went back into the theatre. Then I met a buddy of mine who had been in my squadron. He had been a professional gambler and had won a lot of money during the war so he came back-stage one day and said, let's go into business together. So we started a documentary film company. We made a number of documentaries over the years – for the State Department, the Ford Motor Company and so on, and we won some prizes. Then I made a film for the International Ladies Garment Workers Union called *These Hands*. It was a feature spanning fifty years of the union which was good enough to be released theatrically, and it got very good reviews. I was even nominated for an Academy Award which brought me to the attention of Hollywood. Universal gave me a contract with them as a director and I started working for them in 1950.

'The first film I directed for them was *Girls in the Night*. Originally it was called *Night Flowers*, but they gave it that exploitation title which I didn't like. It cheapened the picture, I thought. It was a pretty good film about the slums of New York and the kids who live in them. It did fairly well and then they started giving me Westerns to do. I spent over seven years at Universal doing every conceivable kind of film. It was in that period that I started making the science fiction films. *It Came from Outer Space* started because Universal had bought a story by Ray Bradbury with that name. They thought it could be successfully adapted to make a 3D picture. 3D had just come out and Warner Brothers had released a picture called *The House of Wax*, which was a hurriedly put together thing, in order to throw objects at people in 3D. So Universal assigned it to me and it was quite successful.

'So from there on I made all their science fiction films, and the more I did of these films the more I liked it because the studio left me alone. No one at that time was an expert at making sf films so I *claimed* to be one. I wasn't, of course, but the studio didn't know that so they never argued with me, no matter what I did. In most of my sf films I tried to create an atmosphere because I think if you shoot an imaginative film – a film in which you ask an audience to believe things that are bizarre – you have to *make them believe* it. You can't do this with the story or actors alone, you have to create a kind of atmosphere while shooting it in which the audience's credibility will be suspended to the point where they don't say to themselves: "That's impossible!" And I think the only way you can get an audience to accept the impossible is to get them involved in an atmosphere – a mood, or what the kids today call vibes, a *feeling* of what you're trying to do. That's why I make a lot of use of actual physical locations: I make them work for my story. That's why I like to shoot in the desert, or on the ocean or beaches, locations that will help me to create an atmosphere.

'Most of *It Came from Outer Space* was shot out on the desert; only the interiors were shot in the studio, and also the scenes in the little town which was on the Universal back lot. Everything else was shot out on the desert. The space ship was, of course, a model. We built a full-scale section of it and a crew went out in the desert and dug a big crater for it. Then we matched shots of it with miniatures for scenes of the actual space ship. *Tarantula* was shot in the same area about ten or fifteen miles to the north of Hollywood. Actually it was a place called Dead Man's Curve where there was an outcropping of rocks that I particularly wanted to use. I would just go into the desert and look for something that looked eerie and if it gave me the shivers I would say, right – we'll shoot here. We controlled the spider with air jets. What we did was match the rocks in the studio to the actual rocks out there in the desert, then shoot them in perspective. We'd push the spider about with the air jets until I got the shot I wanted. I would want, say, a leg to appear over the top of the hill first, then the mandibles and so on. Usually after about ten attempts we got the shot I wanted. We'd shoot the spider against a black background then superimpose it into the scenes with the live actors.

'The Creature from the Black Lagoon was a composite creation. Bill Alland, a producer no longer in the business, was assigned to produce these films and he found this story by Maurice Zimm and he called me in on it and we worked together, with a writer as well, and we evolved the story. Then we sold the studio on the idea of making it. We had a lot of fun trying to create the creature, trying to decide what he should look like. We made a lot of tests before we decided on what appeared in the film, and it turned out very good.

'We shot the underwater scenes at Silver Springs in Florida. Very clear water there. I thought there was a mystery and romance to the underwater scenes and also a sense of terror. I think we succeeded in capturing that feeling in *The Creature*. Those scenes with the girl swimming on the surface and the monster looking up at her from below played upon a basic fear that people have about what might be lurking below the surface of any body of water.* You know the feeling when you are swimming and something brushes your legs down below – it scares the hell out of you if you don't know what it is. It's the fear of the unknown. So I decided to exploit this fear as much as possible in filming *Creature from the Black Lagoon*. But I also wanted to create sympathy for the creature – or my little beastie as we called it.

---

* The success of *Jaws* – voted best horror film of 1975 by *Films and Filming* – was based on the same fear.

Finders, keepers – the Creature and the object of his unrequited love, Julie Adams

'I'd gone to Florida to find an underwater swimmer and we found a boy, who was swimming in a show, who could hold his breath for five minutes at a time. He was such a good underwater swimmer that he didn't use air tanks at all during the filming. What we had was an air hose off-scene and when he felt he needed air he would swim over to it, take a deep breath then swim back to the scene. That way he could stay underwater for ages. We couldn't build air tanks into the costume because you would have seen the bubbles. But he was sensational. His name was Ricou Browning. He became a director later on and I believe he's directing a TV series down in Florida now.

'In the second film [*Revenge of the Creature*] we filmed him in a fish tank in Florida. The first one had done very well at the box office so the studio wanted a sequel. We dreamed up a story about the Gill-Man being captured and put in an oceanarium in Florida. When I went down to scout

A scene from the sequel to The Creature from the Black Lagoon – Revenge of the Creature

locations the oceanarium people showed me this tremendous tank full of sharks, barracuda, moray eels, even an octopus. They were fed by divers going into the tank and feeding them by hand. I looked into the tank and said, could you guys possibly screen off half the tank with a net and then take out the most dangerous fish so that I can shoot the creature inside it. I told them I not only had to get the creature in there, but also my leading man and lady. I said if they took one look at those sharks in there I would never get them in. So they assured me that they would but when I returned with the company and we got ready to shoot I saw there was no net. Where's the net, I asked. And they said, you don't need a net – those fish won't bother your actors, they're too well-fed.

'So I was in a fix. How was I going to get my actors to go in there? Now I had this crazy cameraman on that picture – he was *nuts* [Charles S. Welbourne]. He said to me that *I'd* better go into the tank with him to demonstrate to the actors that it was safe. He talked me into it so I put on a mask and air tanks and jumped in. I closed my eyes at first. After a while I opened one eye and there was a damn shark, at least twelve feet long, his mouth open and *looking* at me. And he was only about a yard away. I didn't know what to do. I didn't know whether to make any movement or to stay absolutely still; so I just shut my eyes again. It seemed the best thing to do. Then he brushed by me and I felt his skin, it was just like sandpaper – but he just swam away and ignored me. So I shot to the surface and said, come on in – nothing to it! But the amazing thing is that by the third day, after all our initial reluctance to go into the tank, all of us were so used to the sharks that we were actually kicking them out of the way. The only animal that gave us any trouble was a turtle. It developed a liking for the Gill-Man's costume and kept biting chunks out of it. Finally we had to assign a grip to stay underwater with the sole job of making sure the turtle didn't bother our monster.

'*The Incredible Shrinking Man* is definitely my favourite film among my sf ones. It was the most challenging because it hadn't been done before. They had done a film similar only in the sense that the people were small, that was *Dr Cyclops*, but they stayed one size. Neither did that picture have the atmosphere I thought the situation required – the situation of being so small that the commonplace suddenly becomes bizarre and threatening. In *The Shrinking Man* an ordinary cellar becomes a hell of a place filled with monsters. I wanted to make the audience realize that their *own* cellars were potential hells – that the familiar could become horrible if the circumstances were changed.

'Much of that film was very difficult to make. The only insurance a director has in that situation is to have good actors. When I cast these sf films I tried to get actors who were intelligent, had imagination and were good at their craft. So that if I told them the story and what was supposed to be happening at a given time they were able to reconstruct it themselves. Grant Williams gave a tremendous performance in *The Shrinking Man*. In the scene where he impales the spider after enticing him down from his web I shot the spider first. It's very hard to direct a spider. I used jets of air as I had done previously with *Tarantula*. I would prod him in the direction I wanted him to move with spurts of air. We flew in sixty Panamanian tarantulas because the domestic ones were too small and we couldn't keep a sharp focus on them. We had to get the biggest ones available and they turned out to be in Panama. They were tremendous beasts – six inches in diameter! We used so many of them during the filming because we had to light to such a high intensity they cooked.

'After the scenes with the spider had been shot we built, in Universal's largest sound stage, full-size replicas of part of the wall, the ledge, spider web, pair of scissors, ball of twine etc – all at a size that would make Grant look an inch tall in comparison. Then I would run the film of the spider and cut it the way I wanted. Then with a metronome I counted out beats for the time the spider's actions took. The sound stage was blacked out except for the over-size sets, so I would set up my camera with a piece of negative of the shot of the spider placed in the camera's ground glass and then match up the sets with the scene on the negative – overlaying the two images until they became one. The camera had to be about two hundred and fifty feet away from Grant and the sets so that he would look small. Then I would rehearse Grant in what he had to do. With my

The star of Tarantula *poses for a publicity shot*

The Tarantula in action, thanks to the skills of special effects expert Clifford Stine

count on the metronome we would time it all – at every count Grant would have a different action to perform. He would go up and shake the web – that would last maybe for eight counts, then on nine counts the spider started down; on fourteen counts the spider was down; on eighteen he was coming closer; on nineteen something else had happened and so on. All of it had to match in exactly with the footage of the spider. Grant did it all by numbers, having to imagine what was happening at each point. Then when we had two pieces of film we just married them together into a single piece and there it was. You would swear that Grant and the spider were together on the ledge.

'There was no jiggling at all with our matting technique. Cliff Stine and his effects team worked it all out mathematically. Cliff was a genius. The blue screen process [an automatic travelling matte technique] wasn't in use when we made *The Shrinking Man*. We used a combination of making our own mattes and rear projection. Anyway, blue screen work always looks a bit phoney to me – if you're not careful you often have a green line around people. It's very tricky to do properly.

'Cliff Stine was originally my cameraman but he was made head of the Universal special effects department. He was very knowledgeable and a very good cameraman. We worked very well together. [Stine was brought out of retirement to work on *Earthquake*.] We had a lot of crazy problems to work out while making those films. For instance, in *The Shrinking Man*, apart from the problems of shrinking him down to less than an inch and getting him down into the cellar, we had the problem of making drops of water look large. The drops were supposed to be coming from a leaking hot water unit. Grant was living in a matchbox underneath it. Everything had to be built in proportion on the set to make him look one inch tall but the problem was to make the drops of water look huge in comparison to him. We tried everything. We got up on the top of the sound stage and rigged a device that released water a small amount at a time, but the water would spread out on the way down and look useless. Then I remembered a little bit about my ill-spent youth when as a kid I found a box of contraceptives. I didn't know what they were at the time but I discovered that they made dandy bombs when you filled them with water. I used to drop them on top of people from windows and I remembered that they used to hold a tear-shaped form on their way down. So I got hold of one at the studio – I asked my crew if any of them had one in his pocket. After much cajoling, I said I wasn't kidding and that one of you guys must have one. One of them did, so I said let's fill it up with water, go up there and drop it. It turned out to be the perfect proportion and splattered just like a large drop of water when it hit the floor. So I ordered a hundred gross of the things and we rigged up a treadmill that dropped them at an increasing rate until we opened the gates of the tank and released tons of water on top of Grant for the big flood scene. But the really amusing part came at the end of the picture – the production office called me in to go over the facts and figures of the costs. They told me there was one item that they didn't understand. I asked what it was and they said it was this order for a hundred gross of contraceptives. I said, fellows, it was such a hard picture and we all worked so hard we decided to have a big party at the end of it.

'Grant Williams never did catch on with the public. His looks weren't in vogue in the 1950s. Grant was blonde and blue-eyed, kind of too pretty to be a character actor, but not quite the picture book Rock Hudson or Robert Taylor type that Hollywood wanted at the time. He was short-changed, he never got the right parts. In our films, the science fiction ones, the pictures themselves were the stars, and the special effects, but not the actors. Yet in *The Incredible Shrinking Man* almost three-quarters of the film was silent and it required real acting from Grant. It wasn't just a case of reciting banal dialogue as happened in so many sf films. Grant had to act; and I thought he gave an outstanding performance, but it didn't help his career. Universal didn't put him into an "A" picture as they should have done, they just put him into more "B" pictures. That's happened to us all in this business at one time or another – directors, actors or writers. Lady Luck sometimes sits on your shoulders but other times she's busy elsewhere.

'Actually, though my sf pictures were technically "B" ones, they had relatively large budgets for those days. We spent about seven to eight hundred thousand dollars which was a lot of money for a film in the 1950s. That's what made the difference between our science fiction films and many that followed – such as the ones that American International Pictures made, and the Japanese ones. They just went out to exploit the market without trying to do anything imaginative. But our budgets were fairly good. It wasn't a budget that they would have given to, say, a Lana Turner picture, but it was above average for a "B" picture.

'I never regarded my films as horror films. I would call that film that Warhol made, *Frankenstein*, a horror film. I haven't seen it and I have no wish to see it. I don't relish seeing the guts and innards of someone thrown at me from the screen in 3D. The same applies to *The Exorcist*, which I did see. I thought it was a great special effects film but I hated it. I was offended by the vulgarity and the pornographic quality of it. I found myself saying as a director: "*I* couldn't do that." I couldn't make a fourteen-year-old girl go through the bestial things Linda Blair did. I know they used doubles for some of the worst parts but making a kid say the words she did – no. But I thought Mercedes McCambridge did a sensational job on the voice of the devil and, as I said, the special effects were great. They should have got the Academy Award for the special effects. [No award was given in the effects category in 1974.]

'It was purely an exploitation picture. A film designed to scare, and in that respect it was a hell of a good film, because it certainly succeeded in scaring audiences out of their wits. But it only succeeded in disgusting me and making me feel ill. I think I also expected something more. Blatty and Friedkin got too pretentious with it – they began to think they were making the film of the century and it's hardly that. But that's only my opinion. I'm sure you will find many who will say it's a great film, but for me it was curiously lacking in atmosphere. The child, when she was possessed, was certainly chilling and realistic; but they went out of their way to shock you, instead of creating a horrific atmosphere, which would have been much more effective. And there was no build up to the horror. They hit you right away with it. You should lead an audience up to it slowly so that the horrors begin to compound one another. But with *The Exorcist* they didn't have anywhere else to go, after the scene where she came down and pissed on the floor, except to have her vomit on someone. As a film maker that's my objection to it. I didn't think it was in the same class, for instance, as *A Clockwork Orange*. Now *that* is my idea of a great film. I think the cinema craft of Kubrick is far superior to that of Friedkin's.'

Arnold is still active in the film industry though he hasn't made any science fiction/horror pictures since the 1950s. He later became involved in TV production but has now returned to film making. 'I was the Executive Producer on the *It Takes a Thief* series with Robert Wagner. Now I've formed my own company to make films. I'm tired of doing TV now, too much hard work for too little artistic satisfaction. The money is good but it's like working in a sausage factory. With my own company I've got the financial backing to make three films and I'd like one of them to be science fiction. I want stories that I can create an atmosphere with, but so many sf stories are like technical manuals. I've been trying to get Richard Matheson to write one for me again – he's a beautiful writer. We might get together and see if we can dream up a suitable story. But that's in the future; if my health lasts that long, or *I* last that long. I've got a lot of plans, I just hope I've got enough time to fulfil them.'

6 Hammer

In July 1953 the BBC began a six-part television serial called *The Quatermass Experiment*. A mixture of horror and science fiction, it was about an astronaut who returns from space infected by a mysterious spore that proceeds to take over his body. He is finally transformed into an unrecognizable 'thing' that retreats into Westminster Abbey where it is destroyed by Professor Quatermass, the scientist responsible for the space project. Written by Nigel Kneale, an actor-turned-writer (he later wrote the screenplays for John Osborne's *Look Back in Anger* and *The Entertainer*), the serial was enormously popular with the British public and the following year it was made into a film by a small company called Hammer Films Ltd. Released as *The Creeping Unknown* outside of Britain, the film proved to be as popular as the serial. Even the critics liked it. 'This is the best and nastiest horror film that I have seen since the war,' said Paul Dehn, writing for the *News Chronicle*. 'Exciting but distinctly nauseating,' said the *Sunday Times*. 'The monster proves more acceptably alarming than most "things" in science fiction and in his more human stages Richard Wordsworth's tortured grimace and menacing make-up suggest a pathetic as well as a horrific figure,' said the *Monthly Film Bulletin*. The *New Statesman* said: 'The film does in fact touch the imagination. Its hero, gripped by fantastic horror, hints at tragedy. What we witness in a number of scenes is much extended by what we don't quite see. The doomed hero is frighteningly played by Richard Wordsworth. Val Guest directed and Anthony Hinds produced. None of these, if I may put it so, are classed among our swells, but they have done their job well, and the result seems to be a better film than either *War of the Worlds* or *Them*.'

The film remains a truly horrific one, even today when certain segments have become dated. Richard Landau and Val Guest, who wrote the screenplay, succeeded in retaining the unique qualities of Kneale's original script (Kneale is definitely one of Britain's top talents when it comes to the writing of bizarre horror), but much of the success of the film should be credited to Richard Wordsworth who gave a performance equal to that of Karloff's as the Frankenstein Monster in the way that he combined, as the reviewers noted, the horror with elements of tragedy. In several scenes he managed to convey, with the aid of Phil Leakey's subtle make-up, a real sense of being something utterly alien to human experience. Wordsworth also succeeded in communicating the unbearable loneliness of the character – a once-intelligent man who was still vaguely aware of the terrible thing that was happening to him but helpless to prevent it. This was best illustrated when the creature, attempting to hide in a deserted canal boat, encountered a little girl in a scene reminiscent of the one in *Frankenstein*. Already partially transformed, for his arm had absorbed a cactus plant and changed into a shapeless lump, there still remained enough of the man within the monster to save the girl from himself by frightening her away before he lost control. In a way, it is true to say that *The Quatermass Experiment* was Hammer's first remake of *Frankenstein*, and perhaps its best.

'That film has been with me ever since,' said Wordsworth in an interview with the *Radio Times* in 1972. 'The cactus bit was great fun. My face was covered with rubber solution and I had spikes growing out of my arm. Jane Asher playing the little girl the monster meets. I had to lurch at her and knock the head off her doll. As soon as the scene was finished there she was crying. Naturally I knelt down to say, "There, there," and everybody started yelling at me, "Get back, you fool!" Of course I was terrifying her. I'd quite forgotten what I looked like.

'My part in the film had been over about twenty minutes when the monster attacks Westminster Abbey. In that sequence the monster has become a great round blob of rubber solution draped over everything. A landlady up north said to me, "Mr Wordsworth, you were so good. And in the Abbey scene – your make-up! It was marvellous!"'

The success of *The Quatermass Experiment* had a great effect on Hammer Films Ltd which up to then had been a small, relatively undistinguished company. Very much a family business, its origins went all the way back to 1913 when a man called Enrique Carreras sold his interest in the cigarette firm founded by his grandfather. With the money he built a cinema at Hammersmith called The Blue Hall. Its success led him into building a whole chain of similar cinemas across England, and in 1935 he formed a distribution company in partnership with Will Hammer (real name Will Hinds), a former variety performer. It was called Exclusive Films. In 1939 they were joined by Enrique's son James, after he had had an apprenticeship of several years managing a cinema in Manchester. Four years later James's own son, Michael, joined the company at the tender age of fourteen. To make it even more of a family affair, Will Hammer's son, Anthony Hinds, also became involved in the company.

Exclusive Films made a few low-budget pictures near the end of the Second World War (mainly screen versions of the radio series starring popular secret agent Dick Barton) but it wasn't until 1948 that they changed their name to Hammer Films and went into full-time production.

Michael Carreras – the present head of Hammer Films

By that time James Carreras was in overall charge, Anthony Hinds was producer and Michael Carreras his assistant. Their first film was *Dr Morelle – The Case of the Missing Heiress*, which was directed by Godfrey Grayson. Hammer's output was prolific during the following six years and though the quality of the films may have left much to be desired (many were low-budget adaptations of popular radio series, such as *Life with the Lyons*), the company proved quite successful. This was due mainly to an arrangement they had made in 1951 with an American company, Robert Lippert Productions, to co-produce films, which ensured that Hammer's films received an American distribution. (Hammer was the first British company to enter into such a co-production deal). In 1954, however, the arrangement came to an end when the Americans decided it was no longer worth their while to continue it and Hammer's future looked bleak – until *The Quatermass Experiment*. After the period of inactivity which had occurred during their financial crisis the Hammer team was confident enough to resume production. Two more horror/ science fiction films quickly followed: *X – The Unknown* and *Quatermass II* (released as *Enemy from Space* outside of Britain); and though reasonably successful it wasn't until they made *The Curse of Frankenstein* in 1957 that Hammer really hit the jackpot.

'We found that the "thing" that looked like an oil bubble in *X – The Unknown* frightened nobody,' said James Carreras. 'They are only really terrified by something they are likely to meet in the dark on their way

home from the cinema.'[55] Michael Carreras said : '*The Curse of Frankenstein*
was an extraordinary moment in history and I suppose it stemmed from
the first Quatermass film – remember how the monster in that, even when
it was in Westminster Abbey, had a kind of humanity so that you could
identify with it. That suggested to us the Frankenstein monster idea and
it worked. But the picture wasn't sponsored by a distributor. In fact we
went to New York – my father, Tony Hinds and myself, with it still
unsold. Then we showed it to Warner Brothers, they leaped in the air
and that's how it all started.'

Baron Frankenstein was played by Peter Cushing and the monster by
the then unknown Christopher Lee. 'There was no conscious policy of
creating a Hammer team of actors,' said Carreras. 'It just happened.
Cushing at that time was a big catch for us because he had just won the
Best Television Actor of the Year Award. Christopher Lee just happened
to be six foot four inches tall.' The picture bore little resemblance to any
of the Universal versions, and neither did the characters. Unlike Colin
Clive's neurotic, guilt-ridden Frankenstein, Peter Cushing's was a man
who was cold and ruthless, and who would stop at nothing to achieve
what he wanted. He was in no apparent moral dilemma over his un-
savoury attempts to create life out of stolen corpses – that side of it was
left to his unwilling assistant. And Christopher Lee's Monster was very
different from Karloff's. Lee's was much more corpse-like, though the
overall impression wasn't as memorable as the Karloff version. The
'new look' make-up was partly to avoid copyright problems with Universal but also arose from a genuine desire on Hammer's part to avoid the
cliché that the Frankenstein Monster had become. 'We refused to have
anything mechanical,' said director Terence Fisher. 'Our monster, with
his do-it-yourself stitches, is very different from Karloff's nuts and bolts.
We wanted the monster to fit Chris Lee's melancholy personality. We
wanted a thing which looked like some wandering, forlorn minstrel of
monstrosity, a thing of shreds and patches, but in flesh and blood and
organs.'[56]

The Curse of Frankenstein broke all records when it opened in London
on 2 May 1957, and was soon playing in two West End cinemas. Its
success was mirrored in America and before long Hammer were able to
announce that they had made an arrangement with Columbia to make
three pictures a year. Since then Hammer have never looked back. Not
that *Frankenstein* was unleashed upon the British public without a certain amount of opposition. Most of the critics weren't impressed and
many, such as C. A. Lejeune of the *Observer* (who wrote: 'I put it among
the half-dozen most repulsive films I have ever encountered') were very
much against Hammer's new product, and provided the company with
the dubious reputation it still manages to retain. (In America there was

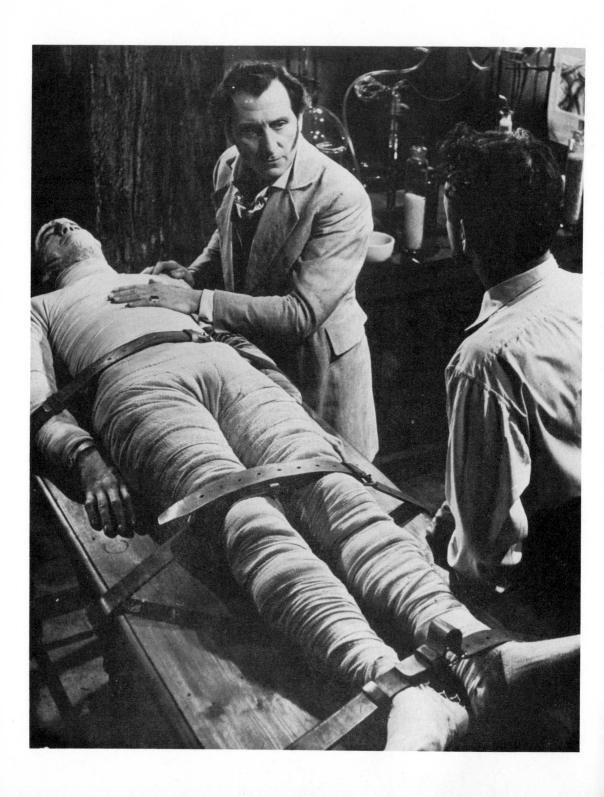

A scene from The Curse of Frankenstein – *the film that had a profound effect on the Hammer company. Peter Cushing as Baron Frankenstein (centre) with Christopher Lee, in bandages, as the Creature*

little adverse comment.)

Of the five pictures that Hammer made in 1957, three were of the horror variety – *The Abominable Snowman* (Val Guest), *The Revenge of Frankenstein* and *Dracula* (both directed by Terence Fisher). It was the latter, released in May 1958, that was to prove to be almost as important for Hammer as *Frankenstein*. As big a box office success, it provoked an even more hostile reception from many critics. 'I went to see *Dracula* prepared to enjoy a nervous giggle,' wrote Nina Hibbins for the *Daily Worker*. 'I was even prepared to poke gentle fun at it. I came away revolted and outraged. From the moment that Dracula appears, eyes bloodshot, fangs dripping with blood, until his final disintegration into a crumbling, putrescent pile of human dust, this film disgusts the mind and repels the senses. Dracula is no legendary, half-man, half-bat as Bela Lugosi was in the original version – he is a handsome, sinister human being in a long black cloak with a sexual lust for the blood of the beautiful women who are his victims.' Hammer's friend at the *Observer*, C. A. Lejeune (it's interesting to note that both the film's harshest critics were women) wrote: 'I regret to hear that it is being shown in America with emphasis laid on its British origins and feel inclined to apologize to all decent Americans for sending them a work in such sickening bad taste.' Needless to say, many Americans welcomed the film with open arms and showed their appreciation at the box office. And the adverse comments

'Dracula is no legendary half-man, half-bat as Bela Lugosi was in the original version – he is a handsome, sinister human being in a long, black cloak with a sexual lust for the blood of the beautiful women who are his victims.' So wrote a shocked female critic after seeing Christopher Lee in Hammer's Dracula

that the film received didn't bother the Hammer executives. On the contrary, they appreciated them. 'In general,' said Michael Carreras, 'those sort of criticisms are highly exploitable.'

Like its *Frankenstein*, Hammer's *Dracula* was very different from Universal's version in 1930 and Christopher Lee bore no resemblance to Bela Lugosi in his portrayal of the character. Lee played him alternately as an icy, aloof aristocrat and a ferocious animal, the latter aspect of Dracula's character being even more disturbing, set, as it was, amongst staid, Victorian surroundings and people. 'Within the bleakness of this world,' wrote a critic later, 'a more athletic, more bestial Dracula cleans up like a fox loose in a chicken coop.'[57] And, as Miss Hibbins noted, Lee's Dracula was a highly sexual creation. There had always been strong sexual undercurrents in the previous Dracula films, as there is within most vampire myths, but Hammer's version definitely brought it nearer to the surface.

Michael Carreras agrees: 'The greatest difference between our Dracula and anybody else's was the sexual connotations. There was no real horror in it, the women were eager to be nipped by Dracula and I think that gave it a fresh look. The other thing, of course, that worked for us was that they were the first Gothic horror films to be in colour. It gave them a new dimension.' It also allowed the blood to be shown in bright red, a colour now associated with the name of Hammer. *Dracula* itself began with a sudden splatter of blood as the credits finished rolling. 'There was only one thing that really disturbed me at that time,' said Carreras. '*Dracula* was such a success when it opened at the Warner theatre in Leicester Square that they covered it on television. They had a camera outside the cinema and they interviewed people who came out. And there was this one very weird gentleman who said something quite frightening – that he loved to see the "blood spurt". He said it with such feeling that one felt for a moment – "Oh Christ." But I've always felt quite honestly that the horror that titillates your adrenalin is something you really do leave behind when you go out in the fresh air, because it's so unreal. It's taking you on a little trip, if you like. I think things like *Straw Dogs* and films of that *genre* are much more frightening and harmful than anything we've ever made. You're not liable to be bitten in the neck by a vampire on your way home, but you are quite likely to be kicked by a thug in a leather jacket.'

Hammer followed *Dracula* by running through the whole gamut of classic horror themes – *The Mummy* (Terence Fisher) and *The Two Faces of Dr Jekyll* (Fisher) in 1959, *The Curse of the Werewolf* (Fisher) in 1960, *The Phantom of the Opera* (Fisher) in 1961, *The Gorgon* (Fisher) in 1963 and *Plague of the Zombies* (John Gilling) in 1965. Interspersed with these were other films of varying types – costume dramas such as *The Pirates of*

Herbert Lom as Erik in
Hammer's remake of
The Phantom of the
Opera

Blood River (John Gilling, 1971), contemporary melodramas such as *Hell is a City* (Val Guest, 1959), war films – *The Camp on Blood Island* (Val Guest, 1957), *Yesterday's Enemy* (Val Guest, 1959), and comedies – *Weekend with Lulu* (John Paddy Carstairs, 1960). There was also a cycle of films inspired by Hitchcock's *Psycho*, which began in 1960 with *Taste of Fear* (Seth Holt) and followed up with *Maniac* (Michael Carreras, 1962), *Paranoiac* (Freddie Francis, 1962), *Hysteria* (Freddie Francis, 1964), *Fanatic* (Silvio Narizzano, 1964) and *Crescendo* (Alan Gibson, 1969).

Yet another cycle of Hammer films was the Stone Age one which began with a remake of *One Million Years BC* (Don Chaffey) in 1965 (an expensive production to celebrate their 100th film), followed by *When Dinosaurs Ruled the Earth* (Val Guest, 1969) and *Creatures the World Forgot* (Don Chaffey, 1970).

David Prowse as a less-than-impressive product of Frankenstein's laboratory (from The Horror of Frankenstein)

Sequels to their most popular Gothic films have been numerous. There have been six Frankenstein films since *Curse of Frankenstein*, five of which have starred Peter Cushing as the Baron; the one exception was *The Horror of Frankenstein* (Jimmy Sangster 1970), a remake of *Curse* which starred Ralph Bates as a younger version of Frankenstein. To date (the end of 1974) there have been seven Dracula sequels made, six of which have starred Christopher Lee (the exception, *The Brides of Dracula* (Fisher) in 1960), the last being *The Satanic Rites of Dracula* (Alan Gibson 1973).

There have also been several other Hammer films based on the vampire theme, such as *Kiss of the Vampire* (Don Sharp, 1962), *The Vampire Lovers* (Roy Ward Baker, 1970) which was based on Sheridan Le Fanu's story *Carmilla*, *Countess Dracula* (Peter Sasdy, 1970) – though the Countess herself was not even a vampire, much less a relation of the Count's. *Legend of the Seven Golden Vampires* (Roy Ward Baker, 1974), set in China, is Hammer's latest vampire success story. Dracula himself also made a brief but disappointing appearance in the film, played as he was by a miscast actor called John Forbes-Robertson in lurid green make-up.

Part of the reason why the earlier Hammer films have a distinctive 'Hammer look' about them lies in the fact that they were made at a small studio called Bray (actually a converted country house overlooking the Thames near Maidenhead), which Hammer used in the years from 1951 to 1968. In the beginning the studio consisted merely of the house itself but over the years various additions were made to it. The exterior of the house and the surrounding grounds often appeared in Hammer productions and most of the members of the Hammer team have fond memories of the place. 'I have a great deal of sentimental attachment to Bray,' said Michael Carreras, 'because I really grew up there. It was a marvellous studio. One thing I do like is a studio where you only make one picture at a time. That way everybody on the lot is concentrating on that one picture, which is good. When you move into a multiple picture studio, as we later did, you tend to get lost and the accounting and everything gets more difficult. But it's not so much that side of it – it was the *flavour* of Bray. It was like a family affair. We used to have a marvellous woman called Mrs Thompson who came in and did the lunch, and the crew used to come down by bus from Hammersmith Broadway. It was a great atmosphere that will never be recreated. But we eventually outgrew Bray, which may sound silly. We had formed a close association with EMI and they owned their own studio, so we moved to Elstree where our production headquarters is still. We have a place there called Little Hammer House.'

Terence Fisher agreed about the pleasures of working at Bray. 'It was excellent for me in the early Hammer days because I was feeling my way – I was young in the game. Being in a small studio one got to know everyone connected with it. The crews didn't change from picture to picture. We also had a brilliant art director there – Bernard Robinson.'

'We had a great team,' said Carreras. 'We had a great cameraman, Jack Asher, a marvellous make-up man called Roy Ashton, who really created all the characteristics of Frankenstein and Dracula. I think he's working for Milton Subotsky at Amicus now. And I must say that the art director, Bernie Robinson, was a major contributor to those films. His stylizing of the sets was tremendous. He really understood what those pictures were about.'

Bernard Robinson, who died in 1970, joined Hammer in 1956. He had first entered the film industry in 1935 as a draughtsman and became an art director at the age of twenty-six. He worked for several major British film companies over the years, including Alexander Korda's. The first film he worked on for Hammer was *Quatermass II*, and this was followed by *The Curse of Frankenstein*, for which he designed Frankenstein's spectacular laboratory. The extent of Robinson's talents are better realized when one appreciates the small budgets that he had to work with. For *Dracula* he was required to create the front of Dracula's castle within the grounds of Bray. This exterior set was built a short distance from the main entrance at Bray and was used again in subsequent pictures, such as *The Revenge of Frankenstein* and *The Hound of the Baskervilles,* suitably disguised by Robinson each time. In *The Stranglers of Bombay* it even represented part of an Indian village. The last film that Robinson worked on for Hammer was *Frankenstein Must be Destroyed,* which was made at EMI's studio at Elstree.

Another person responsible for making the Hammer product a unique one is composer James Bernard. His distinctive themes have provided an extra dimension for many of Hammer's films, including *The Quatermass Experiment, Curse of Frankenstein, Dracula* and *The Devil Rides Out.* 'He's my favourite,' said Michael Carreras, 'and he understands these films too. I think his score for our first *Dracula* has never been bettered and we still use that same motif on all our Dracula appearances. He's a very fine composer in his own right.'

Bernard was born in 1925 and was educated at Wellington College, Berkshire. Always interested in music, he was encouraged by composer Sir Benjamin Britten to have a thorough musical training. He later worked with Sir Benjamin on an opera, Billy Budd. Bernard composed theme music for many BBC plays before being commissioned by Hammer to score *The Quatermass Experiment,* his first film.

Terence Fisher is the director who is most associated with Hammer. He directed all their early Gothic films and has continued directing for them right up until 1972 when he made *Frankenstein and the Monster from Hell.* Though his directing style has always been rather static (he rarely moves the camera) he has now assumed something of a cult status among the newer critics as well as among the horror fans themselves. In his book *A Heritage of Horror,* David Pirie writes:

Once one begins to look at Fisher's films closely, it becomes clear that, unlike almost any other director working in the British commercial cinema, they appear to embody a recognizable and coherent *Weltanschauung.* The universe in which they are set is strictly dualistic, rigidly divided between Ultimate Good and Ultimate Evil, Light and Darkness, Spirit and Matter, while visually the opposition is most often expressed in images of bourgeois splendour juxtaposed with those of madness, decay and death.

Fisher himself is less pretentious about his work: 'I was just a hack director who was asked to direct their pictures,' but is willing to agree that people are at liberty to read what they want into his pictures. 'I look upon

(Above) Terence Fisher (left) on the set of Frankenstein and the Monster from Hell. *(Below) David Prowse in another variation of the Frankenstein monster (from* Frankenstein and the Monster from Hell)

myself, not as an *intellectual* film director,' he said, 'but as an *emotional* film director. I work from emotion and intuition and as far as people are concerned who want to analyse my work – well, a director shouldn't speak for his films, they should speak for themselves. It is no good going into a long spiel of intellectual bullshit about why you do things or why you don't – the only thing that can speak is what you've actually directed, and all you've directed is a visual interpretation of the written word and perhaps bugged it about a bit – given it a few more guts in one direction or few less in another. I'm not going to try and justify anything of mine. But I liked Pirie's book immensely because it has probably taught me more about what I do instinctively and intuitively than I realized myself. But I will continue to work *emotionally*, rather than analytically, no matter what I read about myself. You see, a writer who tries to analyse what someone has done and the person who has actually done it are in two different spheres of approach. It's what *they* get emotionally from what you have done. One gets one thing and someone else gets something different. All interpretations are perfectly valid.'

Fisher was born in 1904 but didn't enter the film industry until the 1930s. 'I was a late developer,' he said. 'I had two other jobs previously. I went to sea at the beginning of my working life; then I went into the rag trade.' He started as a clapper boy with Sir Michael Balcon's company at the Lime Grove studios at the age of twenty-eight. 'I was the oldest clapper boy in the business,' he joked. But his ambition was to become a film editor and before long he managed to get into the cutting room. He was working for Rank as an editor in 1946 when that company decided to start a training school for potential directors at their Highbury studio. 'I thought I'd like to direct so I applied for the course and was accepted. Rank gave all of us in the group three pictures to direct and some of us survived and some didn't. But it would have been very difficult to break into directing within the Rank organization if they hadn't started this training programme. My first film was *Colonel Bogey* in 1947. Another of the three films I did for them was *Public Danger*, which was quite good and is in the British Film Institute Film Archives now.

'I made two more films for Rank then they became a little doubtful as to what they were going to do with me so I started with Hammer. I did a lot of their films [his first one for them was *The Last Page* in 1951] before the so-called ''horror'' cycle started – I hate this word ''horror'' anyway, let's use ''fantasy'' or something else – and for me those early films provided a training ground for learning something about film craft. It was pure chance that I came to direct *Frankenstein*. It was a very small company when I began there. Tony Hinds was the real moving force in those days. The Colonel [Sir James Carreras] whom I have a great deal of respect for, was the motivation – he was the one who had built it all –

but my association was mainly with Tony Hinds who, with Michael Carreras, ran the company.

'We weren't influenced at all by the old Universal horror films when we started ours. I didn't screen them or refer to them at all. I was uninterested in them. I started from scratch. You can't go back and *remake* a film; you can remake a subject but that's different. There was a long period of time between theirs and ours. The whole way of living had changed so it would have been pointless to try and copy them. You can't go back. I have seen Universal's films since then. I think they're melodramatic. I wouldn't call mine melodramatic.' But Fisher disagrees with the suggestion that his films moved *faster* than the Universal versions, though he admits that the Lugosi *Dracula* was a very slow film. 'In my film, when Dracula made his first appearance, he took a long time to come down the stairs but it *seems* a short time because you're waiting to see what he's going to look like. Because, the first time, everybody was ready to laugh their bloody heads off – I've seen it in cinemas again and again – they thought they were going to see fangs and everything. They didn't, of course. Instead they saw a charming and extremely good-looking man with a touch, an *undercurrent*, of evil or menace. But I agree that, after he picked up the bags, my Dracula floated quite quickly up the stairs and Harker had to trot after him, unlike the Lugosi one where the walk *up* the staircase was also very slow.

'Another fast scene is the one where Van Helsing is placing the cross in Dracula's coffin, which was in a cellar, and Dracula suddenly opens the door behind him, looks in, sees Helsing and slams it shut again. I think I'm right in saying that scene was the very last one shot. I was under pressure. They were modest budget pictures and you had to keep to a tight schedule [often only thirty days]. Tony Hinds was breathing over my shoulder saying: "Aren't you frightened, Terry? We're running out of time." That same day I had done the disintegration sequence, as well as the shot of the dust blowing away from Dracula's ring. I didn't shoot the whole disintegration sequence, of course. It went away to the special effects man to do. I did the covering shots for him and he took over.

'But I love *Dracula*. It's one film I really look back on in my mind with affection. It had everything in it. Most important was the sexual attraction of Dracula towards his victims, which is the fundamental power of evil. I can take a certain amount of credit for the style of our first *Dracula*, but the script [by Jimmy Sangster] was important too. Thank God in that one I didn't have him turning into a bat or crawling up the wall or anything else like that. He had the power of evil, of vampirism, but we showed it only through suggestion. He could circumvent the limitations of time and space; he could walk through walls; but you never *saw* him do it. And he also had the power, which was again in line with the myth of vampirism, of being able to control mentally the people he had selected as victims. But since then they've introduced a lot of devices into the films which I think are wrong. You see, you can wring a subject dry to a certain point but you have to reach a place where you can go no further. You can't have Dracula walking up the King's Road in Chelsea and have any sense or feel of the character, and I've said this many times. Alright, it's justified because he can live forever until he's staked, but it doesn't work. Of course Chris is a wonderful Dracula. He moves beautifully. He can express emotion in the simplest physical movements – with just his walk alone. That was the secret of his success in parts where he didn't talk, such as in *The Mummy*.'

Fisher is rather condescending about the Dracula films produced by Hammer's competitors. Of the made-for-television Dracula film that starred Jack Palance, he said: 'It was a textbook example of how *not* to make a vampire film, I thought. It was a shame because Palance could have been alright. But the *direction* – there was all this horrible bloody business with the zoom lens. I got angry and told my wife I was going to walk out of the cinema if I saw any more of the zoom lens. The last third of the picture came to life and gave one a bit of feeling, but the first two-thirds were horrible.'

Another film of his that Fisher remembers with fondness is *Curse of the Werewolf*, which starred Oliver Reed. 'I liked that because of the tremendous interrelation between the characters, between Reed and the girl. Hell, anyone can turn into a werewolf, can't they? But it was his *situation* that made it exciting. The horror of him knowing that this was happening to him and the conflict between this and his love for the girl. An audience, I think, will respond to this because they can understand the emotional pull between people rather than the fact of someone turning into a werewolf, or Dracula wanting to bite someone's neck. Of course Oliver Reed was very good as the werewolf. In my opinion he's never done anything better.

'I liked *The Devil Rides Out* for the same reason. It was full of emotional tensions between the characters. I don't like to read Dennis Wheatley a lot because he fills his books with such a lot of stuff, but if you search within them, all the guts are there – all the emotional conflicts. You've got to wade through a lot of words to find them but he knows what he's writing about.'

One thing that Fisher resents is the accusation that critics have made over the years regarding the use of excessive gore in his pictures. 'I have never used it!' he protested. 'It was a ridiculous thing that some of the critics said of the early films that I used explicit gore! Christ, no gore was shown in the early Dracula films except for the actual moment of staking the vampires. It's that old question of whether you imply things or whether you show them. The staking of the vampires was never an act of destruction at all, it was a *release* for them, but the critics never seemed to grasp this. And it was important that it should be shown what happened to them when they were staked. It was an act that was fundamental to the whole myth of vampirism. Of course you can throw shadows on the wall to suggest what's happening sometimes – I did it once or twice because I thought the stakings were becoming clichés – but usually it was important to show the actual release of the vampire.' Fisher was surprised at the suggestion that the people who do the staking often seem more evil than the vampires themselves, especially in *Dracula, Prince of Darkness* when vampire Barbara Shelley is held down on a table by a group of monks and has a stake hammered into her chest as she writhes frantically in their grasp – a sequence that suggests she is undergoing a kind of monstrous rape. Fisher noted that the scene could also suggest the Spanish Inquisition in its most horrible form.

Another sequence in the same film attracted adverse comment. In his book, *Horror in the Cinema*, Ivan Butler wrote:

In particular the revivification of Dracula was merely disgusting – a recently murdered man's body trussed and hung over a bath, his stomach slit open with a knife, blood splattering noisily on to the ashes spread out below. One either felt sick, or found the sequence boringly incredible.

Actually the 'bath' was a stone coffin, and it was the man's throat that was cut open, not his stomach. 'Come, come. What was horrifying about that?' asked Fisher. 'It was a religious ritual. I said to the actor at the time: "Play it like a religious ritual," and you never saw the throat actually being cut, all you saw was the blood falling on the ashes. And he was supposed to be dead anyway.

'Very little was ever cut out by the censor, even in the 1950s. We did have trouble with one thing in the werewolf film, and that was the rape of the girl by the beggar, who was supposed to be a werewolf. But the censor, after seeing the script, said that we must not combine sex and horror, and he made us remove all references to the beggar being a werewolf. We tried to imply it in the sequence because it was necessary to the story. It wasn't really a horror film anyway, it was rather a grim fairy tale.'

Richard Wordsworth, who had been the monster in *The Quatermass Experiment*, played the old beggar in *Curse of the Werewolf* and remembered the incident well. 'Just before shooting I had to come down to London to get fitted for fangs. When I got to the studio nobody seemed to know anything about it. Anyway, I found someone who knew and he said, "Oh, no. No fangs. The censor says no fangs. You can either have fangs or relations with the girl but not both." Well, Oliver Reed had to be born so we had to choose relations with the girl. Terence Fisher was directing that one. We were just about to start the scene where I rape the girl and he turned to the property man and said, "Have you got the white of egg?" I didn't know what he was talking about and I asked, "Er, what's this white of egg for?" "Oh, this is something we always do," he said. 'You have a mouthful of egg white and when you see the girl just slobber a little of it. But keep it tasteful." '[58]

Fisher hasn't worked since he made *Frankenstein and the Monster from Hell* but has no plans yet to retire. At the time of writing he was waiting to hear whether Hammer had any future assignments for him. 'But I'm not contracted to Hammer,' he said. 'I never have been. I'll do anything for anybody. I have two very good ideas in my head but I'm not saying what they are. But I've loved working with Hammer over the years. They had a certain amount of confidence in me and they did leave me alone to get on with the job. But I had a good relationship with Tony Hinds. I think one of the great associations is that between producer and director, and by producer I don't mean a promoter but a *working* producer. Every director wants to go and cry on somebody's shoulder, and he needs encouragement and advice at times too. Tony Hinds and I understood each other and we worked well together.'

Michael Carreras agreed that the team of Hinds and Fisher had been very important for Hammer. 'I suppose Tony was really the major force, particularly in the horror field. He wrote a lot of them under another name [John Elder], he produced most of them and he had a marvellous relationship with Terry Fisher. I think you'll find that on all the so-called classic Hammer horror films it was a combination of Tony Hinds and Terry Fisher. One thing that stands out on all the pictures they did together, despite, if you like, the ludicrous plots, is that they approached the subjects very seriously, and they were never send-ups. There was humour but it was never a send-up approach and I think that really was the main strength of them. You have to believe in it to do it properly.'

Anthony Hinds, born in 1922, has now retired from the Hammer company though he continues to write scripts under his John Elder pseudonym. A quiet, somewhat retiring man, he went out of his way to avoid publicity during his career with Hammer and rarely gave interviews. One exception was in 1963 when he said: 'To the sceptics who peer at me superciliously and demand to know why I make pictures like *Dracula* and *Frankenstein*, I answer that it is my job – I do it for the money. And to those who depict me as the exploiter of the basest of human tastes and desires for the sake of profit, the answer is equally simple: I don't drive the public into the cinemas. They go because they want to go, but only when there is something they want to see. That they go to see the pictures

I make apparently in their millions surely is pretty strong proof of that. There is no more simple or positive formula to motion picture success than the oldest one in the showman's creed: Give 'em what they want and they'll keep coming back for more. There is no more magic to it than that.'[59]

'We hate *message* films,' said Sir James Carreras in *Films and Filming* in 1959, 'we make *entertainment*.' In 1974 a similar declaration was being made by his son Michael. 'The best film is the one that makes the most money. Our job is to entertain and promote something that is really exploitable. Exploitation is the thing.' Sir James has more or less retired from the company and Michael Carreras is now in charge. Born in London in 1927 and educated at Reading School, Reading, he started with Exclusive Films at a very early age and worked in various departments until he was appointed Assistant to the Producer in 1948. He produced his first film at the age of twenty-three – *The Dark Light*. Now in his late forties he is a distinguished-looking man with an easy charm. Though he maintains that he is a dedicated film fan, jazz is really his private passion and one suspects that he enjoys dealing with the business side of Hammer rather more than he does the creative side, despite having directed several of their films himself (*Maniac, Slave Girls, The Lost Continent* and *Blood from the Mummy's Tomb*, which he completed after the death of Seth Holt).

A scene from Blood from the Mummy's Tomb – *partly directed by Michael Carreras*

Today Hammer appears to be as secure as ever, though there was a period at the beginning of the 1970s when it looked as if the run of success was beginning to falter. At that time Hinds had just retired and Michael Carreras had temporarily left the company (he returned in January 1971). It was during this time that Hammer introduced a more blatant form of sex into their films, beginning with *The Vampire Lovers* and followed by *Lust for a Vampire* and *Countess Dracula*, all of which contained nudity and overtones of lesbianism. On his return to Hammer, Carreras said: 'It's not my particular cup of tea – I would have had Countess Dracula looking for young bucks. But what worries me is not the sex, but that Countess Dracula is nothing like as popular as Count Dracula. The people involved in Hammer since Tony Hinds and I left are not the people involved in the earlier ones, and do not have the same respect for the subject. They lost the Gothic flavour, which is perhaps the major ingredient. At the same time, they seemed to have lost all suspense. They felt it was enough that you had a fairly pedantic plot and every now and then you put in a bucket of blood and moved on.'[60]

As always, Hammer today is mixing its horror output with other types of films. A film version of the popular British TV series, *On the Buses*, was one of Hammer's most successful films in 1971. And Carreras remains optimistic about the company's future. 'As long as audiences demand our films they will continue. I think our horror output will become more limited but on the other hand I hope we'll be able to keep up our standard and our reputation in that area. But as far as Hammer is concerned as a company we must look for areas of diversification, as I think every company should at the moment. In a small way we've already sounded out the record market. The first one was successful enough (with Christopher Lee narrating *Dracula*, and the music of James Bernard) for us to go on to the second, and the third which will be released in 1975 will be *Frankenstein* with Peter Cushing. I also want to go into live theatre, and there are other areas where we could bring in the Hammer image.'

In 1972 Michael Carreras was quoted as saying of critics in general: 'They're full of crap and hot air; they can't write a straight review – one phoney feeds another. One of the worst films I ever directed was said by the critics to reveal so much stuff that just wasn't there. Critics rarely review horror films on the level they're aimed at.' In 1974 he hadn't changed his views on the subject. 'I read many reviews of our films with total amazement. I really do. For instance, when the National Film Theatre in 1971 gave us a two-week season I was horrified. I thought if they made us respectable it would ruin our whole image. When one reads all those criticisms, such as the ones that appear in the NFT programme booklet, and the little ones that appear in *Time Out* magazine when one of our films appears on TV, one is just simply amazed.' As an example,

Ingrid Pitt as Countess Dracula – before and after

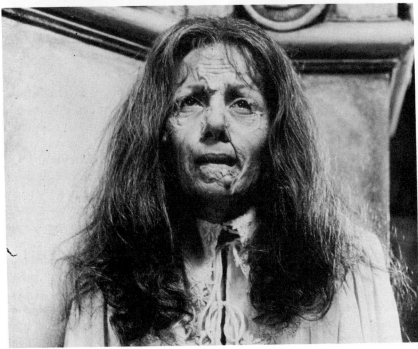

this is how *X-The Unknown*, about a radioactive blob that comes out of the ground, was described in one NFT booklet:

This anxiety-laden thriller shot at the beginning of 1956 conveys the atmosphere of Suez and cold war hysteria more tellingly than a dozen documentaries. In a ghostly Scottish setting, it juxtaposes all the paraphernalia of 'total mobilization' – dark menacing troops, night flying helicopters and 'Police State' notices – with a writhing, chaotic monster which feeds on atomic radiation.

Of critics who manage to discover messages, political or otherwise, in Hammer's product, Carreras said: 'They are reading things in that were never there, or never intended to be there. But let's face it, that is their job. They've got to find things to make themselves clever or to build up their own form of readership and present their own identity. They are, in a way, creating their own films in their own minds. You can't stop them doing it. We've never, of course, made films for the critics as such. I mean, if we get a nice review, that's interesting, but we don't go out of our way for them. The best review I've read in years of one of our films was for *The Seven Golden Vampires* in *Melody Maker* magazine. It was one of the funniest things I have ever read. I mean, the guy tore it to shreds. He put his finger on everything absolutely rightly, and then at the end he says, "Don't let me indicate that I'm trying to put you off seeing this film because I'm going to see it again tomorrow." Well, I think that was a very correct review for the sort of film it was. In other words, it was not meant to be taken seriously. I find a review like that much more interesting to read than the more pretentious rubbish they often write.

'Of course we have been affected by criticism in the past. At one point many years ago we did, in all seriousness, make what I consider to be a very fine film called *Never Take Sweets from a Stranger*. It was based on a play called *The Pony Cart* and we approached it absolutely seriously from our point of view, but the moment the film came out the critics said: "Oh, here we go – look at Hammer taking a social problem about people inter- fering with little children and capitalizing on it." I don't honestly know how they could have thought that of *that* film because it was beautifully made and finely acted and there was *never* any attempt to exploit the subject. We were most careful about the stills, we were most careful about the advertising with the distributor, so I think the critics did a lot of harm to that picture. But you have to expect that sort of thing. We've made serious films since then but nothing of that particular style; but again you've got to go back a number of years to when we were making *Hell is a City* and *Yesterday's Enemy*. I think it was a nice period of film- making for us because we were doing more serious things, but it wasn't

A scene from one of Hammer's failures –Never Take Sweets from a Stranger

what the public wanted from us because our image had already overtaken us. We have to be careful now. If I went to a distributor now with a film that didn't have any obvious exploitation possibilities they'd think I'd gone mad. That's what they look to us for.

'I know the film industry must allow at least forty per cent of its total output to have thoughtful and artistic ingredients, but that is for other producers to provide, not Hammer. But for those other producers to exist and to have the opportunity for self-expression you've got to maintain a healthy industry. We like to think we're helping to keep the industry, as a whole, healthy by getting people into the cinemas; and while they're there they can see the trailers for those other types of films and hopefully they'll go and see them as well.

'Films on vampirism have turned out to be the most popular in the horror field, especially Dracula, but the problem is in coming up with new ways to present him. I mean, we even went into the female Draculas, as well as doing modern ones. I don't think the later ones work so well. They've been successful in terms of public exhibition but I believe that Dracula is much more powerful in his natural habitat – a Gothic or Transylvanian setting. I prefer Dracula films of the Gothic period, and even in the modern ones you'll notice that you always find Dracula in a disused church or graveyard, so that his little world is still a Gothic one though the traffic is going by at the end of the road.

'Of course Chris Lee is no longer enthusiastic about playing Dracula, and quite rightly too, but frankly I think that Chris will always be Dracula as far as the public are concerned. He's grown out of the part now, you could say, and he's also getting a bit too old for it. I think the great strength of Dracula is his sexual image, and though I'm not suggesting that Chris has lost his I think it's time for a change. Actually we are seriously deciding at this moment what our next Dracula will be. There are many ways of doing it – you can have "Son of Dracula," which is the most corny example – but we've got to create a new Dracula with a new actor in the part. I'm of the opinion that we should go back to our 1957 *Dracula* and do a remake. It was the closest to the Bram Stoker original that we ever did, and it was the most successful, so I think we should remake it before someone else does. But it's going to be very difficult to find a replacement for Christopher Lee and to get the public to accept him. It's really going to depend on how cleverly we're able to present him.

'Audiences apparently prefer familiar actors in horror roles. The one criticism we've never had is: "Oh dear, it's Christopher Lee *again*." So a new Dracula isn't going to be easy to come up with. I don't think that we should re-start a cycle but we should certainly go back to the beginning. I am immodest enough to say that since we started making horror films, therefore excluding the Universal and German ones, nobody has made a better Dracula than we have. Not that I've seen, anyway. I've seen hundreds of Spanish and Italian ones and all sorts of others, so I think we should re-examine our own success and stick closely to it.'

When Carreras speaks of a new approach he hasn't in mind the gory and sexually perverse excesses of Andy Warhol's ventures into horror. 'I think Mr Warhol is better at that than we are. I think he understands his own approach. I certainly don't. We've also had the American television companies making *definitive* versions of Dracula and Frankenstein which were, in my opinion, rubbish. It's unfortunate that they turned out the way they did, but they were made for TV so they had to be a bit careful with them and fit them into the restrictions of TV. Nicely made films, if you like, but I don't think they were the public's image of either Franken-stein or Dracula. I also think it was a crying shame that they were shown theatrically in Britain. They were made for TV, and in that medium perhaps they're acceptable; but in the cinemas they were just bastardized versions. Naturally I went to see them both because I thought I might learn something but all I learnt was their mistakes.'

Not surprisingly, Carreras himself isn't a horror film fan. 'As a *film* fan, which I am very much, I don't go to see horror films as my first choice. I naturally see our own a number of times and then I go and see the opposition, or, to be more honest, I get the better examples of other people's horror films in and screen them during the day as part of my working routine. On the other hand, we're up to about the 160th film since we started production in 1948, and the horror films have only been about fifty out of the lot, so it's not as if we sit here concentrating on horror films all the time. But I must admit that, in the pre-production planning stages, they're probably the most enjoyable things to work on because you can let your imagination run riot. I find them stimulating in that way.

'Despite the number of pictures that I've been involved with in one capacity or another, I can still go to the cinema and look at a film as a film fan and not be aware of the techniques. If something really interests me I'll go back and look at it again from a technical point of view. For instance, when I first saw *The Exorcist*, it really frightened me. There were a couple of moments when I really jumped out of my seat. To be perfectly honest, I wish I'd made that film. We are actually into this type of thing. It's not jumping on to anyone else's bandwagon because we have been closely associated with Dennis Wheatley for a number of years. We made *The Devil Rides Out* some years ago and our next film is going to be *To the Devil a Daughter*. Of course somebody will compare it to *The Exorcist*, but it's something that Wheatley wrote a long time ago. Unfortunately I was unable to get the distributors interested in Wheatley until *The Exorcist*. Now, of course, they think that anything to do with the occult is the new scene. So in one way, I suppose, I'm exploiting the general willingness to get into that area now, but it's something we've wanted to make for ages. *The Devil Rides Out* was very successful in this country but it wasn't terribly successful in the major markets outside of Britain. Before *The Exorcist* there wasn't the willingness by the distributors to take our horror films that deviated from the Gothic series. Now audiences worldwide, I think, are much more into the occult.'

Another departure for Hammer was to produce a film in partnership with a Hong Kong company, the Shaw Brothers, who had achieved great success in Western markets with their series of Kung Fu films. The result of the collaboration, *The Legend of the Seven Golden Vampires*, combined vampires, including Dracula, with plenty of Kung Fu battles in a Chinese setting. 'It was interesting to work with the Shaw Brothers, though we were a long way apart in many areas of approach. What we tried to do was get the best out of both approaches and see what happened. I think the first one has turned out exactly as we hoped it would. It's a strange mixture and it was difficult to find the right balance. The Shaw Brothers liked our script and it was Don Houghton, who wrote it, who deserves much of the credit for finding that balance. I think he did it very well.'

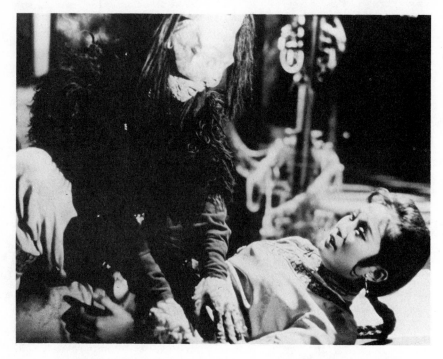

In 1968 the Hammer Company was awarded the Queen's Award for Industry in recognition of the large amount of money that the company had brought into Britain over the years. It was an event that surprised many people at the time. 'It was a marvellous thing for us,' said Carreras, 'because the majority of the British film industry, up to that time, regarded us as a bit of a joke. The Award at least gave us a more respectable image within the industry, but it didn't really affect us in the practical sense.

'I don't have any pretensions about our films but I think they're good, within the areas we lay down. The one thing we never do is make a shoddy film. Even, for instance, a film like *On the Buses*, which can't be anything but exploitation, as we capitalized on the audience from the TV series. But we didn't make it for only £40,000, which we could have done quite easily, we spent a great deal more to try and widen the scope and to give the people who go and see a Hammer film a respectable hour and a half, in terms of visual images as well as just knockabout comedy. I think that one of the reasons our horror films certainly became leaders in the market was that they were always beautifully photographed, the sets were always extremely believable. They've never been shoddy productions.'

7 American International Productions and Roger Corman

AIP was once described in the *New York Times* magazine as having the same status in the American film industry as the man hired to sweep behind the elephants in a circus parade. Despite being America's version of Hammer Films, AIP so far hasn't received the equivalent nod of acceptance from the Establishment that Hammer got with its Queen's Award. But if respectability continues to elude the company, profits certainly don't – like Hammer, it is one of the few *consistently* successful film companies.

Within a year of their meeting in 1954, lawyer Samuel Z. Arkoff and James H. Nicholson formed a small distribution company called the American Releasing Corporation. The following year they decided to move into actual film production and changed the company's name to American International Productions. The new company didn't create any ripples in the film industry at the time, and it's doubtful if many people in Hollywood were even aware of its existence. Their films, with titles like *Apache Woman, The Beast With a Million Eyes* and *Swamp Women*, were of a very low quality but made so quickly and cheaply that they couldn't help but make a profit. The company grew rapidly and so did the output of films – from four in 1955 to twenty-two in 1958. That same year they decided they were established enough to have a studio of their own, so they took out a lease on the old Charlie Chaplin studio on Sunset Boulevard. But by the following year their fortunes had radically changed for the worse and the studio became a liability. So the two men moved to Italy where they made a cheap Hercules-type of film with Steve Reeves. Produced on a very small budget, it grossed $1 million in the USA. AIP was back on top again and more good luck was to follow. Back in America they discovered that comedian Red Skelton wanted their studio because of its associations with Chaplin. 'We would gladly have given him the lease,' said Arkoff, 'but he bought the whole lot. So we got all our money back plus a three-year lease out of the deal, so we could use a little studio there as well as keep our offices. We've never had a studio since. You don't need studios to make pictures. As a matter of fact, you're really better off without one with today's audiences that are visual-minded.

A publicity shot from I Was a Teenage Werewolf. *Under all that hair is Michael Landon*

They want it realistically done, not against cardboard backgrounds and papier-mâché sets.'[61]

The major reason for AIP's success was that they were one of the first film producers to realize that teenagers made up the bulk of the cinema audience in America in the 1950s (with the advent of television older people tended to visit the cinema only very rarely, whereas the teenagers were filling the drive-ins), so they made films aimed directly at the youth market. 'There are some unkind people who say we made pictures that *pandered* towards youth. That's a matter of semantics,' said Arkoff. 'We did make pictures that *appealed* to youth, and in doing so we took a different position from other producers and didn't moralize.'[62] Films where adults rarely intruded, except as villains, were definitely appealing to the teenagers of the late 1950s, and they flocked to see movies like *I Was a Teenage Werewolf, Teenage Caveman, Teenage Doll* and *I Was a Teenage Frankenstein*. AIP repeated their success with the youth market in the 1960s with their Beach Party films and their Hell's Angels series.

Horror and science fiction films had formed part of the AIP output from the beginning, but in 1960 the company took something of a risk by spending $300,000 (a large budget by AIP's standards up to then) to make a rather unusual horror film – *The Fall of the House of Usher*, based on the story by Edgar Allen Poe. To their relief it was a success, and similar

A scene from I Was a Teenage Frankenstein

films followed. 'They didn't have a Poe series in mind to begin with,' said Richard Matheson, who wrote the screenplay, 'but when *Usher* got such a good reception financially and critically they just jumped on the idea. So I started doing more of them. I think *Usher* turned out the best of the ones I wrote. It was the only one that was pure Poe – apart from *Masque of the Red Death* which was written by Charles Beaumont. The rest of them had less Poe to build on. *The Pit and the Pendulum* had one little scene from Poe from which I had to make a whole story. *The Raven* was just a poem, which wasn't much to work with either. In *Tales of Terror* I followed Poe pretty well, but I combined a couple of stories in that. *The Raven* [a spoof on the other films in the series] was fun. The AIP executives had found out that the middle portion in *Tales of Terror*, which had been done for laughs, was very successful so they decided to do a whole funny picture. Anyway, I couldn't have done another serious one. It would have been more than I could stand. I had to do them for laughs by then. I've never had a particular interest in Poe, nor did I develop one while working on those films.

'Working on *Comedy of Terrors* was also a lot of fun. We had Boris Karloff, Peter Lorre, Basil Rathbone, and Vincent Price. [AIP used the old horror stars because they could get them cheaply.] They were all very charming, marvellous people and it really was a delightful experience

Peter Lorre watches as Jacques Tourneur demonstrates how he wants a dance performed during the making of Comedy of Terrors

just talking with them on the set. They loved doing *Comedy of Terrors*. I remember the first luncheon we all went out to, and they were looking forward to doing the picture. It was a good script but it didn't translate all that well on to the screen. I'd finally talked AIP into hiring Jacques Tourneur to direct it – I think he is a marvellous director – but with a two-week shooting schedule you can't spend too much time on anything. That's all the time AIP ever spent on any of those pictures. That's how they made their money.

'I've written other good scripts for AIP that nothing has ever happened with. When I worked for them in the beginning I would write a script for them and two weeks later they would be filming it, but as they got more and more successful they wanted to do more ambitious films. They went through this big artsy-craftsy phase – I think it was Nicholson who wanted to do better things – but though the scripts were good they couldn't get the financial backing they needed because these films wouldn't have made instantaneous money.' Comparing AIP with Hammer, whom Matheson has worked with in London on a number of occasions, he said of the Hammer executives: 'They were very nice people. They were so genteel they made you forget they were just in the same business as AIP – making shlocky films.'

Nicholson, the 'quiet' half of the AIP partnership, died recently, which left Arkoff, who was once described as someone 'who loves to pose, tongue in cheek, as a real crass character', in charge. AIP continues to be successful – in the fiscal year that ended in March 1974, the company showed a profit of $931,000 – and Arkoff is optimistic about the future. 'This business is never as good as people make out, but it's never as bad either. The public have had enough of the kinky picture – *Deep Throat* and so on. They have seen it all, and this is why pictures like *The Sting* and *The Exorcist* are doing so well. We're going through a new phase of the true entertainment film. I take my hat off to Warners: *The Exorcist* is great fun. The public loves to be titillated: out of the mouth of a twelve-year-old girl comes green bile and dirty words. I saw people leaving a cinema twelve minutes after the picture started. Why? Nothing had happened by then.'[63]

Roger Corman, who produced the first picture AIP ever released – *Fast and Furious* (1954) – and who has directed and produced many films for them since, is the one director most often associated with the company. He was born in Los Angeles on 5 April 1926 and graduated from Stanford University, California in 1947 with a degree in engineering, but after a spell at sea in the Navy he became a messenger boy at 20th Century Fox. After working his way up into the studio's story department he left to study Modern English Literature at Oxford. On his return to Hollywood he began to write screenplays, and his first sale was *Highway*

*Director Roger Corman
with Hazel Court and
Jane Asher on the set of*
The Masque of the Red
Death

Dragnet, a picture which he also co-produced (Nathan Juran directed).
He then formed his own company and made *The Monster from the Ocean's
Floor* (directed by Wyott Ordung), followed by *Fast and Furious* (Edward
Sampson and John Ireland). Corman financed these two films by raising
the money himself, but after completing the latter he decided to enter
into an arrangement with the newly formed American Releasing Corporation when he realized he would have a long wait before getting a
return on his investment. 'They wanted to take my picture,' said Corman,
'and I said that I would let them have it if they would give me an advance
against the release of the picture, and also make a deal for a series of
subsequent pictures in which they would give me advances on every
one. That way I could make a series of pictures and get at least a portion
of the negative costs back and not have to go through the wait.

'By and large I'm happy with AIP. They don't normally interfere with
my pictures though they have done a few little things – such as in *The
Wild Angels* when they inserted a shot that turned a church into a funeral
home. They got frightened by the big orgy scene. The insert was badly
exposed and grainy which I thought was good because the thing looked
so ridiculous that anybody who saw it would know instantly that it had
been done by an idiot.'[64]

Corman achieved a reputation for making films with almost unbelievable speed and on very small budgets. The majority of his early films
were done on shooting schedules of five to ten days and on budgets that

ranged from $40,000 to $100,000 (*Monster from the Ocean's Floor*, which he produced in 1954, was made for $12,000). Of course the budgets on his more recent films, such as *The St Valentine's Day Massacre* (1966), *Bloody Mama* (1970) and *The Red Baron* (1970), were much bigger (though relatively small compared to most Hollywood productions) but he retains his reputation of being a fast worker.

A competent but mediocre director, he has, like Terence Fisher, been elevated to cult status by the new generation of film critics. As a result Corman is now probably one of the most overrated directors in the history of the cinema. For example, in the book *Roger Corman*, contributor Paul Willeman writes:

In looking beyond surface meanings, we discover that Corman's entire *oeuvre* represents a series of comments and variations on the theme of sacred time, largely expressed in terms of the Myth of the Eternal Return.

Willeman then proceeds to divide Corman's films up into a number of categories. Films like *Attack of the Crab Monsters* and *Teenage Caveman* are in Group A, which deals with the period 'after the millennium'. Group B, containing films like *The Fall of the House of Usher*, deals with the period 'leading up to the millennium' and so on through to Group D. Willeman then writes:

Corman's treatment of the sacred and profane throughout Groups A, B, and C, and the references to the religious attitude to time in Group D, varies somewhat from E. R. Leach's basic scheme, which graphically represents profane time as a horizontal line, interrupted vertically by sacred time. He describes the sacred intervals as rites of passage. The graphic representation of Corman's view of the flow of time requires a downward inclination in the profane intervals, and a hypothetical point M, signifying the millennium which must logically follow. The sacred intervals before the millennium are, in fact, symbolic rehearsals of the final, total destruction of the world, though they are never quite complete enough to prevent another cycle or interval from following on from the catastrophe.[65]

No director, no matter how good or bad, deserves to have something like *that* said about his work. Corman wouldn't be human if he wasn't affected by such criticism, so it's not surprising that he, too, has become slightly pretentious when talking about his films. 'The primary forces – fire, water, the elements – symbolize certain natural powers and drives, and there may be a cleansing element in there as well,' he said in an interview in 1970. 'For instance, in the Poe pictures I used fire a number of times; so many times, in fact, for the necessary destruction of the house, that when I came to do *The Terror* I said: "We're going to *flood* this house." ' I don't think I've ever analysed what these uses stand for, other than natural force, on the basis that (to quote certain religions) we are all one, and we come out of natural elements.'[66] But Corman remains, essentially, a commercial director and seems to be aware of the dangers of taking himself too seriously. 'I've been quoted as saying that I'd like to go back to the quicker way of shooting. And that probably means going back to a more fun way of making motion pictures. When we did the little comedies – *Little Shop of Horrors* in two days and one night of silent shooting, *Bucket of Blood* in five days, *Creature from the Haunted Sea* in six, everybody worked hard. We took the work seriously but we weren't overwhelmed by it, unless overwhelmed by the schedule. So there was an air of camaraderie and pleasantness on the set in those days. I like the films. They're unpretentious, they're amusing, they're nice.'[67]

Talking of working with veteran actors like Karloff, Lorre and Price, Corman once said: 'They all have this great ability of giving you all you can ask for and more. With so many actors you have to keep working on them to get them to give enough to come out with the really big effect. But with them they will let you have the lot all at once, and then if necessary you can scale it down.'[68] Karloff himself gave a different impression of Corman's working methods: 'James Whale was a brilliant technician with the camera and all the rest of it, just as Corman is. That, I think, is Corman's strong point. But I think Whale had the advantage because he was an older, more experienced man – Whale had a background in theatre and was used to directing actors. Corman expects an actor to get on with it himself. I've worked with him twice. The first time was on *The Raven* and I know that Vincent Price, Peter Lorre, and I had to find our own way, because Corman had all he wanted. He said, "You're experienced actors, get on with it. I've got the lighting and my angles. I know how I'm going to put this together." And if you asked him about advice on a scene he'd say, "That's your pigeon. Go on. I'm busy with this." '[69]

Richard Matheson agreed with Karloff: 'Corman was very good with pace and giving the things an interesting look but he didn't work with actors, and the actors in the Poe films were not usually very good. There were exceptions in each film – Price always did a professional job – but in *The House of Usher* I think all three of the other people were not particularly good, and that was the whole cast! The leading young men were usually pretty wooden. Jack Nicholson's first picture was *The Raven*, but of course it wasn't his style, as time has proved. But David Frankham did very well in several of them because he was a British actor and had the feel for it.' Of the Poe/Corman series of films as a whole Matheson said: 'They were alright. Not that special. But the art director always did marvellous sets. His name is Daniel Haller and he's a television director now, and as a matter of fact he's one of my neighbours. He did marvellous stuff with very little money.' (Haller directed *The Dunwich Horror* and *Pieces*

A scene from The
Raven *with a young
Jack Nicholson on the
left*

of Dreams in 1970.)

Of Haller, who was art director on fifteen of his films, Corman said:
'We would discuss the sets and Dan would kind of sketch them out on a
napkin at lunch and that would be it. When I went to 20th Century Fox
it was really a surprise: all these draughtsmen drawing things out and
the sketch artists and everything else. Dan used to walk out on the set
and he'd take a piece of chalk, make a mark, and say, "Start it about here."
And I think he was totally correct, because they got themselves so wound
up at 20th in such needless detail on sets. It means nothing whatsoever
in a motion picture. The set will change with every lens you use, anyway.'[70]

Both AIP and Corman have been instrumental over the years in giving
young film-makers, as well as actors, a chance to enter the industry, not
from altruistic reasons but because they came cheap. Recently, for instance, the talented John Milius directed *Dillinger* for AIP for a very small
fee. A successful screenwriter (e.g. *The Life and Times of Judge Roy Bean*),
he wanted a chance to direct; so when AIP approached him with the idea
of *Dillinger* he agreed to do it for a fraction of his usual fee. Other now-
famous names that were boosted by their association with AIP and Corman
include Peter Bogdanovich, Francis Ford Coppola, Dennis Hopper, Jack
Nicholson, Peter Fonda and Monte Hellman.

Bogdanovich described his start in the film industry: 'I met Roger

Corman at a screening in 1964. He had read my stuff in *Esquire* and he said, "You're a writer – do you want to write for pictures?" So I said, "Sure I'd like to write for pictures – what do you want me to write?" He said, "Well, I'd like you to write me a combination of *The Bridge on the River Kwai* and *Lawrence of Arabia* – but inexpensive to produce." '[71] Bogdanovich got his first chance to direct while working as Corman's general assistant during the making of *Wild Angels* (1966), a Hell's Angels picture that starred Peter Fonda. 'Really it was a paid, though not very highly paid, course in the making of films,' said Bogdanovich. 'Roger fell behind schedule because the Hell's Angels in the picture didn't like him and kept sabotaging their own motorcycles. So Roger said, "We're going to have to create a second unit." And I said, "Who's going to direct it?" He said, "I don't care who directs it. My secretary can direct it. You can direct it." He was rather angry that day. So I said, "Alright, I'd love to direct it." And then he was pleased with the work I did on that and he gave me the opportunity to make *Targets*. The financing came right out of his own pocket.'[72]

Debra Paget and Vincent Price are menaced by the victims of black magic in The Haunted Palace

Monte Hellman, who has received critical acclaim for his pictures, especially *Two-Lane Blacktop,* said: 'The first film I ever did was for Roger, and before I started making films Roger lost $500, which he invested in a stage version I did of Samuel Beckett's *Waiting for Godot,* so I thought I'd better pay him the money back by doing some films for him. He has artistic aspirations but I think his desire to be commercial outweighs his desire to be artistic. He has attempted serious films on a couple of occasions but they didn't do very well, so he kind of became discouraged; but if he thinks a serious film can be successful, then he'll back it or he'll attempt to make it himself. He certainly has helped a lot of people to get started. There was nobody else in Hollywood at that time who was giving jobs to, say, film students directly out of school as he has done. It wasn't entirely out of kindheartedness that he helped us all in the beginning – he recognized a kind of fresh talent that wasn't very expensive. Nobody else was doing that, so you have to give him credit for that.'[73]

To conclude this chapter one can do no better than to quote the plain-talking Mr Arkoff again: 'When you come down to it, I don't think there are any of us in the film industry making anything today that will be of more than passing historical interest fifty years from now. There are times when, probably, if we at AIP were a little more pompous and a little more serious about the sheer earth-shattering importance of what we're doing we'd be better off – because most people in this business are so fornicatingly serious about the importance of these little ships that pass in the night. But I love this business. This is the most enjoyable and entertaining business of any – though sometimes it's a pain in the ass.'[74]

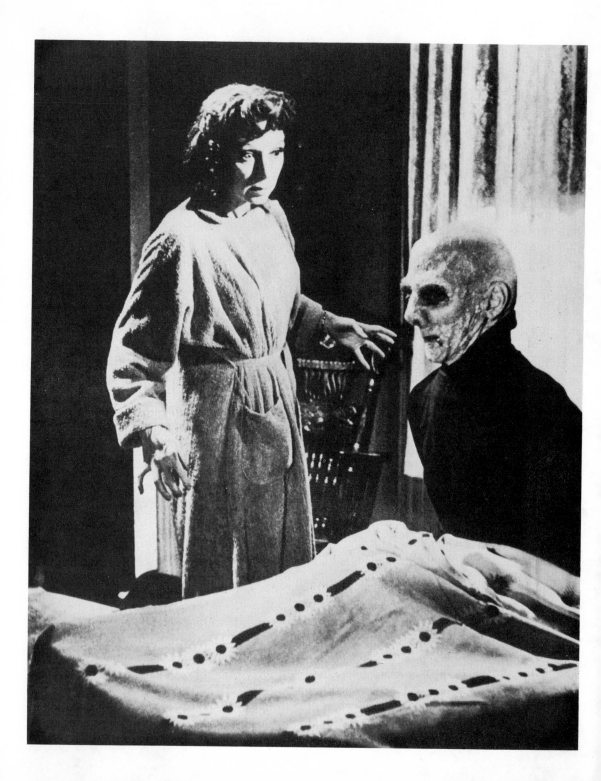

8   William Castle

William Castle, with his ever-present cigar and his sumptuous office on the twelfth floor of a Beverly Hills glass tower, resembles the archetypal Hollywood producer. His cockiness, his vitality, and his fondness for using superlatives reinforce the image; but though Castle is more famous for the way he *promoted* his horror films, rather than for the films themselves, there lies beneath all his flashy showmanship a desire to be regarded as a serious film-maker.

'I have always been interested in horror ever since I was a kid,' said Castle. 'I think it started when I was about six years old. One day, while I was playing along Riverside Drive, [New York] where I lived then, I saw a man pick up, from the side of the road, what looked like an innocent mushroom but was actually a poisonous toadstool. He ate it and before long he was writhing in pain and agony. I stood there watching him until the ambulance came and picked him up. By that time he was quite purple. And that incident left an indelible impression on my life and possibly it went very, very deep into my unconscious mind – creating an obsession with the frightening aspects of horror. Why else does one devote a whole career to scaring the pants off people? This is what I have been doing, and doing very successfully for years, not only in manipulating audiences and giving them nightmares but also in terms of the box office.

'I'm very much like Alfred Hitchcock, not that I am comparing myself to him – he is a master – but we've both devoted our lives to a certain type of film: the shocker. The times that Hitchcock strays and makes a non-shocker he usually has a flop. *Lifeboat*, for instance, took him away from his established formula and it flopped. And the same thing has happened to me when I've strayed away from the thriller/shocker film. All my real successes have been with horror films, so I will keep on making them.'

Castle started in show business in 1929 as a bit actor in New York. Three years later, when he was a mere eighteen, he became a stage manager. The first play he directed was *Dracula* with Bela Lugosi – a revival of the original Broadway production. 'I'm the same age as Orson Welles,' said Castle, 'and when he came out to Hollywood to do *Citizen Kane* I took over his Stony Creek Theatre and produced and directed

A disturbing moment from Castle's The Tingler

William Castle (with cigar) and his cast during a break in the filming of The Tingler

plays. As a result of the successes I had that summer Harry Cohn of Columbia Pictures brought me to Hollywood to direct films. I was in my twenties then and I've been here ever since.

'Harry Cohn was a very misunderstood man. He was rough, tough but he was a contradiction. I adored Harry Cohn. I think he was a tremendous force in this industry. He was dynamic. He was cruel and ruthless at times but if he liked you, and thank goodness he liked me, there was nothing he wouldn't do for you. There were many things that he did for people that I know have never been in print and that he never admitted. He was a strange enigma of a man. He was apparently harsh but underneath there was something that was very, very soft. The books about him have never hit the real Harry Cohn.

'But I had no freedom at all when I was working for him. I had the freedom that Harry Cohn would allow, and in those days that was *none*. You were completely told what to do. When you directed you were given the freedom of direction and if he liked your work he would leave you alone; but if he didn't like your rushes he would pounce on you and make life miserable. But he also liked you to stand up to him. Several people did and they were allowed a certain amount of freedom. It was only when I had grown intellectually, as well as artistically, that I allowed myself to grab this freedom. I had complete freedom when I made *When Strangers Marry*, one of Robert Mitchum's first films, because I was on loan-out from Columbia and I consider it one of the best pictures that I ever did. I used a hand-held camera for the first time in America – I'm not saying I invented it, it came from the Germans – and I had a real ball making that. I realized that true expression needs freedom and one must be free to create.

'It wasn't until 1957, when I went into business for myself with my own production company, that I started making horror films. Before that I did everything from musicals to Westerns to soap operas – I've made every conceivable type of film. Most of them were made for Columbia, though I went out on loan a number of times. In those days I only wrote and directed, never produced. I decided to go into business for myself after I did several TV series, which I hated. The reason that I became a producer as well as a director was that I *hated* producers. I hated the

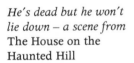

He's dead but he won't lie down – a scene from The House on the Haunted Hill

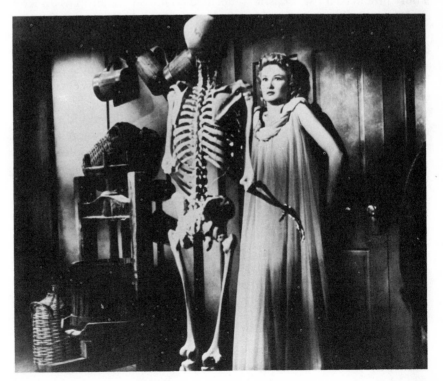

interference. I wanted the autonomy of creating what I wished, and in order to have that I had to become a producer myself and wear two hats. That way I got the freedom of directing the way I wanted to.'

Macabre in 1957 was the first of Castle's horror films and the first to receive his extravagant brand of promotion; he insured each member of the audience for $1,000 with Lloyd's of London against death by fright. *House on Haunted Hill* in 1958 featured a skeleton on a wire flying out from the screen and over the heads of the audiences. For *The Tingler* (1959) he arranged to have some of the seats in the cinemas wired to give a mild electric shock and in *Homicidal* (1961) he created the 'fright break'. 'During the last sixty seconds of the film my voice would be heard saying "Ladies and Gentleman, this is William Castle. You are cordially invited, if you're too frightened to see the end of this picture, to go to the box office and get your full admission price refunded." We did actually refund the money but very few people took up the offer. Those who did just wanted to see if we would, but it was a great gimmick.'

After ten years of making often entertaining, but basically exploitation, films Castle decided to produce a film that would prove to Hollywood that he wasn't just a gimmick-maker but a film-maker. The result was *Rosemary's Baby*. 'It was the first film of mine that I haven't directed: I only produced it,' said Castle. 'I decided on Roman Polanski as director and I'm not sorry I did. He has a real talent and he and I got along famously. He learned a great deal from my past experience and I, of course, learned a deal from his. He says I am the only producer he has ever worked with that he was able to cope with and enjoy working with. I must say I was very close to Roman and he listened to what I had to say. We had many disagreements at times but they were quiet and private. On the whole we had a tremendous rapport between us. *Rosemary's Baby* would not have been possible if it hadn't been for the close collaboration between Polanski and myself. We did, in fact, fight off many unpleasantries together, not only from Paramount but also from Mia Farrow and Frank Sinatra who were quarrelling at the time. We worked very closely together and managed to keep the whole world shut out. We were constantly consulting each other and spoke to each other at least a dozen times a day and at night. Of course he had all the freedom he wanted as far as directing was concerned. He directed that picture, I didn't. Every idea, every nuance, in the film is Polanski's. I will always be grateful to him.'

Rosemary's Baby was a box-office success but Castle wasn't able to enjoy it. 'I went through several experiences on that film that can be put down to coincidence or the occult, depending on which side you're on. Many unexplainable things happened. It was quite phenomenal.' Among the things that happened was the sudden death of the film's

Mia Farrow in Polanski's Rosemary's Baby, *which Castle produced*

thirty-five-year-old composer, who went into a coma and died, and Castle himself had to be rushed to hospital with uremic poisoning. After four operations he was released from hospital but then experienced a nervous breakdown. 'After all the peculiar things that had happened I just fell apart. I was recuperating in San Francisco when I saw the headlines about the Sharon Tate murders. That was all I needed. I drove right down to Los Angeles, went to Paramount where Roman was and just fell apart again.

'Roman is a strange man. He believes in nothing except what he sees, whereas I believe in the occult and evil forces. He pooh-poohs this. After we finished the picture there was an interview with him in the *New York Times* and he was asked whether it was due to the occult and to evil forces at work during *Rosemary's Baby* that there were a lot of mishaps and that I became ill. He said, ''No, the only thing it was due to was that Castle couldn't stand success, and it was all the success and the making of so much money that went to his head.''

'That sort of thing had never happened on any of my other horror films, but the ones I made before *Rosemary* were on a superficial level. They didn't deal with the devil or the occult, they were cheap, *fun* films. But I am superstitious and I do believe in the devil. If one believes in God, and I do very strongly believe in God, one must automatically believe in the devil. And I do believe that the film, which I lived through and almost *died* through, was controlled by some unexplainable force which was rather frightening. And having spoken to the people who worked on *The Exorcist* I heard that apparently the same thing happened there.' (Max Von Sydow's brother died on the day Sydow arrived for his first scene, Jack McGowan dropped dead one week after his death-scene in the picture, an entire set burnt down and when it was rebuilt the sprinkler system broke down and flooded it out, among other incidents.)

'On the drawing board of William Castle Productions at Paramount is a sequel to *Rosemary's Baby*. It will be called *Rosemary's Baby Part 2*. I have a marvellous script for it but I have been seriously debating with myself whether or not I should actually make it or just forget the whole thing. I am very tempted to forget it. I don't want to tamper with the occult again, not on that level. My family is absolutely against it, but my creative instinct urges me sometimes to do the sequel because it would be very challenging. But I don't know – the whole thing is up for grabs. I strongly feel that I will not make another film of that type.

'As for *The Exorcist* itself – what can you say? How can you argue with success? It's just an amazing phenomenon. It pricks the hidden nerve of people's fears about the nature of evil and their fears of the devil. Actually the manuscript was originally submitted to me just after I had completed *Rosemary's Baby*, and I didn't want to follow it up with a film that had so many similarities that quickly. Also I thought it would be unpalatable as far as censorship was concerned at that time. Don't forget that when *Rosemary's Baby* was released in 1968 it was considered to be very shocking. It was way ahead of the new wave – we had frontal nudity in it and used the word "shit" on the screen for the first time. Yet it's tame now compared to today's standards. I think each picture finds its own level in its own time. Obviously 1974 was the right moment for *The Exorcist*; whether it would have worked as well as it has a few years later or a few years earlier is debatable. I think the director, William Friedkin, did a Herculean job of manipulating an audience. The only quarrel I have with the film is why it cost as much as it did. I don't see where $12,000,000 went on that film. I think it was rather ridiculous to spend that much; it was wasteful self-indulgence on their part, though the film did prove many times the negative cost.

'I've watched the film five times. I was fascinated by it. The first two times I watched the film; the next three times I watched the audience to see why they were so frightened. And they *were*, not only women but young men. I spoke to them and questioned them and they were definitely affected by it, so there was something in the film that worked. It was compulsive viewing – effectively portrayed horror is always compulsive.

'I wasn't offended by it in any way, but many of the people I talked to were very deeply offended. But many people were deeply offended by *Rosemary's Baby*. Audiences line up for hours to see a film and then tell their friends not to go and see it because they'll be too frightened! Myself, I thought it was well-done and proved again how one could manipulate an audience. As Hitchcock says, and it's something I've followed, give the audience a little piece each time and slowly build it up. Give your first little jolt, then retreat, lull your audience into a false sense of security, then build a little higher and retreat, build a little higher etcetera, and on the fifth one you throw the book at them. That's audience manipulation.

'With *The Exorcist* you were lulled into a complete false sense of security for the first half hour. It's debatable whether that opening sequence in Iran was necessary. I understand that Blatty, though he had it in his book, didn't write it in his original screenplay and it was only there on Friedkin's insistence. I found it rather good though a lot of people said it was slow and dull. But I thought it was rather exciting because during the first half hour you wondered what all the talking and the fanfare was about, then you were sucked in. And *I* was sucked in, I really was. Having made so many of these type of things I couldn't get too emotionally involved because I knew how the effects were done, so I watched it very clinically but I must admit that Friedkin did a very good job.'

Castle's latest film is *Shanks*, which stars Marcel Marceau. 'I hadn't directed for several years because I was too busy producing and writing, but this film I decided to direct because it was a challenge. In the arts I've only met three geniuses in my lifetime: one was Orson Welles who was a partner of mine in the early days – we did *Lady from Shanghai* together; the second was Charles Chaplin who, though I never had the privilege of working for him, I knew quite well and I used to watch him direct and act. The third is the great Marcel Marceau, who is the reason I decided to direct *Shanks* myself. I think he is just absolutely a genius in his field. *Shanks* is a very provocative and outrageous film; I broke every rule that a director can break – it's full of black comedy, pathos and is an extremely *visual* film. There are only twenty-five lines of dialogue in the whole film. It should have appeal in every country because there is no language barrier. Marcel Marceau plays a puppeteer who manipulates people, and there was a great deal of improvisation. The best way to describe it is as a grim fairy story. But it is also hilariously funny and unlike anything I have done before, though it does have a touch of the macabre. But the interesting thing is that older people do not relate to it – they don't understand it – but the 15 to 30 age group *do* relate to it and like it. I've hit a nerve there and I'm rather glad of that because eighty per cent

of film audiences all over the world are comprised, these days, of youth.

'Later I'll be shooting a film which will be called *The Hyphestus Plague* [eventually released as *Bug!*], a horror piece that I acquired in novel form. It's the story of ten-inch-long cockroaches that come out of the bowels of the earth during an earthquake. And there are actually cockroaches that big, so we don't have to make them, we can use the real thing. They come from the jungles of South America, and are actually ten inches long, and very frightening.'

Castle, like other horror directors, has acquired a cult status over the years, something he accepts with equanimity. '*The House on Haunted Hill, The Tingler*, all those early films of mine are being studied by university students. I even get letters from universities in England asking why I did certain things in certain sequences of my early films – were they done just for sheer shock or were there deeper, symbolic meanings? Who knows what's in our subconscious? It is possible that with those films I was trying to say something that was buried deeply within my subconscious mind.' But despite this unexpected intellectual respectability Castle has not forsaken his talent for showmanship. 'I've pulled many stunts and I still will pull many stunts. In the new film, *The Hyphestus Plague*, I'm planning a "feelie" gimmick which comes from Huxley's *Brave New World*. During the screening of the picture the ten-inch roaches will get loose in the theatre – we're working on something which will enable the audiences to feel the roaches actually *crawling* over their legs. [This gimmick was later dropped!] It's the same with *Earthquake* and the gimmick of creating the sensation of being in an earthquake which is produced by high frequency sound – you *need* this sort of showmanship these days. It's all coming back. Showmanship is an integral part of the entertainment world – you must have it. Of course, as Mr Shakespeare said, "The play is the thing" – you must have a story and a fine cast, but you have to sell and merchandise a picture and this is why I started my gimmicks. I had no cast and no money so I had to do something else to compel audiences to come into the theatre. Not having stars or a high budget I had to do something different and I became, in effect, the king of the gimmicks. I know I'm a darned good showman; no one could top my gimmicks.'

In a William Castle film you never know what you're going to find in the bath (from The Tingler*)*

9 Vincent Price

'Emerging, usually on the wan side, from a Vincent Price film,' wrote a critic in a 1964 issue of *Films and Filming*, 'I always have to fight down the inclination to send him a telegram reading: "Congratulations, you've done it again." Punk scripts, bad handling, limp co-stars, mangy sets, choppy editing, old Vincent takes them all in his stride. In his own way he's quite a stylist. No matter what piece of junk he appears in, he never seems embarrassed or uncomfortable.'

As noted earlier, there are two types of horror stars – those who make a name for themselves in horror films and move on to better things, such as Oliver Reed; and those who find themselves typecast in horror roles after enjoying a more varied career, such as Peter Cushing. Vincent Price is definitely in the latter category. After a moderately successful career as a character actor on both stage and screen he has, during the last decade and a half, become established as *the* major horror star, ranking as high as Karloff and Lugosi with the horror film fans. It's a situation that, understandably, he slightly resents. 'I think of my career and I'm always amazed when people say, "Well, you do horror pictures." I do one horror picture a year. I also do about seventy-five television shows a year and a lot of radio, as well as writing articles.'[75] Price is also known as an art expert and collector. He was one of the founders of the Modern Institute of Art in Los Angeles and is a patron to several contemporary artists. At one time he was the leading buyer of art for the giant Sears-Roebuck company and had a permanent float of $1 million to spend on art treasures for their mail-order business. He has written two successful books on the subject as well as many articles. He has also written books on cookery, another passion of his (for a time he had his own cookery programme on British television – something that surely only his most avid fans could have willingly endured to watch). His other interests include archaeology and anthropology, and he spends much of his time lecturing on these and other subjects, such as art. Not surprisingly, he is one of America's highest paid lecturers.

As an actor, one way Vincent Price has coped with the horror tag is by putting his tongue firmly in his cheek and leaving it there. That way he usually gives the impression that he is sending up both the film and him-

A young Vincent Price in Otto Preminger's Laura

self. This tactic of rarely playing a horror role straight is sometimes a source of annoyance to the dedicated horror fan, as well as to the people he works with. 'He's fallen into acting habits,' said Richard Matheson. 'The first time he ever snapped out of it was when I wrote *The House of Usher* for him. He liked the script so much it shook him out of his usual style and as a result he did a very commendable job on it. But as he did more and more of the Poe pictures he started sliding back into the same thing.'

'I must confess,' said Price, 'that it's hard for me not to break up with laughter when we're doing some of these pictures. Once, during *The Fly*, Herbert Marshall and I had to examine a spider's web which held a small fly which was supposed to be my brother – and it took us a whole day to film it. We kept laughing ourselves sick. In the end we had to film back to back – we couldn't look at each other's face.'[76]

'It was difficult keeping a straight face through some of the scenes,' said actress Valli Kemp, who was Price's co-star in *Dr Phibes Rises Again* (Robert Fuest, 1972), 'because just before a shot Vincent is likely to pat me on the bottom and joke with me when I'm supposed to go on and be serious. I did one scene with him where I was playing the violin and he took a grape from the fruit bowl and shoved it in my mouth. He then took another grape and shoved that in my mouth so I had two grapes in my mouth and daren't swallow them because if I did I would have burst out laughing. Then he picked up a pineapple and went to put that in my mouth as well, but then shook his head when he realized it was too big. This has all been left in the film and it's hysterical because it was completely improvised and I didn't know anything about it.'[77]

Vincent Price was born on 27 May 1911 in St Louis, Missouri. The son of the president of the National Candy Company, Price had a secure, upper-middle-class childhood. After graduating from Yale, where he had studied art history, he became a singing coach and apprentice teacher at the Riverdale Country School in New York. While at university he had become interested in acting so in his spare time he made the rounds of various New York theatrical agencies – with no success whatsoever. He then decided to become an art historian and went to London where he studied for his Master's degree at the University of London. (It was his third visit to Europe – at the age of sixteen he had spent five weeks touring the art galleries in many of the major European capitals, and while at university he had visited Europe again as a member of the Yale Glee Club.) In London he was an avid theatre-goer, which rekindled his interest in acting. He began to audition for parts and was eventually hired, mainly for his American accent, to play a policeman in the London production of the play *Chicago*. This was in 1935. His next part was a bigger one – that of Prince Albert in *Victoria Regina* – and later that same year he found himself back in New York when the production moved to Broadway. He was hailed by New York critics as a 'talented new discovery'.

More stage roles followed and he spent a period with Orson Welles's experimental Mercury Theatre Workshop before making his film debut in 1938 in a comedy called *Service Deluxe* (Rowland V. Lee). That same year he married Edith Barrett, granddaughter of Edwin Booth's acting partner, Laurence Barrett. (This marriage ended in divorce in 1948 and in 1949 he married Mary Grant, a former fashion designer. He is now married to British actress Coral Browne. He has two children, a son from his first marriage and a daughter from his second.) In 1939 he signed a contract with Universal after making one film for Warner Brothers – *The Private Life of Elizabeth and Essex* (Michael Curtiz), the costumed soap opera that starred Bette Davis and Errol Flynn (Price played Sir Walter Raleigh). His next film was another costumed melodrama – *Tower of London* (Rowland V. Lee), and his co-stars were, significantly enough, Boris Karloff and Basil Rathbone.

He did three more films for Universal before his contract expired in 1940, including *The Invisible Man Returns* (Joe May, 1940), the first of the many sequels to *The Invisible Man*. It was a role in which he used his smooth, velvety voice to good advantage, as had his predecessor, Claude Rains.

In 1940 Price moved to 20th Century Fox where he made *Brigham*

Young (Henry Hathaway), playing the part of Joseph Smith, the founder of the Mormon religion. The following few years were probably the best for him as far as his career as a 'straight' actor was concerned. During this period he appeared in *The Song of Bernadette* (Henry King, 1943), *Wilson* (Henry King, 1944), and the now classic *Laura* (Otto Preminger, 1944) in which he played the weak-willed fiancé of Gene Tierney. Also in 1944 he appeared in *The Keys of the Kingdom* (John M. Stahl) which starred newcomer Gregory Peck. More good roles followed in films such as *A Royal Scandal* (Otto Preminger, 1945), *Leave Her to Heaven* (John M. Stahl, 1945), *Shock* (Alfred Werker, 1946) (the villainous role in the latter was a foretaste of things to come) and *Dragonwyck* (Joseph L. Mankiewicz, 1946). In *Dragonwyck* he again worked with Gene Tierney and gave a fine performance as her husband.

In 1947 his contract with Fox wasn't renewed, and this marked the beginning of a decline in his career. Most of the films that he appeared in during the next six years were forgettable, with the exception of *The Three Musketeers* (George Sidney, 1948) in which he played Cardinal Richelieu. Memorable as an oddity rather than anything else was *The Baron of Arizona* (1950), a Samuel Fuller film about a man who tried to lay claim to the state of Arizona by means of forged Spanish land grants.

It was in 1953 that a major turning-point in his career arrived. This was when he was offered the simultaneous opportunity to do a Broadway play directed by Jose Ferrer, *My Three Angels*, and a film, *The House of Wax*. Price chose the film. 'I would have loved to have done that play,' he said later. 'It was an enormous success, but so was the film.' A remake of *Mystery of the Wax Museum* (Michael Curtiz, 1932), *House of Wax*, directed by Andre de Toth, was the first Hollywood feature film to be made in 3-D. The plot, about a man hideously scarred in some catastrophe who returns to wreak revenge on his enemies, was similar to that of *Phantom of the Opera* and is still serving today in such Vincent Price films as *The Abominable Dr Phibes*.

'*The House of Wax* was very demanding,' said Price, 'as I had to get to the studio every morning at 5.30 a.m. to put that make-up on. It took three hours to put on and it was agony, absolute agony. Because it was the first 3-D film it was made with two enormous cameras photographing in a mirror, so that you could get two tracks, and because of that unwieldy camera I had to do my own stunts. They couldn't do a close-up of me and then cut to a double. The most difficult stunt was at the very beginning, when the fire starts in the museum, and I run under this balcony that's in flames just before it falls. I actually did that. I worked it out with a stunt man. Anything on the floor that I might trip over or slide on was moved away and we figured out a course for me to take around these burning figures so that I could get into a little tiny closet when this

Price in one of his first big horror roles – that of the sculptor in House of Wax

3,000 lbs of burning balcony fell. It was scarey.'[78]

Full of 3-D gimmicks, *The House of Wax* isn't very impressive when seen today. Price gives an adequate performance as the mad sculptor, but in his appearances as the mysterious murderer, a figure all in black, he unfortunately adopted a peculiar, pigeon-toed way of walking – with ludicrous results. The following year he more or less repeated the role in *The Mad Magician*, a cheap 72-minute Columbia picture directed by John Brahm. Though by this time he was already typecast as a villain, Price didn't appear in another horror film until 1958 when he made *The Fly*. During the intervening years he made an uncredited appearance in *Casanova's Big Night* (Norman Z. McLeod, 1954), a Bob Hope vehicle, played Omar Khayyam in *Son of Sinbad* (Ted Tetzlaff, 1955), a talent scout who discovers Mario Lanza in *Serenade* (Anthony Mann, 1956), and a newspaper editor in *While the City Sleeps* (Fritz Lang, 1956). He also had parts in two more illustrious productions (though neither of them were as entertaining as any of the above) – Cecil B. DeMille's *The Ten Commandments* (1956), in which he played a villainous slave driver who is strangled by Charlton Heston's Moses, and Irwin Allen's typically preposterous *The Story of Mankind* (Allen is now better known for his science-fiction TV series and the currently popular disaster films such as

The Poseidon Adventure and *Towering Inferno*). The latter featured just
about every available actor and actress in Hollywood at the time,
including the Marx Brothers. Price played the Devil who had a verbal
duel with the Spirit of Mankind, played by Ronald Colman (Charlton
Heston was apparently otherwise engaged).

The Fly (Kurt Neumann) was a lavish-looking production in colour and
wide-screen, which was unusual for horror films in those days. The story
concerned a scientist (Al Hedison) who invents a matter transmitter and
then goes and gets himself mixed up with a fly during an experiment. He
ends up with the head and arm of a fly (suitably enlarged, of course)
while the fly ends up with *his* head and arm. For some reason, never made
clear, the scientist's personality remains with his body, despite the switch
in heads. Much of the film is taken up with him trying to conceal this
drastic turn of events from his wife. He keeps his head concealed under
a napkin at first but his wife suspects something is very wrong when she
hears him slurping a saucer of milk up through his proboscis (at least
Hedison wasn't required to rub his legs together). A totally ludicrous
film but a very enjoyable one, especially since the cast manage to appear
to take it all so seriously. It was no wonder that Price, who plays the
scientist's worried brother, had so much trouble in keeping a straight
face during the shooting.

In 1959 Price made *The House on the Haunted Hill* for director/producer
William Castle, who has since specialized in horror films (see Chapter 8).
Castle now claims credit for 'resurrecting' Price's career though by then
the actor was already in demand for horror roles. That same year he also
appeared in *The Return of the Fly* (Edward L. Bernds), and *The Bat*
(Crane Wilbur) as well as in one of his last non-horror pictures for some
time (though it depends on one's definition of the word 'horror') – Irwin
Allen's *The Big Circus*, in which he played the ringmaster.

The following year he made another Castle film – *The Tingler*, which,
like *The House on the Haunted Hill*, was slightly tongue-in-cheek. Price
played a pathologist who evolved a weird theory about acute fear causing
a jelly-like growth on the spine which can kill if it isn't alleviated by the
act of screaming. He is able to prove this theory when an associate con-
veniently arranges to scare his wife – who is deaf and dumb – to death.
The sequence where he does just that is quite effective, though the
remainder of the film is unmemorable.

That same year he made the first of the Corman/Poe films – *The Fall of
the House of Usher*, which was closely followed by another Matheson-
scripted production, *Master of the World* (William Witney), based on two
books by Jules Verne. The script was fairly intelligent; Price, as Robur the
Conqueror, was very good, and the picture could have rivalled the similar
Twenty Thousand Leagues Under the Sea if it hadn't been made so cheaply.

The large amount of stock footage spliced into it was laughably obvious, and often not even of the right era. For example, when Robur's charmingly quaint airship bombs turn-of-the-century London it is a scene of *Elizabethan* London that one sees through the bomb-sight.

Next came another Poe/Corman film – *The Pit and the Pendulum*, in which Price was at his hammiest. The film is still good fun, though it's obvious that Matheson had some trouble in working the actual pit and pendulum into his screenplay. That same year, 1961, Price made three pictures in Italy. Two of them were non-horror subjects but the third, *The Last Man on Earth* (Sidney Salkow), was based on Matheson's classic horror novel *I Am Legend* about a solitary man in a world full of vampires – the ultimate paranoid fantasy. But Matheson wasn't happy with the result (see Chapter 12) or with Price's performance. 'Price, who I like as an actor, was completely wrong for the part,' said Matheson.

The following year Price had two straight roles, in *Confessions of an Opium Eater* (Albert Zugsmith) and *Convicts Four* (Millard Kaufman), as well as appearing in Corman's *Tower of London*, a remake of the film that he had appeared in twenty-three years before (the years brought him a promotion – this time he played Richard the Third, the part that Rathbone originally had). Also in 1962 he appeared in another Corman production, *Tales of Terror*, which consisted of four Poe stories adapted by Matheson.

Nineteen sixty-three was a busy year for Price. He made five feature films as well as narrating a documentary about the life of the artist Chagall. His films included *The Raven*, a spoof which Price's customary acting style suited perfectly, *Diary of a Madman* (Reginald Le Borg), the film that produced the reaction in *Films and Filming* quoted at the start of this chapter, and *Beach Party* (William Asher), the first of AIP's successful 'teenagers and sand' pictures with Price making a guest appearance as Big Daddy among such luminaries as Frankie Avalon and Annette Funicello. Probably his best film that year was *Comedy of Terrors* (Jacques Tourneur), the Matheson-scripted comedy about a group of undertakers. The cast included Karloff, Lorre and Rathbone. Sadly, Price is the only one alive today.

In 1964 he made *The Haunted Palace*, another Corman picture that successfully combined Poe with H. P. Lovecraft, and it remains one of the best of the Corman horror series with a better-than-usual performance from Price in a dual role. Then came *Masque of the Red Death* and *The Tomb of Ligeia* (1965), the last of the Poe/Corman films. *Masque* is probably the most pretentious of all of Corman's films, but *Ligeia* is very impressive, the last half hour in particular. (It contains a number of unforgettable sequences, such as when Price's young wife, Rowena, becomes entangled in the shroud of the dead Ligeia – whose arms seem to grip the girl tighter as she struggles to escape; and the duel between

Price and the black cat, possessed by Ligeia, which succeeds in clawing out his eyes before he can kill it.) Both films are beautifully photographed and Price gives a good performance in each.

City Under the Sea, also known as *Warlords of the Deep* (Jacques Tourneur 1965), was a very poor AIP cheapie built around a single line from one of Poe's poems. About the only memorable thing about it was the unusual sight of David Tomlinson sharing his diving helmet with a chicken. Much more fun was *Dr Goldfoot and the Bikini Machine*, an AIP film that spoofed the company's own teenage and horror products (the climax is lifted from *The Pit and the Pendulum*). Directed by Norman Taurog, it gave Price the opportunity to indulge his natural inclination for broad comedy.

After a forgettable sequel to *Goldfoot* in 1966 (made in Italy), and an equally forgettable German/Spanish production in 1967 – *The House of A Thousand Dolls* (Jeremy Summers) – Price returned to England in 1968 to give one of his best performances for a long time in *Witchfinder General* (released as *The Conqueror Worm* in the USA so as to give the misleading impression that it was based on one of Poe's works). Playing Matthew Hopkins, the notorious witchhunter of Cromwellian times, Price was persuaded by the young director Michael Reeves (See Appendix) to forgo all his usual mannerisms and play the character absolutely straight. The

. . . then it's all smiles as the principals take a short break between takes

result was a masterly portrayal of evil that serves to remind one that, when he wants to, Price really can *act* – a fact often forgotten when one observes him doing his familiar mugging routine in film after film.

His next three films – *The Oblong Box* (Gordon Hessler, 1969), *Scream and Scream Again* (Gordon Hessler, 1970), and *Cry of the Banshee* (Gordon Hessler, 1970) – were all rather disappointing after *Witchfinder General* (though *Scream*, a strange mishmash of horror themes – vampires, artificially-created people and so on – is becoming something of a cult film). In 1971 he made *The Abominable Dr Phibes* (Robert Fuest, 1971), one of his most successful films in recent years. Fuest, a former set designer, produced a stylish spoof that combined humour with a number of grotesque murders. Phibes, played by Price, was a madman whose face was so badly disfigured that it resembled a naked skull and who could only eat, drink or speak by artificial means. It was a fairly easy role for Price, apart from the discomfort caused by the make-up, and he repeated it in the sequel *Dr Phibes Rises Again* (Robert Fuest, 1971), which was just as amusing as the first, though not nearly so successful.

Price prepares to lower the boom on his victim in The Pit and the Pendulum

AIP parodies itself with this scene from Dr Goldfoot and the Bikini Machine, *which Price also starred in*

The perfect host – Price entertains his guests, Frankie Avalon and Dwayne Hickman, with a knife trick in Dr Goldfoot

Similar in plot was *Theatre of Blood* (Douglas Hickox, 1972) in which Price played, with obvious relish, a bad Shakespearian actor who murders all the critics who had attacked his performances in the past, basing his murder techniques on those described in Shakespeare's plays. Rather sick, perhaps, but very entertaining. And the revenge motive was used yet again in *Madhouse* (Jim Clark), also known as *The Revenge of Dr Death*, which Price made in 1973 though it still hasn't been released at the time of writing. From all accounts it is a rather mediocre film, which may account for the delay in its release (though that's never stopped anyone before). Price's last film appearance to date was a small one in the so-called British sex comedy (it was neither funny nor erotic) *Percy's Progress* (Ralph Thomas), in which he played one of his favourite real-life roles, that of an art collector.

Though in his mid-sixties now, Price has no intention of retiring: 'They'll have to bury me before I retire and even then my tombstone will read "I'll be back!" Besides, I can't afford to retire. I've got to keep working. I've got ex-wives, and wives and mothers-in-law and children to support.'

Like most actors who have become associated with horror films he is defensive about their effect on people. 'These macabre exercises are

An unusual view of Price as he jokes for the camera with co-star Jane Asher

pure escapism,' he said, 'and to claim they harm children is the veriest nonsense. For them they are simply fairy tales, no grimmer than the Grimm their Grandmothers used to read at bedtime. I also believe children can rid themselves of feelings of hatred and violence while watching us on the screen, instead of taking it out on their parents, friends, and schoolteachers. And besides, these horror films are pure fun. People love them because they love being scared. But for us actors and the technicians involved, making films like these is a very serious business indeed. We would be lacking in all responsibility to our public if we allowed ourselves to say that they are rubbish. Making a horror film is far harder, in fact, than making many so-called straight films. We have to make them believable at all times. This can be damned hard work.'[79]

'With the death of Karloff,' said Forrest Ackerman, 'I would say that Vincent Price has ascended the throne of Mr Nice. He really just seems to be an absolutely sincere, sweet, nice person. There's no snobbery or anything like that about him. I was on the set as Creative Consultant when they did the Horror Hall of Fame TV special and I watched him in action from nine in the morning until eight at night and he was kind and pleasant to everyone all day, from the lowliest person on the set on upwards. He worked very hard and was willing to do anything.'

10   Christopher Lee

'As far as I'm concerned, the horror film, now [October 1974] and in the foreseeable future, is for me a thing of the past,' said Christopher Lee, somewhat vehemently. 'That is not to say that I will never do another, and it doesn't mean that some of those that I have done have not been very good, but it does mean that now I have a far wider choice of roles I am going to be much more diversified in the work that I do. But as I've said in public many times, I feel that, with few exceptions, the standard of the ''horror'' film – a dreadful word, incidentally, which is neither accurate nor appropriate – is steadily deteriorating. People are finding it too easy to make rubbish that will still make a profit. And I, like every other actor in the world, have been obliged to appear in pictures that have been less than good in order to make a living. But that era, as far as my career as an actor is concerned, has served its purpose and is now ancient history.

'When you look back at the pictures I made for Hammer! I started with *The Curse of Frankenstein*, which was certainly a ''horror'' film (though I prefer to call them fantasy pictures, or morality plays, or fairy stories, all of which they are in clearly defined terms), I then did the first *Dracula* and played, immediately afterwards, the romantic lead in *The Hound of the Baskervilles*, followed by *The Mummy* – which certainly wasn't a horror film either. Nor was *The Man Who Could Cheat Death*, in which I played the hero. I played *Rasputin*, and that wasn't a horror film. So where is the typecasting? In the mind of the press, not the public. The press keeps on using the word ''horror'' actor or Dracula every time I'm mentioned. They won't let it go because the press like to put a label on you and put you in a pigeon hole. But I won't conform and I never have.

'I am, if you like, typecast as a heavy in the way the late, great Humphrey Bogart, to name one of many, was typecast as a heavy. But how many different *kinds* of villains did he play? Claude Rains, Conrad Veidt, Sydney Greenstreet, Peter Lorre, Basil Rathbone – so many of them played heavies but how different they were. They put the stamp of their own personalities on to the parts they played – an actor has to do that – but they weren't the same characters or the same parts. And that's my position at the moment. If one can be called a successor to anybody I was, for a time, the successor to Chaney, Karloff and Lugosi, but now I am, to

Christopher Lee as Dracula

my mind, the successor to Rains, Rathbone, Veidt and many others, but this is not typecasting. The people who write to me and the people who come up and talk to me – very few of them mention the horror films. Ninety-five per cent of the people who write to me from all over the world say they like to see what I do as an *actor*, not as a horror star. There may be some who only like to see me do horror films but they are not the majority, they are the five per cent. But I am popular as the *villain* and I am quite content to go on playing villainous roles. They're the best parts – they're the ones everybody remembers. They're the most entertaining to do and I will probably play the heavy for the rest of my life, and this I am

'At last, no more typecasting!,' Lee seems to be saying in this scene from The Wicker Man

perfectly prepared to accept. It doesn't worry me at all because there are so many ways of doing it. But I am not typecast as a horror star! How can I be, after *The Wicker Man, The Three Musketeers* and *The Man With the Golden Gun?*'

Despite Mr Lee's protestations to the contrary, he is still synonymous with horror roles, particularly with Dracula, as far as most people are concerned, and it is going to take a long time for him to shake off this image. For example, during the making of the James Bond film *The Man With the Golden Gun* in which he played the villain, Scaramanga, Lee told an interviewer that: 'Guy Hamilton [the director] got something out of me in this picture which I've never been able to show on the screen. In his own words, he got the spook out of me. He got the Dracula out of me. Because, obviously, I can become very menacing, rather heavy, if I'm not careful.'[80] But on the film's release one reviewer wrote: 'Lee brings an authority to the part from his Dracula background that evens up the confrontations between him and Bond.' And another said he played Scaramanga as 'a Westernized, Draculaesque Fu Manchu'.

To be perfectly frank, Dracula is one role that Lee has really excelled at. He is a competent actor, but in many of his parts he has seemed rather inflexible and he admits himself that he finds laughing, as an actor, rather difficult to do. His main advantages are, naturally, his saturnine good looks and his height, which make him perfectly suited to standing around and looking aloof and dignified, ideal for the role of Dracula (the most common thing said about him by the critics for years was that he had 'a commanding presence'). But as Dracula he has brought to the character a certain vitality, particularly in the scenes where Dracula is at his most active, that was often lacking from his more conventional roles. He has often succeeded in communicating, usually by facial gestures and body movements alone, the presence of sheer evil. With this sort of exaggerated mime it would be very easy to overstep the mark and turn the character into something of a clown. To his credit, Lee has never done this (with the exception of one brief scene in *The Scars of Dracula* when, unexpectedly confronted with a crucifix, his reaction gave the impression that the Count was smelling something very bad rather than being threatened by the power of Light and Goodness). And, though he denies it, he does seem to have an affinity with the character. By means of his unique interpretation, he has made the role well and truly his own.

A handsome man who towers six feet four inches, a descendant of both Emperor Charlemagne and the Borgias, a former secret agent, an expert swordsman, a linguist, an opera singer – Christopher Lee couldn't be ordinary if he tried, and it is this larger-than-life quality that he possesses that worked against him when he began his acting career. He didn't fit into the rather staid world of the British film industry in the late 1940s and early 1950s: he was either too tall or too Italian looking for most of the parts he auditioned for. So, in effect, he was obliged to wait for the British cinema to change to the extent that it could accommodate him with the larger-than-life roles he was most suited to. And that didn't occur until 1956.

He was born Christopher Frank Carandini Lee in London on 27 May 1922 (the same day and month as Vincent Price and Peter Cushing). The Carandini part of the name came from his mother's side of the family. The Carandinis are among the oldest of Italian families and claim to date back to the Holy Roman Empire and Charlemagne. They also, at one time,

Lee prepares himself for a death scene

The finished scene from Dracula AD 1972

intermarried with the dreaded Borgias. Lee's father was a Colonel in the King's Royal Rifles and he wasn't pleased when his son announced his intention of becoming an actor. 'He was a tough army officer,' said Lee, 'who became the army's fencing champion. He wanted me to make the army my career. He was speechless when I told him I wanted to act. He had taught me how to shoot, fence and ride, and these accomplishments came in very handy when I got into films.' Lee made his first stage appearance at the age of nine in a school play – he played Cassius to Patrick MacNee's Brutus – but he didn't really consider becoming an actor until after the war (though part of his background was theatrical: his great-grandmother founded the first operatic company in Australia and took her daughters touring around the mining camps in a covered wagon while her husband worked as an actor, singer and dancer). Before the war Lee had to leave college prematurely when the family ran into financial troubles, and for a while he worked as a messenger boy for a shipping line in the City for the huge salary of £1 a week. At the outbreak of war he volunteered for military service and found himself serving in the RAF in Rhodesia where he trained as a bomber pilot. But his grasp of five languages ensured him a posting as an Intelligence Officer with 260th Fighter Squadron in the Western Desert.

It was one of the Carandini cousins – actually Italy's first post-war Ambassador to Britain – who suggested that he take up professional acting. He then introduced Lee to Filippo del Giudice, another Italian who was the head of Two Cities Films, a division of the Rank organization. Within weeks of the interview Lee was given a seven-year stock contract with Rank and that same year, 1947, appeared in his first film, *Corridor of Mirrors*, which was directed by Terence Young, who later became famous for directing many of the James Bond films. Lee's part in the picture was a small one and he had only one line of dialogue. He appeared in eleven films during his first eighteen months at Rank, and most of them were little more than walk-on parts. Among these films was Laurence Olivier's *Hamlet* (1948), in which, ironically enough, Peter Cushing also appeared, though the two of them never actually met until almost a decade later.

The parts were small but there were enough of them during the first few years of his career for him to live as a full-time actor. Unfortunately, in 1950 the British film industry entered a very bad period, caused mainly by the advent of television, and less work became available, although that same year Lee did land a role in his most prestigious picture up to that time – *Captain Horatio Hornblower RN* (Raoul Walsh). Lee's part, that of the captain of a Spanish man o'war, wasn't very big, but he did have to fight a duel with the star of the picture, Gregory Peck. The following year, however, his contract with Rank was allowed to expire and he was forced to become a freelance. The next few years were hard for Lee. He continued to get a number of small parts but was obliged to supplement his income by undertaking stunt work.

'In those days I was glad of a chance to double for stars in duelling and riding scenes. Often it was dangerous work. One of my first jobs was in a swashbuckler with Errol Flynn [*The Warriors* – also known as *The Dark Avenger*, made in 1954]. I had to duel all over the set, doubling for several actors, including Flynn. The director, Henry Levin, hired me as an expert who would make sure none of his stars, particularly Flynn, got hurt. In one scene I doubled first for Flynn, and when he stepped in for close-ups I switched over to take the place of his opponent. I fought for hours! During the final take I could hardly raise my aching arm. When I did, Flynn ran his sword into it. Just above the elbow. Everyone said

An early publicity photo of Lee

how wonderfully realistic it was. Everyone except me. As they bandaged my wounded arm I gritted my teeth and vowed I'd never double for anyone again.'

Lee as the Frankenstein creature in The Curse of Frankenstein

In 1955 Lee actually got the title role in a film – *Alias John Preston*, a short film directed by John MacDonald which didn't attract any attention when it was released and has apparently disappeared completely now. It was a psychological thriller in which Lee played a man who had a recurring dream about the murder of a young woman. After that it was back to the small roles again. He was now in his mid-thirties and naturally feeling rather depressed about the way his career was going. It was eight years since his screen debut and he didn't seem to have progressed very far.

The following year, among his usual minor supporting roles in films like *Battle of the River Plate* (Michael Powell), *Storm Over the Nile* (Terence Young and Zoltan Korda) and *Ill Met by Moonlight* (Michael Powell), he also appeared as the Frankenstein monster in *The Curse of Frankenstein*. At the time it was just another part and Lee did not attach any importance to the film at the time (even now he regards it as 'a terrible film'), but it was significant that for once his impressive height, instead of being a handicap as it had been up to then, was responsible for landing him a role.

The Frankenstein film didn't automatically lead to his getting the role in *Dracula* the following year but it did serve to keep his name in the minds of producer Anthony Hinds and director Terence Fisher. A number of actors were auditioned for the part but finally it went to Lee. 'He was an obvious choice, when you think about it,' said Michael Carreras. 'He had absolutely the right features, the commanding presence, and that fantastic voice. I'm quite sure if anybody at all had been sitting in that office and they saw six actors, one of whom was Christopher Lee, they would have chosen him as Dracula too.'

It was *Dracula* that set the seal on Lee's long association with Hammer though strangely enough they didn't take proper advantage of him for many years. His contribution to the success of *Dracula* was apparently overlooked, and instead of giving him similar roles that utilized his unique sexual attraction he was relegated to a series of supporting roles in films like *The Hound of the Baskervilles* (Terence Fisher, 1958), *The Man Who Could Cheat Death* (Fisher, 1959) and *The Two Faces of Dr Jekyll* (Fisher, 1960). Even more surprising, when Hammer made their first sequel to *Dracula* (*The Brides of Dracula* in 1961) Lee wasn't even included in the cast. They *had* cast him as the mummy in *The Mummy* (Fisher, 1959) and, despite being buried under all the usual make-up, Lee managed to invest the character with a certain amount of sympathy (his disjointed way of walking was particularly effective). But after *The Mummy* Lee decided

that he wasn't going to play any more heavily made-up characters. Unlike Lon Chaney Snr he 'didn't want to go through all that misery'. That's quite understandable considering that he was paid far less than Chaney had been for suffering for his art. Lee has also made a point of saying how irritating it was for him to have to wear the red contact lenses in the scenes where Dracula's blood-lust was up. 'They make me cry and I have to put water inside to lessen the irritation. I can only see hazily when I have them in. The coloured part doesn't cover the pupil of the eye, so I don't actually see red.'[81] Even more annoying was the eye make-up he had to wear when he played the slit-eyed Fu Manchu. The plastic strips took ninety minutes to apply each day and were extremely uncomfortable to wear, and they also hindered his portrayal of the character. 'I couldn't look up, I couldn't look down, I could only play, so to speak, from side to side. I had to rely entirely on the inflection of the voice and the "lack" of movement to put over the character.'[82]

Despite the regularity of his appearances in Hammer films the financial rewards weren't very high and in 1959 he temporarily left England to make the first of many continental horror films – *Tempi Duri per I Vampiri* (directed by 'Steno'), an Italian spoof that was released with the English title of *Uncle Was a Vampire*, though the correct translation was the more apt *Hard Times for Vampires*. Oliver Reed, who donned Lee's rejected heavy make-up to play the werewolf in *Curse of the Werewolf* (Fisher, 1961), recalled that Lee used to earn extra money during his early days at Hammer by loaning out his white Mercedes and his services as a chauffeur to fellow actors for five shillings at a time.

In fact it wasn't until 1965 that Lee's career began to improve. (In the meantime he had married, in 1961, former Danish model Birgit Kroencke and two years later his daughter, Christina, was born.) 1965 was the year he first played Fu Manchu in *The Face of Fu Manchu* (Don Sharp). Lee was the perfect choice for the oriental villain and had, in fact, once tried to interest Hammer in the idea, but without success. Made by Hallam Productions, it was cheaply done though competently directed by Sharp, and turned out to be a financial success. This resulted in a number of quick, even cheaper, sequels, that rapidly deteriorated in quality. But by 1965 Hammer had also realized the value of Lee and demonstrated this by starring him in both *Rasputin the Mad Monk* (Don Sharp) and in *Dracula, Prince of Darkness* (Terence Fisher). In the former Lee gave what many consider to be one of his best performances but the vastly inadequate script was too much to overcome. *Prince of Darkness* was almost as good as Hammer's first *Dracula* (in fact a few sequences were almost exact copies from the original, such as the occasion when Dracula first appears with his blood-lust up). His scenes were kept to a minimum, which served to make his appearances more im-

Lee as the Oriental arch-fiend Fu Manchu (from The Brides of Fu Manchu*)*

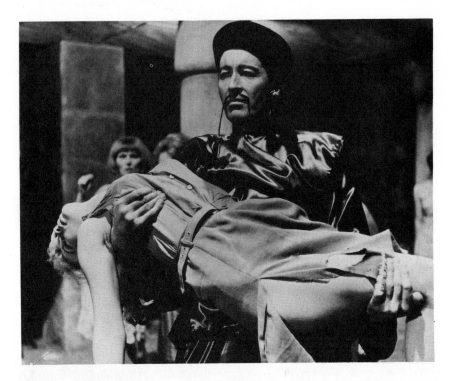

pressive, but this time the Count was without a line of dialogue, apart from the odd snarl. This didn't completely please Lee: 'In the book he hardly ever stops talking. I think he should say something in these films, though when he does speak it has to be something worth saying.'[83] Another difference was that now Dracula sported a cape with bright red lining instead of his original all-black one. 'Hammer like a bit of colour,' was Lee's explanation.[84]

Prince of Darkness was very successful but it was another three years before Hammer made another Dracula. Directed with real flair by Freddie Francis, *Dracula is Rising from the Grave*, despite the title, is probably the best of all the series. One highlight was a sequence where Dracula, asleep in his coffin, was staked through the chest but was able to rise up and pull out the stake because his attacker, the young hero of the picture, was an atheist and therefore unable to say the necessary prayer to complete the ritual. It was an amusing and surprising twist but the vampire fundamentalists weren't happy about it. Even Lee himself said: 'It was all wrong that Dracula should have been able to remove the stake. Everyone knows a stake through the heart is the very end of a vampire. I objected at the time but it was overruled. It was an extremely gruesome sequence. The blood came pouring out.'[85] Also gruesome in a majestic sort of way was the climax of the film when Dracula was impaled

Dracula is impaled on a giant crucifix at the climax of Dracula Has Risen from the Grave

on a giant cross and forced to stagger about with it protruding from his back until a handy priest arrived on the scene to deliver the appropriate prayer, at which point Dracula settled back on the cross and expired gracefully with tears of blood streaming down his face. (Not surprisingly, the young hero, faced with this demonstration of the power of prayer, announces in the film's closing moments that he has found religion.)

Dracula Has Risen from the Grave was even more successful than its predecessor, which caused Hammer to start churning out more *Draculas* at a faster rate. *Taste the Blood of Dracula* (Peter Sasdy) followed in 1969, *The Scars of Dracula* (Roy Ward Baker) in 1970, *Dracula AD 1972* (Alan Gibson) in 1971 and *The Satanic Rites of Dracula* (Alan Gibson) in 1972. But with each film Lee grew more unhappy about appearing in them. In 1968 he said of the character: 'Dracula is a great role and very difficult to play. I find it a stimulating challenge to make him convincing to today's cynical, worldly audiences. I see him as aloof, dignified and austere, exploding into tigerish activity when necessary.'[86] Four years later he complained: 'All I get to do is stand around on unhallowed ground, sweep down corridors and make the odd pounce or two. Nobody can write dialogue for Dracula. Time and time again I have suggested that they go back to the original Bram Stoker novel. In the new film [*Dracula AD 1972*] I have one original Bram Stoker line, but that's yelled out at a

*Dreams of world
conquest go up in
flames for Dracula in*
The Satanic Rites of
Dracula

distance of a hundred years. I've told Hammer that unless certain conditions are met, I shall not play the role again.'[87]

Whether or not those 'certain conditions' were met, Hammer succeeded in getting him back in harness, and cape, for *The Satanic Rites of Dracula* which had Dracula occupying an office penthouse in modern-day London (he had been in modern London in the previous film but had remained inside an old church). 'I thought that was very wrong,' said Lee, 'and I told them so at the time.' Actually *Satanic Rites* was rather entertaining and a vast improvement on the previous one, but Lee is now adamant about never playing Dracula again. 'I will *not* play that character anymore,' he said recently. 'I no longer *wish* to do it, I no longer *have* to do it, and I no longer *intend* to do it. It is now a part of my professional past, just one of the roles I have played in a total of 124 films. Four other actors have played him in the past year [1974] – Jack Palance, Udo Keir in Andy Warhol's film, John Forbes-Robertson in the new Kung Fu Dracula, or whatever you want to call it, and David Niven in *Vampira*. I am now one of the many actors who have played that part.'

Despite his determination to have nothing more to do with the character he still looks back on the first Dracula film with a certain amount of pride. 'The first *Dracula* was a very good picture. I was with Franco Zeffirelli recently and he said it was, in its way, a classic, which it certainly was. But the reason for that is extremely easy to see. It was the nearest to the book, and when you have a story that is world-famous, and indeed a story of great power and imagination, and you transfer it to the screen with a certain fidelity to the author's intention, it will obviously work. If it's done properly with efficient and competent technical work, with good production and direction, obviously it's going to have tremendous impact. But if the standard of that story progressively degenerates over the years because people find it so easy to turn out cheap rubbish (and I'm not just referring to the Dracula films), because it will always make a profit for somebody, then I, as an actor, do not wish to be associated with it. I agreed to do the Spanish version of Dracula, *El Conde Dracula* [Jesus Franco, 1969], for one reason only. It was the only opportunity I ever had for portraying Stoker's character physically on the screen exactly as he described him – as an old man dressed in black and getting progressively younger during the story, which was the whole point of Stoker's novel. The film itself was a disappointment because it was done cheaply, without due attention to script, production or anything else. Put it on the screen, get it in focus and it will make money somewhere, if not a lot. But I don't accept this any more. Fortunately I am now in a position (and today who knows how long this sort of position lasts with anybody, in any business or profession) where I am able to choose the work I do. Obviously I have no intention of making another picture which doesn't have good production values.'

As far as the film industry is concerned, if not the public, Lee does seem to have succeeded in escaping the horror star tag. This process began in 1970 when Billy Wilder cast him as Sherlock Holmes's brother Mycroft in *The Private Life of Sherlock Holmes*. 'That really started the break for me,' said Lee. 'After all, my contention was that if one of the greatest directors in the history of the cinema was prepared to choose me to play one of the leading parts in his film, where is the type-casting?' After that he appeared in a Western with Raquel Welch, *Hannie Caulder* (Burt Kennedy, 1971), in which he played a bearded, scruffy-looking gunsmith. In 1972 he made *The Wicker Man*, a rather upper-class horror film scripted by Anthony Shaffer of *Sleuth* fame. Lee played Lord Summerisle, a pagan aristocrat on a remote Scottish island, who lures a Christian policeman (Edward Woodward) to a particularly unpleasant death. Lee's portrayal of the character, at least until the climax of the film, was something of a departure from his usual style in that Summerisle came across as a jovial type of person given to outbursts of song. Another departure from the usual Christopher Lee image was the sight of him, wearing a dress and long wig, high-kicking his way through the countryside as he led his pagan followers in a fertility rite.

'I was very much involved in *The Wicker Man*,' said Lee, 'because the writer, Anthony Shaffer, the producer, Peter Snell, and I did it for

Lee, the figure on the extreme right wearing a dress, as Lord Summerisle leading his people in a fertility rite in The Wicker Man

nothing. Of course we'll get a percentage of the profits if the film makes money but we did the picture for nothing at all, such was our belief in the subject and the story. Unfortunately, something like fifteen to twenty minutes was cut out of the film, which, in my opinion, spoiled it. But even with that amount of time cut it is still, to quote one newspaper: "One of the most original and unusual British films in years." And a magazine said: "There is still hope for the British film industry when it is capable of making films of this kind." It was the best part I've ever had as far as the script was concerned. It was a brilliant script, with wonderful lines. What more can an actor ask for?'

To set the seal on his escape from Dracula, Lee then appeared in Richard Lester's *The Three Musketeers* in 1973 (originally it was one film but extra footage was later shot and it has been released in two parts, the second being *The Four Musketeers*) as Rochefort. 'Of course that was a lovely part too, as Rochefort is on the screen a lot of the time in both pictures. A good action part and in a funny sort of way, quite a romantic part, and yet he is a villain of the deepest dark. But it was a strenuous film to make. The greatest injury I've ever had was during that. I tore the ligaments in my left knee and I couldn't walk properly for three or four months. That happened, unfortunately, at the beginning of the picture in the first fight that I did. Oliver Reed got hurt too – he was stabbed in the wrist, and Michael York nearly lost his eye. We all got knocked about on that picture.

'In the Bond picture I again played a villain, a very evil and wicked man, absolutely lethal and dangerous, but also charming, witty and amusing – even attractive according to the way he's presented on the screen.'

During the making of *The Man With the Golden Gun* Lee and director Guy Hamilton decided that the villain, Scaramanga, should be a little like Bond himself instead of the rather conventional thug of the novel. 'When I first read the script,' said Lee, 'I visualized Scaramanga as a straight-down-the-middle heavy. The villains are always the centre of curiosity in Ian's books, but I must agree that Scaramanga is not one of his most impressive murderers. So Guy and I decided to make him into a sort of counter-Bond. The fastest gun in the East. When we were filming in Thailand Guy kept saying to Roger Moore and myself, "Enjoy it, enjoy it! Lightly! Lightly!" And enjoy it we did. With the exception of Billy Wilder, no one has given me more help on a picture than Guy.'[88] Fans of the Bond films will probably say that Hamilton succeeded *too* well; *The Man With the Golden Gun* is so light it threatens to float away. But despite Hamilton's efforts to make Lee seem as bland as Roger Moore, Lee manages to retain enough of his old characteristics to make Scaramanga a memorable villain. (And Hamilton didn't completely avoid utilizing Lee's Dracula image – one of the film's better sequences, a sinister confrontation between Scaramanga and his mistress, begins with Lee asleep in bed in a very Dracula-like pose.)

In 1973 Lee formed, with producer Anthony Nelson Keys (an old Hammer regular), his own production company called Charlemagne Productions Ltd (named after Lee's illustrious ancestor). The company's first film was a mediocre thriller called *Nothing But the Night* (1973) which starred Lee and Peter Cushing. 'It wasn't as successful as we hoped it would be,' said Lee. 'We are about to put another one together which will be about witchcraft and the occult. We do own all the rights to Dennis Wheatley's black magic stories. I did one for Hammer, *The Devil Rides Out*, which was a very good film and we're hoping to do something equally as good from a book of Wheatley's called *To the Devil a Daughter*.* Wheatley's books are hard to transform into a film script because he paints such enormous canvases and his books are very detailed and long,

* Presumably Charlemagne Productions will be making this in conjunction with Hammer Films, who have also demonstrated an interest in the same book.

and very difficult to condense into an hour and a half or two hours.

'As far as directing films myself, I have no intention to at the moment. I don't consider that I have enough technical knowledge to do so. I have a fair amount, I think. Obviously one doesn't make 124 movies with one's eyes closed so one can't help but learn a lot. From the point of view of directing artists I don't think that would be any problem, but as far as camera set-ups, lenses, cutting, etcetera are concerned I would have to concentrate and work extremely hard for quite a considerable period. One would have to spend three to four months in the cutting room, which I would be prepared to do if it was the right kind of subject. You see, too many people take the easy way out. I've never done so. Unfortunately I'm a perfectionist, and that's a terrible thing to be. One very seldom lives up to one's own demands on oneself, let alone other people's, therefore I'm not prepared to do something unless I can do it well; and that is hopefully better than what other people do. That is not conceit – it's determination, and belief and faith in oneself which you must have, particularly if you're an actor. Actors are always in need of help and assistance. We're all basically, I suppose, quite insecure people who need to be reassured.

'One of the problems with me is that I've been associated with – not exactly B pictures or C pictures, or whatever you'd like to call them – but a *cheaper* kind of picture. They can be very good and make a lot of money, but this association with them has prevented me, until about three years ago [1971], from doing the work I wanted to do and the pictures I should have been in – the type that I'm in now. So, as far as I'm concerned, the horror film was merely a phase in my career which is now, for the most part, finished. They were a tremendous launching pad for me, no question of it, but people have said that because I won't do another one I'm con-demning the pictures I've made. This is totally incorrect and untrue. I have never said that. I have always said that my relationship with companies like Hammer have been excellent ones. We have, at times, agreed to disagree, but that is as it should be. I have always said they helped me but I have long ago fulfilled my obligation to them. I'm not, and never have been, under contract to them. And it's not a question of me saying thanks very much and goodbye, because if Hammer ask me to do a picture, and it's a good story and a good part and I want to do it, I will do it. But very few horror scripts are sent to me now. I always make the proviso before they are sent that I will never play Dracula again, I will never play a vampire again; and I will not do the conventional type of horror picture which is made for a quick buck.

'I have been more fortunate than some actors who have been in horror films, I know. It was a shame that Boris Karloff was confined to the play-ing of one type of role because he was too good an actor. But Lon Chaney, the most brilliant actor of them all, was not confined to playing horror parts. Far from it. Very few of his roles were horror ones. You can't call *The Hunchback of Notre Dame* a horror film.* I would define the Chaney character in the picture as a very sad and pitiful one, which of course so many of these characters are and that is the way they should be presented. Even Dracula is a sad creature, drained and weak in the daytime, doomed to live forever because he is so wicked he can never die and be at peace. Audiences, I think, are more shocked by a sad vampire than by a ferocious one. But comparisons are odious. You can't say that you are like a particular actor because you are *you*. I have tried, and I will continue to try, to carry the banner so superbly held for so many years by all those great actors like Chaney and Karloff; but that doesn't mean I am prepared to remain in one area. And you must remember that in those days they had a far higher standard of production – those pictures were made as major productions. That's what Karloff said to me – they had top directors, top writers and they were made as top pictures before the war. That is, alas, not the way it is today, apart from a very few exceptions like *Rosemary's Baby* and *The Exorcist*.

'*The Exorcist*, by the way, is definitely a horror movie. You can't possibly call it anything else. I haven't seen it and I have no desire to see it. I don't say that I disapprove of it, it's just that I have no particular desire to see the possession of a very young child, with her using that kind of language and doing those sort of things. That kind of thing revolts me. I'm not saying it's wrong and I'm not adopting a high moral tone about anything. There are a lot of pictures I don't go to see because I don't *want* to see them, not because I disapprove of them.'

While giving a lecture at the National Film Theatre in London in 1971 Lee said that he considered the violence in the Bond films to be more harmful than that in the horror films he had appeared in. Now, after appearing in a Bond film himself, it's not surprising to learn that he has modified his opinion on the subject.

'When I made that remark I thought what I said was absolutely true. There was less real, *copyable* violence in the sort of picture that I had appeared in at that time than there was in the Bond pictures of the period, when there was a lot of violence and some of it was very sadistic and sickening. But there isn't any more. The Bond violence is fantasy violence now. I mean, in *Live and Let Die* the violence was very minor and the same applied to *The Man With the Golden Gun*. There's practically none in the latter. Of course people get killed but they don't dwell on the gory details. A man is shot, he falls over and he is dead – they don't make a great banquet out of it for several gory minutes. They take the curse off the violence by treating it with a light touch. As to the suggestion that might

* I can.

Dracula punishes his servant, Patrick Troughton, in a scene from The Scars of Dracula

be even more dangerous, well, that's a paradoxical statement, in a way, and one could argue about it forever. The violence in a Bond film now is not made attractive, but it's not made as unpleasant as it really is. But as I said at the lecture three years ago, there is less *real* violence in the horror films that I've made than in many other pictures which, in my opinion, do have an effect, and sometimes a harmful effect, on people. In the Dracula films when there's all that blood spurting about it's not real because you know that the character can't be killed – the violence is happening to a supernatural creature – and that's why it's never damaging. 'People enjoy it because it's escapism. I mean, who's going to go rushing around trying to drive a stake through someone's heart after seeing a Dracula film?

'I do believe in a limited form of film censorship. I've always felt that certain films should be shown to adults and certain films should *not* be shown to younger people. Children should be protected from excessive copyable violence, and from eroticism taken to the extreme where it becomes obscene and perverted. That's what I don't like about pornography (not that I'm in the habit of looking at pornography – in fact I've never seen a blue picture in my life and have no desire to) that it takes something which in itself is a beautiful act and makes it filthy, dirty and obscene. It's not that I disapprove of pornography, but I feel that children should not be allowed to see pictures in which the sexual element is so blatantly perverted that it destroys a beautiful thing. That sort of censorship should exist. A film like *Deep Throat* certainly should not be seen by young people. And I don't think some pictures with excessive violence, violence that could be copied, should be shown to young people. By young I mean under fifteen years old. If you show everything to young people you are showing it to them far too soon. Let them retain a few illusions about life – there aren't that many left. Why throw them this Niagara of sewage and sickening brutality at an early age? They'll begin to think everyone is like that. As for censorship for adults – I'm not really in favour of it. If you're grown up you can make your own judgments. "You don't have to go," is the classic phrase.

'I can't recall ever making a film myself that was excessively violent. It is true that we sometimes made two versions of the same scene in early Hammer films for overseas markets – we made them more horrifying, a bit more gruesome perhaps. But then again it was made gruesome for audiences in a part of the world who would not be unduly affected by it. People who had probably lived with that kind of thing so often they expected to see it on the screen. Countries like Japan. But to my knowledge that kind of thing doesn't happen any more, and there were very few instances where I've ever actually shot an alternate scene. Today it's nudity usually, but in those days it was elements of the gruesome rather than sex.'

Despite his break-away from the horror film *genre* as an actor, Lee remains personally interested in the occult and a large portion of his 12,000-strong book collection is devoted to it. But he claims that he never involves himself in any way with the practice of magic, black or white. 'It's too dangerous,' he said. In 1971 he made his first trip to Transylvania, legendary home of Count Dracula, while making a television documentary called *In Search of Dracula*. This traced the roots of the Dracula legend to Prince Vlad Tepes Dracula, an actual historical figure of the fifteenth century who was famous for his excessive cruelty (he was called Vlad the Impaler due to his favourite method of execution). Lee appeared as Vlad in the documentary and, suitably enough, there was an uncanny resemblance between the actor and portraits of the once-dreaded Prince.

In certain circles Lee has a reputation for being a rather cold, humourless person ('Christopher Lee can't be funny,' said one producer, 'He's such a dead serious person. He hasn't an ounce of humour in him,') but this is not the picture of him that most of his friends and aquaintances have. According to Peter Cushing: 'Christopher has a delicious sense of humour and wit, plus a deep personal kindness. Some are awed when first meeting him in person, but they should know that beneath his outward aloofness and dignity lies a very *human* being: sensitive, warm, and oft-times suffering from nerves which he goes to great length to conceal.'[89] Robert Bloch said of him: 'Christopher Lee has a great sense of humour. He stayed with us for about two weeks when he came over to L.A. a few years ago and when you have a man like that living in your home you begin to realize that there is far more than just the public persona. He has a great singing voice, and when you hear him doing Wagner excerpts in the shower that's really something. He's a fine athlete, a great linguist, an avid golfer and cricketer, and there are many other aspects to him that he doesn't generally display.'

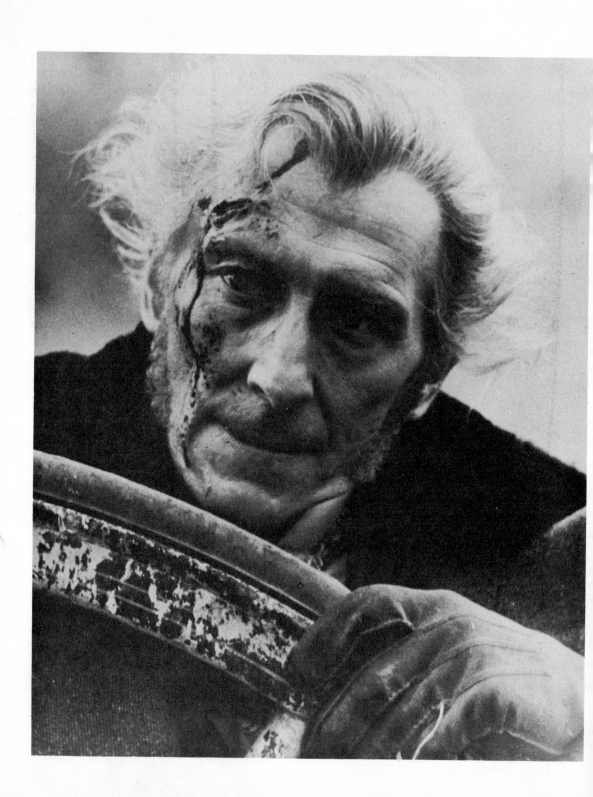

11   Peter Cushing

In Chapter 9 Forrest Ackerman said of Vincent Price that he had inherited the crown of Mr Nice after the death of Boris Karloff. There is another strong contender for this crown, and his name is Peter Cushing. One could question every member of the British film industry without discovering anyone with a bad word to say about him. Invariably the stories told about him reflect only his kindness and charm. Typical was the story of how Cushing insisted that his stand-in, who had been with him for several years and was recuperating from a serious operation, should do no work. Instead he made sure that his employee was always sitting down and comfortable, and when Cushing wasn't working or standing in for his own stand-in, he spent all his spare time making him cups of tea.

But Cushing, apart from being one of the most pleasant people one is ever likely to meet, is also a very fine actor; and it's something of a tragedy that in recent years he hasn't had many roles that can make full use of his talents. Cushing, though, takes it all very philosophically: 'I have been awfully lucky in the amount of work that I have been able to do. There have been long periods when I haven't worked, which is called resting because it's so unkind to say that an actor is out of work. But every week something I've been in seems to be on television and I'm happy just to keep on working. I don't think I'll ever retire. I don't think *any* actors ever retire. They can never afford to.'

Cushing takes all his roles very seriously and puts a tremendous amount of work into them, no matter how bad the script. Before a film begins he spends an enormous amount of time in preparation – he sketches out his entire wardrobe and selects every single prop that he's going to use, from a ring to a walking stick, making sure that both clothes and props will fit in with the character that he is playing.

Peter Cushing was born in 1913 in the town of Purley, Surrey. His interest in the cinema began when he was a child and spent many hours in the Electric Palace watching Chaplin, Keaton, William S. Hart and Tom Mix; all of whom fired his ambition to become a film star. When he left school he announced his intention of becoming an actor to his parents who, in the manner of most parents faced with such news, were not im-

Peter Cushing as Van Helsing, Dracula's perennial adversary, in a scene from Dracula AD 1972

pressed. Cushing compromised, at first. During the day he worked as a surveyor's assistant for the Coulsdon and Purley Urban District Council, but his nights were spent with the local amateur dramatic societies. Eventually he gave up the surveying and joined the Worthing Repertory Company; the same company, incidentally, that Christopher Lee later joined. Then, after four years with them, he decided to go to America.

'I had this great passion to go where Tom Mix lived, he was my hero, you see. So I went to America. My Dad, bless him, bought me a one-way ticket. No one knew me as an actor so when I went to Hollywood it was really a case of a fool stepping in where angels feared to tread. But I was frightfully lucky and did remarkably well. I'd armed myself with two addresses and I just went to Edward Small's studio where I heard they were making this picture and I got to see the casting director. "Do you fence?" he asked me. And I said, "Oh, yes. I've fenced all my life." So I got the job. Then he said I'd better go and polish it up with the fencing master who said, as soon as I took the sword, "You have fenced before?" And I said, "No, dear fellow, never, but I had to say yes to get the job." He said, "Now that you've been truthful I will teach you to become one of the best swordsmen in Hollywood." (And don't forget that we had Errol Flynn to contend with.) He said I'd taken hold of the sword as if it had been a knife so he knew immediately I was a novice.

'I didn't have any dialogue in my first scenes, I just had a fight with Warren William who, I remember, was playing one of the three musketeers in this film called *The Man in the Iron Mask* (1939). But they were quite pleased with what I did, so I had another small part where I rode up on a horse and said: "The king wants to see *you*!" Louis Hayward was playing twins in this film and the director, James Whale, was looking for someone who could play opposite Hayward for the split-screen scenes. Naturally all their scenes would end up on the cutting room floor after both scenes of Hayward had been spliced together; but it was better than just having someone, like the continuity girl, reading the lines from the script, as it's very off-putting for an actor not to have someone to play against. Like playing tennis, you need someone at the other end of the court. Anyway, that's the job I landed. I was on the picture three months playing all these scenes with Louis. I played both parts and was able, in so doing, to learn a great deal about filming. I don't really like the word but it's a very *technical* medium. Why I say I don't like the word – I don't like to think there's a technique of acting because to me there isn't, you either can or you can't. The greatest compliment is that it all looks so easy. But as a *medium* it is very technical. You've got not only to remember your lines and the character but also where you're standing, whether your foot's on a mark, and getting your own key light and trying to keep your shoulder out of the leading lady's light – there's a great deal on your mind for those few seconds that you're filming. That's where the mental strain comes in. You've got to remember a lot at very short notice and you get very little rehearsal time in films.'

After *The Man in the Iron Mask* Cushing had a small role in a Laurel and Hardy comedy, *A Chump at Oxford* (Alfred Goulding, 1939), and then landed the second male lead in *Vigil in the Night* (George Stevens, 1939). 'I got it because I could manage the Lancashire accent required.' The following year, after more roles in films like *Women in War* (John H. Auer, 1940) and *They Dare Not Love* (James Whale, 1940), Cushing decided to return to England. 'I got fearfully homesick because war broke out almost upon my arrival. It wasn't because I wanted to fight, or anything, I'm not really a fighting man – I'm sure hundreds of people weren't – but I did want to be at home. It's a strange thing but I think it's a natural instinct. There was quite an exodus of British actors from Hollywood at that time. We all had our medicals and my results were pretty low because of some old wounds I'd sustained at rugger. Those of us who were not a hundred per cent were told to stand by, but I couldn't wait for that and I decided to get back on my own. It was extraordinary – I offered my services to everyone and everything but I was too old for this and too old for that. I was getting desperate. Eventually I got up to Canada and from there to Liverpool. It took me eighteen months altogether to get home. And within a month of arriving back I was with ENSA. I think the troops called it Every Night Something Awful, but the real title was Entertainments National Service Association. I got into that because the actor playing Noel Coward's part in *Private Lives* was suddenly called up and they were desperately looking for someone to take over. And I said, ''Oh yes, I can learn that part in two days.'' Anything to get a job. I played it and was very glad I did for all sorts of important reasons. Sonya Driscoll, who had been playing the Gertrude Lawrence part for about a year and a half, was absolutely exhausted when I joined. The little leading lady who took over from her, Helen Beck, I married. I owe everything to her. She was a tremendous help to me in everything, not just my career. I always say that I was born in 1913, I started to live in 1941 when I met Helen, and I died in 1971 when she died.

'I was actually invalided out of ENSA. After a year and a half I got bronchitis or something. But it was a marvellous experience. I think the troops liked the play. It was a very good play. They had to be marched in at the point of a bayonet but once they realized it was a comedy they enjoyed it, especially the part where there was a fight and I was hit over the head with the gramophone record. In the war the props men had to get what they could in the way of properties. They got bundles of what were supposed to be 75s [sic] – big, old records that shattered easily – but amongst them there were some that were unbreakable. So sometimes when Helen hit me over the head with these things they wouldn't break. It was a bit unfortunate but the troops loved it. But apart from that one went into all sorts of the most beautiful country houses. They were commandeered for the duration so we were able to stay in these marvellous places. Mind you, they were stripped to the bare bones and all the wonderful banisters had sacking over them. We slept on navvy beds which were always too short. We used to move these little camp beds into the vast bedrooms which had the posts of four-poster beds but no bed between them. We put our little beds between them and tried to pretend we were sleeping in a four-poster. I adore England, and apart from doing a job I liked I was able to see a lot of the countryside. Of course one had to guess where one was because there were no signposts. But I found it all absolutely wonderful and the general atmosphere was pretty marvellous.

'When the war finished I said to my dear Helen, "I suppose I go back to repertory now." And she said, "Oh no, don't do that. Aim for higher things. You've done your training in Rep." So after the war I did a lot of work at a theatre called the Kew Theatre. You got very little money there – I think it was £5 for the two weeks, the week of rehearsal and the week of playing, and as I always demanded two weeks' rehearsal it wasn't very much financially – but it was a great shop window where you could try out plays with the possibility of them being transferred to the West End. But more than that, you were often seen by theatre managers who came down from the West End, and it was through that indeed, that many things stemmed. It was Helen who suggested that I go to Kew for those very reasons.

'I can't speak any languages at all but Helen spoke several fluently. She was born in St Petersburg and spoke Russian perfectly. She taught me to speak French, and it was while I was playing a Frenchman in a play called *While the Sun Shines* at Kew that I got the part in the film *Hamlet*. Prior to that I had been to see Laurence Olivier, as he was then, and his right-hand man Anthony Bushell, when they were putting on a play called *Born Yesterday* and were looking for someone to play the part that William Holden had played in the film. So when I arrived to see them they asked me if I spoke American and I said no. Laurence said, "But you've been to America." And I said, "Well, I've been to Lancashire too but I can't really speak in a Lancashire accent. I don't like to do anything that I feel I can't do properly but I need a job *desperately*." And they said, "Well, that's very honest of you. You haven't wasted our time and we will keep in touch." I thought this was just a polite way of saying goodbye but sure enough, a week after I did this play at Kew, I got a phone call from Tony Bushell saying that he and Laurence would like me to consider playing something in the film of *Hamlet*. So I said, "I suppose Hamlet's cast?" And he said, "Yes, Laurence is playing that." I said I didn't know

Cushing as Osric in Olivier's film version of Hamlet

many of the other characters and he said, "Well, the only one left is Osric." And I said, "Well, that's me, obviously." He told me that the only reason they had chosen me was that they had been down to see *While the Sun Shines* and Laurence had said that the Frenchman was awfully good and later on they discovered it was me.

'During the filming of *Hamlet* Laurence asked me if I'd like to go to Australia with the tour of the Old Vic that he was taking there; and I said I'd obviously like to very much indeed, but that I wouldn't go anywhere without my wife as we'd had too many partings during the war. "I don't know what I can offer Helen," he said, "but she can certainly come along, even if it's just for the ride." But he did find her work which was splendid. We were in Australia and New Zealand for nearly a year. I worked with Laurence again in 1951 when he was doing his Festival of Britain season at, I think, the King's Theatre. Then he was taking it to America but I didn't want to go, so that was that.

'Prior to that I went through a low period in my career when I almost gave up acting, or rather it was giving *me* up. I hadn't worked for two years and I was in such desperate straits. During that time someone said that if you want to look at it from a purely financial point of view you're almost forty and a failure. It was true. I had nothing. Absolutely nothing. In fact I always say I married Helen for her money because when I met her she had £12 10s. while I had only £9. I've still got this terrible thing about being in anyone's debt and I think it all stems from that period when I was out of work. I eventually got a job designing ladies' head-scarves – they were worn a lot in those days and were selling like the proverbial hot cakes. For that I was paid a magnificent amount – £10 a week, more than I'd ever earned before in my life, and it was much more than anyone was getting in the theatres. I did that for nine months. I said to Helen that I think I'll stick to this instead of acting, because at least we're sure of something coming in; and she nodded, but of course she knew I'd go back to acting.

'Around about 1951 I said to Helen – "Now what?" And she said, "The thing of the future is going to be television and we shall get into that." So she got a copy of the *Radio Times* and got all the names of the producers from the programme credit lists and wrote a sort of round-robin letter saying that Mr Peter Cushing finds himself unexpectedly available and is free anytime you would like to offer him work. And I said, "Darling, this is *awful!*" And she said, "Perhaps you're not very well known with the public, but you've done enough work with enough well-known people for your name to be known in professional circles." And she was absolutely right. She had an incredible instinct about these things. I got wonderful letters back, one in particular from Harry Clayton who said that he knew my work and would be delighted if I would play the leading part in a play recently done at the National Theatre. It was *Eden End* by J. B. Priestley. And it was in 1951 that I did my first television play.

'It was laughingly called "live". My heavens! You rehearsed three weeks, which is as much as you would do in the theatre, and then gave this "live" performance, then three days passed and you repeated the "live" performance on the following Thursday. That was a pure form of torture, because your nerves carried you through on the first night and afterwards you had people ringing up and saying that was marvellous and so on, so that you had to be as good as they thought you were, or try to be better, on the second performance. And I got into such a state that I felt afterwards each time as though I had walked into a plank of wood. I couldn't hear my own voice, I was so shaking with nerves. It didn't show, mind you. But Helen went to a doctor and said that my living was jeopardized by my shattered nerves – what can you do about it? And the doctor gave her some pills for me to take just before a show was to start. Actually what he had given her were little purple hearts – pep pills – and this was long before they were in the news. Well, he rang up one day and asked Helen how I was getting on. "Fine," she said, "he took ten of those little pills before the last play." And the doctor said, "Is he still alive?" Helen said, "Yes, the only trouble is he's not sleeping." So I had another lot of pills – these to put me to sleep. I took so many pills I began to rattle.

'But it was terribly hard work. It really was. The strange thing was that people would congratulate you for playing hysterical scenes and bursting into tears but oh, it was so *easy*, compared to playing someone who was cool and calm. Usually in those television plays I was always playing people who were in control of the situation and that was difficult. But it was certainly a wonderful thing to have happened to me because overnight I was known in England. It was a big audience, even in those days, at least a million sets, and at that time there was only one channel so there was no competition. I did that for several years and it was through all this TV work that I got back into films.'

One of the first films that he appeared in during the 1950s was *Moulin Rouge* (John Huston, 1951). This was followed by *The Black Knight* (Tay Garnett) in 1954 in which he played the villain (Alan Ladd was the hero). 'One film company kept ringing my agent saying they wanted Peter Cushing to make films for them. That was Hammer. It started after I did the television play of Orwell's *1984* which caused a bit of a furore at the time. Soon afterwards, James Carreras, as he was then, started to ring my agent once a week almost regularly saying, "When's the boy going to be free? We must have him." So then I read in the papers that they were going to remake the Frankenstein pictures, which I remembered being very thrilled by as a boy, so I rang my agent and said if they're still interested I'm free now as this is the one I'd like to do.

'They very kindly showed me their recent film – *The Quatermass Experiment* with Brian Donlevy, and I thought it was a splendid film. No-one at all connected with the Frankenstein film realized where it was going to lead to. It was just a picture in a group of five they were doing that year. They had no idea it would start this incredible snowball. But it looked absolutely marvellous and they had wonderful people working on it, such as Jack Asher who was a wonderful lighting cameraman, and of course Terence Fisher who was a first-class director. In America's eyes the whole thing looked, as they used to say, like a million dollars. And it wasn't, of course. My heavens, it was a ridiculous budget – £65,000. As a budget for a film that was nonsensical. But it made a fortune for Hammer and everyone else, so they spent a little more on the next one, *Dracula*. It's never stopped since.

'I have a tremendous amount of affection for Baron Frankenstein for all the obvious reasons. I based the original character on Mary Shelley's novel, which I'd never read until I knew I was doing the film. You couldn't put all of Mary Shelley's novel into an hour and a half's screening but it was adapted very well, I thought, by Jimmy Sangster, and there was a certain amount of the original character I could bring into it. In the

Cushing in his last appearance as Frankenstein to date – a scene from Frankenstein and the Monster from Hell

Cushing as Baron Frankenstein – apparently wondering where he left that new brain (from The Evil of Frankenstein*)*

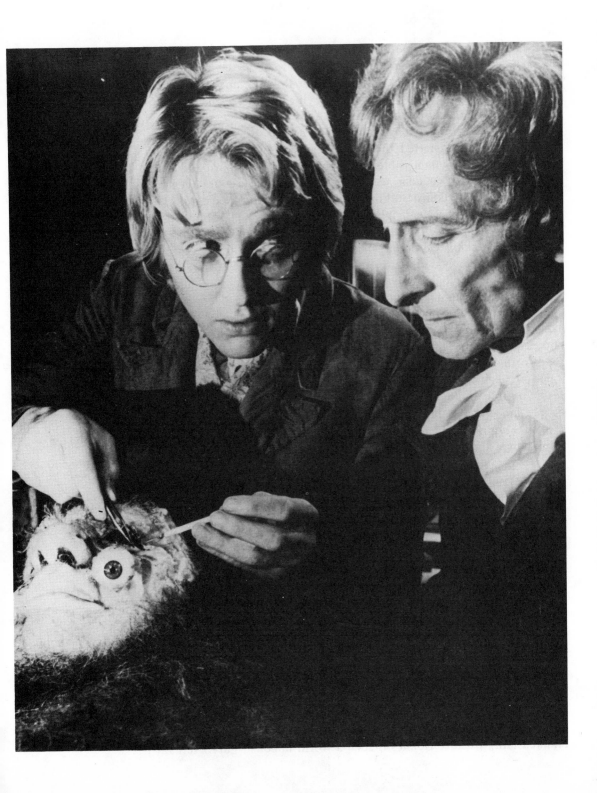

subsequent films he became more ruthless. You see, you couldn't just let him be a do-it-yourself merchant – there had to be a reason behind his actions, so I more or less based him upon Dr Robert Knox, the famous anatomist who went to terrible trouble trying to get the medical profession to allow him to use cadavers. So he shut his one eye as to how Burke and Hare got him bodies – he didn't care where they got them from. Of course when we started these films Frankenstein's activities were still considered to be impossible, but along comes Dr Barnard and starts doing the real thing. Oh dear, we said, this means our days are over, but it wasn't so. As Frankenstein I'm still one jump ahead of Barnard – I've transplanted a brain! Not frightfully successfully I will admit, but at least Frankenstein has done it. I'm sure Dr Barnard will catch up. But I try to base Frankenstein on a man who is, fundamentally, trying to do something for the good of mankind, as indeed Knox was, but against all odds because the villagers always seem to come and knock on his door and shout, ''You beast! You beast!''

'I don't mind being known as a horror star. My heavens, that would be like socking a gift horse in the face, or whatever the saying is. It doesn't bother me at all. But I don't think people should be called either comedy actors or horror actors or whatever, they're just actors. One should be, if one is true to one's trade, able to do it all. I don't say that *I* can but one *should* be able to. But horror films have such a sensational impact upon people and prove so popular that one is naturally associated with this sort of thing more than the many other things that I've done. But I think horror films are marvellous. To me a real *horror* film is something like *The Godfather* or films about the war. They are things that have happened to people, and do happen, but basically ''horror'' pictures are fantasies that take people out of themselves. People can go and enjoy them – they can laugh at them if they want, as long as they enjoy them.

'But I do the parts now that I think the audiences want to see me doing. Who wants to see me do Hamlet? Very few. But millions want to see me as Frankenstein, so that's the one I do. Audiences are the most important thing to an actor. On the other hand I won't just do anything that comes along in this type of film. The people who see horror films are very critical and they don't like just any old nonsense. But as long as the people are going to be entertained, and if the part's good, I will do it. One does turn down more scripts than one goes ahead with, but it's not a question of being very choosy – I will only play the parts that I can see myself in, and that's the way that I've always regarded parts. Actually I'm better known as Sherlock Holmes to many people than Frankenstein (and I only made one film as that character, and did a TV series of sixteen stories for the BBC, which doesn't compare with the number of times I've played Frankenstein), because Holmes is such a world-famous figure. Actually

Cushing as the sad old man in Tales from the Crypt *who is hounded to death by a ruthless landlord*

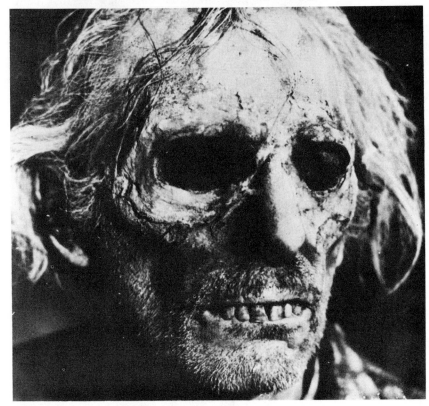

Cushing on his return from the grave to claim revenge, transformed by make-up expert Roy Ashton

I have played very few real villains during my career.'

Which, despite his villainous image, is basically true. In films like *The Skull* (Freddie Francis, 1965), *Night of the Big Heat* (Terence Fisher, 1967), *The Vampire Lovers* (Roy Ward Baker, 1970), *Tales from the Crypt* (Freddie Francis, 1971), *The Creeping Flesh* (Freddie Francis, 1972) his roles have been sympathetic ones. Of course in the *Dracula* films he plays Van Helsing, Dracula's continual adversary who represents the forces of Goodness. He has even, in two films, appeared as *Dr Who*, the benevolent scientist created in the BBC's long-running children's serial. But one of the outstanding things about Cushing is that no matter how mediocre, or downright dismal, the script may be, he always manages to give the character he is playing that something *extra*. He breathes life into characters that would be mere cardboard in anyone else's hands. It's one thing to turn in a good performance when there is an excellent script to build on but it's the mark of a real actor to create something out of very little material. Cushing also has a very wide range – one has only to compare his part in *Tales from the Crypt* in which he played a lonely old man who was victimized to death by his landlord (it being a horror film, naturally the old man returned from the grave to claim his revenge) to his role in his latest film to date, *Legend of the Werewolf* (Freddie Francis, 1974), as a jaunty, sardonic pathologist, the type who is seen munching happily on his sandwiches while surrounded by the grisly evidence of his profession.

The one actor whom he has been most associated with during his horror career is Christopher Lee. They met on the set of *Curse of Frankenstein* in 1956. 'I always say that I met him first in his creature make-up and when he took it off I screamed. He's been such a dear friend. And it's taken tremendous courage on his part to break away from horror films and succeed in something different. It takes a great deal of courage in this business to turn away from something that's sure and try something that isn't. But I think he will play Dracula again if and when a definitive version is done. He just doesn't want to keep on playing in the sort of Dracula films he has been playing – "Dracula in the Dark", "Dracula Meets Frankenstein", "Search the House for Dracula" and that sort of thing. As he said, the Van Helsing character, even though it's the same character, is more interesting; but all he has to do as Dracula is stand in a corner, show his fangs, and hiss. I do see his point, but if a good one comes along he'll do it, I know he will.

'We've made a lot of pictures together since the first *Frankenstein*. The picture we made for his own production company, *Nothing But the Night*, was our twenty-first together. Another one we did together during the last few years was *Horror Express* (Eugene Martin, 1971). I adored doing that. We did that in Spain and Christopher was so kind because

Cushing, accompanied by Patrick Wymark and skull – a scene from The Skull

it was one of the first things I did after I had undergone a personal trauma. It was an enjoyable film to make and Christopher was marvellous during it because he's so good with languages – he speaks about ten, bless him. It's very tricky working in a foreign country when you're so used to English ways. I can hardly speak English, much less Spanish, but they were all so sweet during the making of that. It took just a little more time, naturally, for the Spanish to get across to me what they were after – and vice versa – but Christopher was, as always, a tower of strength. It was indeed a very happy film to make. He and I had some nice exchanges of dialogue – we always work on those together, with the director, of course. And I thought it was so clever of the producer who bought the two model trains used in the film *Nicholas and Alexandra*, (to have them built especially would have cost a fortune) and then wrote a script around them. It was wonderful – all they had in the studio in Spain was a carriage on one sound stage and a carriage in another sound stage, so we worked in one which was dressed up as the guard's van, and the other one would be dressed up as, say, the dining car, and when we were finished in the guard's van we went and did all the scenes in the dining car. In the meantime they altered the guard's van into something else. It was a picture I very much wanted to see when it was completed but I was in France making another one when it came out.

'I get quite a lot of fan mail. I always answer the initial letter but I cannot carry on a correspondence because, of course, I haven't got the time. But I do have a fan club and they have a questionnaire section and if any of the letters come with questions they're answered within this journal that the club puts out regularly. Most of the letters are usually from people who write saying we love your films and can we have a photograph, but one or two are a bit odd. The oddest was from a fellow who wrote – "I've read in a newspaper that you have died. Would you please write and tell me if this is true." I don't know how he expected me to answer it if it *was* true but I wrote back and said, "As far as I know, not yet." '

12   Writing Horror: Richard Matheson and Robert Bloch

Many film critics are in the habit of analysing films in a way that suggests the films sprang fully-formed from the minds of their directors, totally ignoring the writers' contribution. The *auteur* theory in regard to directors may be perfectly valid in some cases but it can equally apply to writers, and often with much more justification. One example of this is the work of Richard Matheson. Many of the films for which he has written the screenplays have been highly regarded but usually most of the credit has gone to the various directors concerned, in particular Roger Corman. Matheson's horror/fantasy films include *The Incredible Shrinking Man* (Jack Arnold, 1957), *The Fall of the House of Usher* (Roger Corman, 1960), *Pit and the Pendulum* (Roger Corman, 1961), *Tales of Terror* (Roger Corman, 1962), *Burn, Witch, Burn* (which he wrote in collaboration with Charles Beaumont – directed by Sydney Hayers, 1962), *The Raven* (Roger Corman, 1963), *The Comedy of Terrors* (Jacques Tourneur, 1963), *Die! Die! My Darling* (Silvio Narizzano, 1965), *The Devil Rides Out* (also known as *The Devil's Bride*, directed by Terence Fisher, 1968), *Duel* (Steven Spielberg, 1971), *The Night Stalker* (John Llewellyn Moxey, 1972), *The Legend of Hell House* (John Hough, 1973), *Scream of the Wolf* (Dan Curtis, 1974), and *Dracula* (Dan Curtis, 1974). The last five of the above titles, with the exception of *Hell House*, were all made-for-TV films, but both *Duel* and *Dracula* have been given a theatrical release outside of America. Matheson was also one of the major contributors to the excellent television fantasy series *The Twilight Zone*.

'I've read fantasy all my life and have always been interested in it,' said Matheson, 'but when I wrote my first story, *Born of Man and Woman* I was told it was science fiction. I thought of it as a little horror story but at that time there was a big boom in science fiction magazines so I decided to investigate the field. After that I sold quite a few stories to the science fiction magazines but I've never really cared for science fiction. Most science fiction is not interesting to me at all, whereas fantasy still appeals because it covers such a wide spectrum.

'I didn't sell my first story until 1949. I had just got out of college and was unable to get a job on a newspaper or magazine in New York, where I lived at the time, but an editor at *Esquire* suggested that I work at night and write during the day. So that's how I was able to write and sell my first story; and after that I slowly began to sell one after another. My first novel was called *Someone is Bleeding*. It was a mystery novel and I wrote it because when I came out to California in 1951 the first person I stayed with was a mystery writer, and everyone I met through him were mystery novelists, so I just decided I would try one too. I wrote two of them before I did my first science fiction novel, which was *I Am Legend,* and after that came *The Incredible Shrinking Man*.

'I became involved with film-writing in 1955 when Universal wanted to buy *Shrinking Man*. Although I had always wanted to be a script-writer I had never attempted to break into the business until they wanted one of my books. I used their desire to film *Shrinking Man* as a wedge to get myself into the industry by saying they couldn't have it unless I was allowed to write the screenplay. It's really the only practical way to break in, even to this day, otherwise you can batter your head to a pulp and never get anywhere. Of course you have to be able to succeed at it after you get in.

'They revised my screenplay for *Shrinking Man* but not to the extent that it was no longer my work. But I can't say that I was satisfied with the way the film turned out. Only recently have I come to enjoy watching it. I like the visual part of him being small – that's interestingly done – but the relationship between the central character and his wife wasn't cap-tured, I think. As a matter of fact the first time I ever really enjoyed it was after my son pointed out that it was very unusual for films of its time in that it didn't have the usual story line – the usual happy ending – actually it had no particular story line, it was very picaresque, it just wandered on. I didn't have anything to do with the shooting of the picture except to go in and watch once in awhile. But I suppose it must be pretty good if everyone says it's a classic.'

Matheson's nightmarish book *I Am Legend* has been filmed twice but neither time was he involved with the writing of the screenplay. The first version was *The Last Man on Earth*, directed by Sidney Salkow in 1964. 'I thought it was terrible,' said Matheson. 'That's about the only way you can describe it. I had written a good screenplay but they had someone rewrite it and made it abysmal. At first I wrote the screenplay for Hammer Films but they told me that the English censor wouldn't pass it. Then a company over here bought it. I did the script again and made it even better because I was told that Fritz Lang was going to direct it, but it turned out otherwise.' The second version was *The Omega Man* (Boris Sagal) made in 1971. 'The first one was very poorly done,' said Matheson, 'but it did follow the book. *The Omega Man* bore no resem-blance at all to my book, so I can't comment on it. I had absolutely nothing to do with the screenplay but they did pay me a very small remake fee.

A scene from the first film based on Matheson's ultra-paranoid novel I Am Legend – The Last Man on Earth

A similar situation in the second version – The Omega Man

I don't know why they bothered really. I still think it would make an interesting film. Dan Curtis has spoken about making it sometime, maybe in about five to ten years.'

After his success with the Corman/Poe series of films made by AIP in the early 1960s (see Chapter 7) Matheson did a number of screenplays for Hammer Films, including the much-praised *The Devil Rides Out*. 'It was pretty good for Hammer. Of course it could have been a lot better. The casting was terrible with a few exceptions. Christopher Lee was his usual professional self and the fellow who played the villain [Charles Gray] was good but the hero and heroine, I thought, were just dreadful. And of course they had to cut financial corners which always damages a film. The whole sequence at the end where they are defending themselves against the forces of evil in that big room could have been done a lot better. But by and large it wasn't bad, and they got across a good period feeling. Dennis Wheatley was very happy with it. He wrote and said it was the best screen adaptation anyone had ever done on one of his books. I don't know why more films aren't made of his books. Hammer wanted me to do *The Haunting of Toby Jugg* but nothing ever came of it. It wasn't too difficult adapting his book for the screen. The story line was all there, it was mostly a case of excision.'

One of Matheson's more recent successes was *The Legend of Hell House* (1973) which was based on his own novel, *Hell House*. 'When I first saw it I disliked it intensely. Then people told me how good it was so

Pamela Franklin, Clive Revill and Roddy McDowall experience a ghostly manifestation in The Legend of Hell House, *based on Matheson's novel* Hell House

I went to see it again with a more tolerant view. It's not bad really. People have expressed disappointment that it doesn't hew strictly to the book, which would have made it like *The Exorcist*, and I don't think I would have cared to have it *that* graphic. Actually a producer, Stanley Chase, and I were to set up our own production of *Hell House* at one time but I ended up selling it because we weren't getting anywhere. But I thought the special effects were marvellous, and so were the performances, though I didn't care too much for Clive Revill; but the other three were great, especially Pamela Franklin and Roddy McDowall. The film, I think, was too short. They had to simplify the whole puzzle which was much more complicated in the book. If you thought about it when you saw the picture you would wonder why it took them so long to work out the mystery of Hell House because it all looked so simple the way the film presented it. And I thought the ending was absurd, really absurd.

'I haven't seen *The Exorcist* and I don't want to see it. I don't know whether it will be good for the horror film business or not. Of course they've been trying to present it as a straight motion picture and not as a horror film, but that's what it is. But I don't believe in sickening horror. Frightening someone through their minds is one thing, but to just batter them down with sound and horrible sights of blood and vomit – to me, *that* is *horror*, and I don't care for it.

'As far as I know I haven't been approached by people wanting me to do scripts that imitate *The Exorcist*. My agents, knowing my desires, put up a wall between me and people. Often a producer or someone will come up to me and ask me why I didn't want to do such and such a script and I will say I didn't even know anything about it. I don't really want to do the horror sort of thing any more. In fact the most successful thing I've had in the past year or so was a Dick Van Dyke television film about an alcoholic. It was called *The Morning After* and it worked out very well, Van Dyke was even nominated for an Emmy. But I don't want to be confined to one area, whatever it is. I've more or less finished with theatrical films and I concentrate mainly on television. You reach millions on television but very few people see your films in theatres. And television is becoming more and more challenging, it's not bland and insipid any more. I couldn't work on a television series though. I've had many chances to become part of a series, and there's a lot of money to be made out of them, but I couldn't stand it. I get too bored if I'm on the one thing too long – I like to go on to something else.

'I don't write short stories any more, there's really no market now, outside of *Playboy* magazine. There's no point in writing them for the science fiction and fantasy magazines. To spend a lot of time writing something that will sell for just $50 is hardly worth the effort. Besides, most of the ideas I've had at one time, and which I've kept on file, I just

Vincent Price despatches an unwilling vampire the hard way in The Last Man on Earth

don't care for any more. Unless something really appeals to me that will suit that format I think I will just as soon stick to novels. My latest book is called *Bid Time Return*, which is a time travel story. It's just a romance really, no horror – no spooky stuff at all.'

'I have the heart of a little boy,' Robert Bloch is fond of saying, 'I keep it in a jar on my desk.' But Bloch's public persona, that of someone who relishes the horrible side of things, is a total contradiction of the man himself – a warm, friendly person, well-known among his friends and associates for his overwhelming kindness. Bloch didn't receive wide public attention until the release of Hitchcock's film *Psycho* in 1960, which was based on one of his novels; but since the 1930s his name had been a familiar one to the readers of horror, fantasy and science fiction magazines. In these rather 'closed-shop' literary circles he is just as famous for being a humorist as he is as a horror writer, and his witty speeches have long been a highlight of American science fiction conventions.

'It was through *Weird Tales* magazine that I became involved with writing,' said Bloch. 'That was in 1934. I had sent my first fan letter two years previously, when I was fifteen, to H. P. Lovecraft. I wanted to know if there was any way that I could get to see his earlier stories. Remember, in those days there were no paperbacks, and there were no reprints of weird fiction in hardback, nor were there any original anthologies – it was just looked upon as a sub-division of the flourishing pulp magazine market. Anyway, Lovecraft wrote back offering me not only all of his stories but also a look at any of the volumes in his library. This really impressed me so I started to correspond with him, and in his third or fourth letter he said he detected something or other in my letters that led him to believe that I might be interested in trying my hand at writing myself. So he said, why don't I? He'd be very glad to read and criticize anything I wrote. So with this encouragement I started to write. I sent him my first two or three stories and he didn't criticize them really, he was just very flattering and encouraging – which was what a teenager needed, particularly in those Depression years. So I persevered. I graduated from high school when I was seventeen and two months later I sold my first story to *Weird Tales*. That was how I got in, and I've kept it up ever since.

'I corresponded with Lovecraft from 1933 to his death in 1937, but I never did get to meet him. August Derleth, who lived in Wisconsin, as I did at that time, planned to bring him out for a visit in the summer of 1937 but he died in March of that year. Lovecraft was certainly the major influence in my life. I rate his work just under Edgar Allen Poe. I did then, and got hooted down in English classes when I dared to bring up his name. No one had ever heard of him and none of the critics took him seriously. When he died Derleth decided to put out this memorial volume – *The Outsider*. I believe he issued 1,250 copies at $5 a copy, $3 a copy for an advance order, and only a few hundred copies sold. It took him several years to dispose of all of them, so that shows the status of Lovecraft and his peer group at that time. But through the years he has very steadily and slowly won an audience and has become a great seminal influence on many people who are writing today. He was recognized in France of course, before he was recognized in America, as Poe was. But I know of no other writer whose style has influenced the field of fantasy writing as Lovecraft's has since the days of Poe.

'*Psycho* was the first novel of mine to be sold for filming but it had nothing to do with my entrance into screen writing – nothing whatever. *Psycho* was sold blind by my agent in New York to MCA [the agency] who wouldn't tell him who was buying it. Subsequently I heard that Mr Hitchcock was going to do it, which was interesting but really didn't mean much to me as I was living in a small town in the mid-west of Wisconsin. I learned later from Herbert Colman, who had been Hitchcock's associate producer on *North by Northwest*, that Hitch had asked whether I was available to do the screenplay and the gentleman he asked immediately said no, I wasn't available. The gentleman he asked was an MCA agent who wanted to sell one of his own clients. So that's the way that worked out because I was two thousand miles away.

'I came out here to Hollywood as a result of very special circumstances. A friend who was in the business arranged for me to get an assignment from a syndication outfit called ZIV which was then making many TV shows and selling them across the country. This friend not only got me the assignment, he said come out, stay at my home and try your hand at this sort of thing. If you find that you like it, fine – it could be a new vocation, if not, you've had a three weeks' paid vacation. So I came out, I did the assignment and ZIV bought it immediately and asked for a second one as soon as possible. I began to get the message. I acquired an agent and moved into an apartment – my family were still in Wisconsin – and then the next thing I knew the Hitchcock TV show asked me to do an adaptation of one of my own stories. So I took on that assignment and several others, and in the space of several months I had six or seven things going – whereupon the Writers' Guild declared a strike!

'I was left dangling in limbo out here in Hollywood for five and a half months. So I went back to fiction and waited for the strike to end. By that time I had met Hitchcock, I had been out on the set of *Psycho* while it was being filmed, and I attended the first rough-cut screening of it with Hitch, Janet Leigh, Bernard Herrman and the other people. I remember I watched *their* reactions because they hadn't seen it before either and that was interesting. I was very, very pleased with the film. I certainly wouldn't have thought that anyone could have done it better than Hitch did – and since they practically filmed the book without changing the plot or introducing any new characters I had no reason for complaint on that score. That's something that seldom happens, and it was something that Hitchcock has seldom done in his work in the past, such as *The Thirty-Nine Steps* which bears little resemblance to the Buchan book.

'One must remember that at the time *Psycho* was, initially, a very

Anthony Perkins as the twisted murderer in Psycho, *based on Robert Bloch's novel*

dubious proposition. Hitchcock had a contract with Paramount for a certain number of films which gave him a choice of material, and *he* wanted to do *Psycho*, but Paramount didn't. They put every obstacle in his way that they possibly could. They said there was no room at Paramount so he had to film it at Universal. They kept his budget down, down, so that Hitchcock, who had been making films with stars like Cary Grant and Jimmy Stewart, had to make do with a skimpy cast and was also forced to use his television camera crew and film in black and white. Now today the story is that he chose black and white because he thought it would be much more effective – I think it was, and so does Hitch – but that was *not* the reason he filmed it that way, it was because there was only $900,000 in the budget. Everybody fought the picture. They didn't like the title and many of his associates tried to persuade him out of it.

'At that time if I had said I had written *Psycho* it would have meant absolutely nothing to anybody – it would have been a negative factor. So by the time *Psycho* did appear and was successful I had already done six or seven teleplays and had five or six more assignments. *Psycho* started to affect me within the following two years, but not through my own efforts. The people who were putting out the novels, and their blurb-writers, started this "author of *Psycho*" thing – they pasted that label on my forehead and for a while I fought it because I didn't think it was something I wanted to live with. But then I realized that I'd have to live with it, so I decided I might as well accept it without protest. It's just one of those things, but it never led to much. The gentleman who made the screenplay adaptation got far more out of it than I did. That's the way things work out here. That was Joseph Stefano and he became involved with *The Outer Limits* on the strength of *Psycho*. For some time he went around claiming he was the author of *Psycho* but my agent gently dissuaded him, and so did a few other people, from making that claim. I breathed a sigh of relief that he hadn't adapted the Bible.

'I've never worked directly with Hitchcock. On the TV show he was merely a figurehead. He came in, read the lines that were written for him and did a number of those introductions back to back [i.e. Hitchcock filmed the introductions to a number of different episodes all at once]. He had nominal story control. But I did have an opportunity to work with him once – he offered me an open-ended contract to develop a story with him, which was very flattering. So I went over and had lunch with him in his bungalow, which was a little disconcerting because his tape-recorder was going all the time. He tape-records everything, as far as I know. I don't know whether he ever erases any of it or deletes the expletives. It was fascinating to talk to him, of course, but I got to thinking after I got home that it was a rather strange contract. The substance of it was that he and I would work together until we arrived at something that was mutually satisfying. That's all very well but I could have been submitting ideas for six months or more, tied up exclusively to him, and it was a luxury I couldn't afford. I asked my agent to explain this and bowed out, much as I would have enjoyed the opportunity.

'My first screen credit was *The Couch* for Warner Brothers in 1961. It was a "B" picture – they were still making "B" pictures in those days. Shirley Knight and Grant Williams, who had done *The Incredible Shrinking Man*, were the nominal leads. It was a psychological suspense story. After that I was involved in *The Cabinet of Dr Caligari*. It started out very well but the gentleman who was directing it decided that he was also going to produce it too. Then he decided, unknown to me, that he was going to rewrite the screenplay and become a writer as well. Well, he couldn't take away my screenplay credit but I wish he had. He managed to effectively destroy what it was I tried to do.

'It was agreed that we couldn't re-do the original but I did try to keep the *spirit* of the original. What I had done was a screenplay which involved an apparently normal person in an apparently normal situation but with a great deal of mystification. Only in the end does one discover that this normal person is fantasizing and that everything that is interpreted as a threat or horror has a realistic explanation because she's a patient in an asylum. But by rewriting the dialogue, a very simple matter, and making the psychiatrist a menacing figure as well as the fellow patients etcetera, the whole spirit was destroyed. It was no longer a mystery/suspense vehicle with a surprise ending but was just something that was obvious from the beginning, though confusing. So that's a credit I have that I don't really take any credit for.

'Then I did *Straitjacket* for William Castle with Joan Crawford and after that I did *The Nightwalker*, for Castle again, with Barbara Stanwyck and Robert Taylor. Both enjoyable experiences for me to work with those people. And then Amicus bought something of mine, a short story that was originally called *The Skull of Marquis de Sade* which they filmed over in England as *The Skull*. Milton Subotsky, I think, did the screenplay, then they asked me to do an original screenplay for them, which I did. Subsequently I did a number of those omnibus films for Amicus, such as *Torture Garden*, *The House That Dripped Blood* and *Asylum*. I never actually worked in England, I did my scripts here in Hollywood and sent them over. Sometimes they were changed, which, of course, was beyond my control.

'I would say that there's never been a screenplay that's been left completely untouched, but there are screenplays that have large areas left alone. Naturally I prefer it when my work isn't tampered with, but I must say that in a few select instances there have been elaborations that I have approved. The touches of humour in the final sequence of *The House That Dripped Blood* I cannot take credit for but I heartily approve of them.

'In *Asylum* the director, Roy Ward Baker, stuck very, very faithfully to the script throughout, which pleased me, although the producer requested that they reverse the sequence of two of the stories. That didn't please me very much. I'd had what is now the first sequence and the third sequence and it built up a little better that way. I had thought it should start on a more pedestrian note and gradually work up to more physical horrors. But with the exception of that they did best by me in *Asylum*. And there are some lengthy stretches in *Straitjacket* that were left untouched and, I think, worked well. I hope it's not egocentricity on my part but I often find myself quarrelling with the definition of what constitutes horror and suspense. In many cases it seems as if directors working with low budgets, without sufficient time and working under various other handicaps, find it expedient to substitute a sudden shock effect for something that is built up or arrived at. Or they will stint on characterization – they use one of the most foolish words in the industry but one which is constantly used – they say: "The *pace* is too slow. We've

Patrick Magee is about to get it in the neck in this scene from Asylum, *scripted by Robert Bloch*

got to step up the *pace*.'' Who needs that explanation or that little bit of byplay? Incidentally, I feel that this is something that British films of the '40s and '50s excelled at. They'd have these little vignettes, little asides – all of a sudden some minor actor would come on and do a scene that was almost a non sequitur but was so charming and natural it fitted in and gave you the feeling that you were actually observing something that was real, other than a very mechanically constructed, *paced* vehicle.

'That's the trouble with these omnibus films because each segment is so short and only exists to build up to a shock. I would much prefer a feature-length film. But there's not much latitude today because the present pattern is one of episodic butchery. Someone decides to revenge himself and then there are eight or nine killings, each more fantastic than the last. The *Dr Phibes* and *Theatre of Blood* sort of thing. Actually I thought that the first *Phibes* was very well done because there was tender loving care exercised in building up the background. It was more or less a tongue-in-cheek thing. Vincent Price described it to me as the *No, No, Nanette* of horror films. And it was, it wasn't outright camp but it was definitely tongue-in-cheek; and while some of the murders were gruesome they weren't gore for gore's sake. *Theatre of Blood* followed the same pattern and I thought that Price's performance was exceptional – he had the opportunity to do some very nice Shakespearian bits – but the film was just downright nasty. It reminded me of boy scouts sitting around a campfire telling stories to see which one can out-nauseate the others. And this seemed to win appreciation from a certain segment of the audience, but it made me shudder a little. When I was watching it in the theatre and I heard this ghoulish, sadistic laughter when someone's heart was torn out from his living body – Oh, no, this is sick, I said to myself.

'As to where I draw the line in my own scripts – first of all, attitude. I do not believe that revenge should be glorified. Taking the law into one's own hands isn't something that should be extolled, yet it has been in many recent films. I've never written a film in which the evil-doer, who is usually mentally deranged, is shown to be a happy person, a fulfilled person or someone who is happy in his or her existence. Quite the contrary. I don't think that anybody who saw *Psycho* wanted to be Norman Bates or would be inclined to emulate him as such. I think the incentive to violence comes from films in which violence or violent action is shown to be desirable, or shown to be rewarded. This is what makes an impression on minds susceptible to possible psychotic behaviour, so I don't care for it.

'In my own films I much prefer to have the gore off-screen. For instance *The House That Dripped Blood* – that title was dreamed up by the producer, but there's *no* blood in that picture. The title was supposed to be an exploitation one but it actually worked *against* the film. I noticed when

Edgar Allan Poe lives on in this scene from a segment of Torture Garden, *based on Bloch's story 'The Man Who Collected Poe'*

it was shown on TV in America they had it on at 11.30 at night, but it was milder than much that's screened in prime time.

'I haven't seen *The Exorcist* so I'm not really qualified to pass judgment on it but I would say that primarily it would come under my dictum of going too far. Judging by audience reaction, the main thing it seems to create is nausea – which to me is not entertaining. If you want to go in that direction why not do "A Day at Auschwitz", or "Fun in Bangladesh"?'

'My own personal favourite fantasy film, and Christopher Lee agrees with me on this, is *All That Money Can Buy*. That was a tremendous film. The alternative title was *The Devil and Daniel Webster*. It was made in 1940 at RKO and starred Walter Huston, Edward Arnold and Simone

Simon. It was a very unusual film about a New Hampshire community where a farmer sells his soul to the devil. I was also very pleased with portions of the Lorre film *Mad Love*, and a much more obscure Lorre film, *The Stranger on the Third Floor*, which he made for RKO in 1941. And of course I'm fond of *Dead of Night*; and there was another British omnibus film called *Three Faces of Murder*. The first sequence was called *The Picture* and to me it is one of the great, shock, fantasy sequences of all time, but it has not received any attention whatsoever. It is well worth hunting up. And I believe *Island of Lost Souls*, against the context of its time, was a most unusual and most daring film. But I always have to keep that in mind, having been there, and having seen these films exhibited in a theatre, under the proper circumstances with an audience, not of film students, critics or nostalgia buffs, but a fresh, receptive audience not prepared for anything of this sort by a million subsequent imitations. The impact of *Frankenstein* and *Dracula* has been lessened because of the tremendous number of imitations, the copying of every sequence, of every attitude, of every character – finishing up on TV in something like *The Munsters*. But originally they were fresh and new and they had a really sensational effect. And they were the result of many creative imaginations at work in concert on these projects.'

Unlike Matheson, Bloch is not happy about writing for television and believes that the strictures of the medium make it difficult to produce horror/suspense subjects effectively. 'I'd done this script for a made-for-TV horror film and at a late stage they changed the leading lady and brought in a rather big-name star. So I had to do a certain amount of rewriting, just to make sure that the new characterization didn't clash with the fantasy elements of the show. So I did that. *Then* they decided that since she was a star the story would have to change. That is to say she would have to be introduced up front rather than in the second act. Now the normal course of the story called for her introduction in the second act but no, I had to write in a sequence that would introduce her at the beginning. So I restructured it, there was no other way around it, but it destroys the careful build-up in a suspense story when you have to arbitrarily change things. The ludicrous thing is that this big star didn't play the role after all but they still had to shoot it that way. And they had cut out a great deal of what I had written because it was running too long, they said, but when they shot it they discovered that they were twelve minutes short. Twelve minutes short out of seventy-two – one-sixth! If they'd left what I had put in so carefully, all the little touches, the little atmospheric things that were necessary to the build-up, they would have had a perfectly realized script. But they discovered this when they saw the rough-cut and by then the sets had been struck, the actors who had been hired on a per day or week basis were gone – and they had to add twelve minutes. So they recalled two actors and they had part of one set left and part of another; then they contacted me and said that they were shooting in two days time and wanted twelve minutes of script. And do it, they said, in such a way that it integrates with the story and doesn't affect the flow! I did it but it certainly didn't improve the story. And that sort of thing happens all the time in television.

'This is a characteristic of executive thinking which is used in Westerns where, say, you have a fight in a bar in the script and they say, well, the budget won't allow us to have breakaway furniture and a big bar set, so put the fight outdoors. What difference does it make? And in that kind of thing it often doesn't make a difference. The same with a private-eye TV show which consists mainly of someone going around asking people questions. It doesn't matter if they scrap an elaborate set where one suspect was going to be questioned and put him somewhere else. But they don't realize that if you do that with a mystery/suspense story, or a fantasy, it destroys the mood. It's the same with comedy, and that's something that Buster Keaton taught me. I knew Buster when he was doing TV commercials in the early 1960s and he said to me: "I always try to direct my own commercials though I don't take the credit for them. Look at it this way. I know that in comedy camera placement and timing are all-important, but people who don't do comedy don't realize this. I'll have a situation where I have to fall down the stairs, and I know that if I put the camera *here* in such an angle, it's funny; but if I put it over here at this angle all you get is a picture of an old man taking a nasty tumble down the stairs, and it's sad." And horror and comedy are opposite sides of the same coin; both depend on the unexpected, the grotesque, on the dislocation of seemingly natural events, and both depend on timing and tempo that sucks the audience into a scene.

'Another thing wrong with television is that when you get a series in the field of horror or fantasy the most unusual scripts are those done by a writer-director or a writer-producer. He is in a position, working with the company, to come up with something over the lunch table which seems very outrageous and they say, let's do this! But if an outsider comes in with the same idea – oh no! We can't do anything like that. It's too far out! So an outside writer is often handicapped because he or she must come in with something fairly conventional, or *accept* something fairly conventional. This is not a personal grudge, this is something that is readily seen.

'As the writer has no autonomy in Hollywood whatsoever, many people who want to get ahead in the business decide to become directors or producers to protect their own properties and also to promote themselves. The Writers' Guild now has an increasing number of what we call hyphenates – writer-directors and writer-producers. But it calls for certain characteristics which I fortunately, or unfortunately, don't possess. Boris Karloff told me once that he was in one of the first talkies that MGM ever did and it was the first directorial effort of Lionel Barrymore, who, at the beginning of the 1930s, wanted very desperately to break out of acting and become a director. He did, but only for one film or so because he kept falling asleep on the set. He was already in his fifties and it was a gruelling job, even in those days of the big studio. He just couldn't work a sixteen- or eighteen-hour day, he didn't have the physical stamina, so he went back to acting. Well, I'm of a comparable age and I don't have the physical stamina either. Now the other characteristic is a certain aggressiveness, a certain ability for self-promotion which I've never possessed and which a producer or a director needs. It's necessary for survival and I recognize that but I just can't be that way. I'm not comfortable in that role.'

13   Directing Horror: Freddie Francis and Roy Baker

Roy Ward Baker is well known to horror fans for films like *Quatermass and the Pit* (1967: also known as *Five Million Years to Earth*) *The Scars of Dracula* (1970), *The Vampire Lovers* (1970), *Dr Jekyll and Sister Hyde* (1971), *Asylum* (1972), *And Now the Screaming Starts* (1973), *Vault of Horror* (1973) and *Legend of the Seven Golden Vampires* (1974) but his earlier, more prestigious films, are often overlooked. These include *Morning Departure* (1950), which caused him to be hailed as one of England's greatest young directors at the time, *Don't Bother to Knock* (1953), one of Marilyn Monroe's early films, *The One That Got Away* (1957), a controversial film about a German airman who manages to escape from a British prison camp during the Second World War, and *A Night to Remember* (1958) about the sinking of the *Titanic*.

Baker was born in 1916 and decided to enter the film industry when he

Roy Ward Baker (left) with producer Anthony Nelson-Keys on the set of Quatermass and the Pit

was still at school. He started with Gainsborough Films in 1934 at their Islington studio as an errand boy for the production department. 'It was a marvellous piece of luck,' he said, 'because in those days you could dodge about from job to job and learn everything. I was a stills man and a location manager by the age of nineteen. I was never out of work – if there wasn't anything on the floor they still carried the whole crew. Unimaginable today, of course. It was marvellous, I worked on forty pictures in six years. I worked my way up to being a director through being third Assistant, second Assistant and so on. It didn't take me long to cotton on to the idea that the director's job was the one to have.

'I was still with Gainsborough when the war broke out and I was called up within two months. Eventually I ended up in one of the army's three film units. It was called the Army Cinematography Corps and it was located in the old Wembley studios which used to be owned by 20th Century Fox before the war. We made technical training films to begin with, then we went over to propaganda, and towards the end of the war we went on to making instructional films for soldiers coming out of the army. They were interesting pictures to make because we had everything – sets, actors and so on. First of all I was taken on as a production manager but within six weeks I got myself the job of directing a picture which was a whole nine reels long, almost a full-length feature. It was to teach the Home Guard all about house-to-house fighting in case there was an invasion. It was fascinating to do because we had half of Battersea at our disposal – the area had been flattened by the bombers and so it made a marvellous wreck; and what wasn't already wrecked, *we* wrecked. We could do anything we liked, pull buildings down or blow them up. It was all quite extraordinary, thinking back on it now.

'We were a very informal group because we were all old buddies from the film industry and we more or less ignored military conventions between ourselves. I'd have to keep reminding myself to salute at times. There were a number of older army gents, who were too old to go into action, in the administrative side of the unit and we drove them absolutely to distraction because, as far as they were concerned, we didn't fit into the right army mould. We were scattered all over the place, everybody lived where they liked – I had a flat in Tottenham Court Road – providing they got into the studio in time. It was ridiculous, really, it was just like having a job. I had a very good war, as they say. But one day the army people decided to have a church parade to shake us up, and it was a turning point in my life because during the parade I was introduced to someone who was working with one of the other film units – and that was Eric Ambler, the novelist. We became fast friends and we began to talk about working together after the war. Near the end of the war he was commissioned to write a script for the Two Cities Production Company and was told that he could also produce the film himself when he got out of the army. He asked me to direct it and that was how my directing debut came about. That was *The October Man* in 1947. I was launched.

'My career went from bad to worse after the success of that film, until I was offered two properties a few years later. One was *God Protect Me from My Friends*, which never got off the ground, and the other was *Morning Departure*. The latter came out to the most fantastic reviews you've ever seen – I was the new hero, the greatest director England had ever laid eyes on – which was wonderful! It was extraordinary to read these things that were written about me and I still can't believe them. They were obviously the reason why I was asked to go to Hollywood. I worked for three years over there and it was a marvellous experience, particularly at that time because it was just about the end of the old Hollywood, which had each studio making so many pictures a year. I went back there recently and saw the 20th Century Fox lot and it was enough to make you weep – if you could have seen it as it was in the old days!

'I was under contract to Fox all the time I was in Hollywood so I didn't get the opportunity to work for anyone else. I had a very happy time there and I made a lot of friends. It was the experience that turned me into a professional – up to then I had been a very lucky amateur. You can go on being one of those for a long time in Britain, but you can't do it for five minutes in America.

'One of the pictures I did in Hollywood was *Don't Bother to Knock* with Marilyn Monroe. There's now a sort of Marilyn Monroe industry in existence which I think is disgraceful, but it was bound to happen to her because for some reason she never attracted anybody except parasites – and I don't care who you include in that department! She never managed to find anybody who would do something for her for nothing. But that was her fate, it was very strange.

'She was absolutely unique, which is what made her a star, and she was unquestionably a sort of uncertifiable lunatic, but you couldn't help falling in love with her. I never saw anybody who came near her, man or woman, for the first time, who didn't have to touch her. Not just to see if she was real but because she had that extraordinary quality of real magnetism. As an actress she wasn't as experienced as people have said. She had done a lot of work previously but she was frightened to death and you had to drag a performance out of her line by line. But I was dealing with a very special personality that needed very special treatment so I gave it to her. Richard Widmark was a tower of strength during the making of that picture. He was wonderful, because it is very difficult for an actor or actress to play a scene with someone when they don't quite know what the timing of the next line is going to be, or whether the line is coming at all. Very difficult to keep your concentration in those circumstances, And of course Marilyn's part in the film was totally wrong for her. Both the producer and I protested violently to Darryl Zanuck about it. "Oh, you're both just prejudiced," he said. "You don't understand how big this girl is going to be!" We said, please listen and try to understand. We agreed about her potential, having met her and seen the bits and pieces that she had done, but we tried to point out to him that this was a story that depended entirely on a girl who is going dotty because her fiancé has been killed in an air crash; and her real fear is that, because she's rather plain and ordinary, she'll never manage to get another man. That was the motivation for the whole story. She's left alone in the hotel bedroom with the little child she is minding, and she dresses up in the mother's clothes and make-up to try and make herself pretty. Well, of course you didn't have to *try* to make Marilyn Monroe pretty and it knocked the bottom right out of the story from the word go. "I don't give a Goddamn about that," said Zanuck. "You can dress her down for the first couple of sequences."

'I came back to England with no more than an ordinary reputation out of Hollywood. I'd done well – one miss, one indifferent and two hits, so that wasn't bad batting. They hadn't lost money on me or anything. But when I came back here to England I more or less had to start all over again. I went back to Pinewood and my biggest success was *The One That Got Away*. It caused a certain amount of controversy at the time. I did it largely because I was sick and tired of seeing caricature Germans on the screen. I stuck my neck out, though I didn't realize I was doing it at the time, but the picture came out, got marvellous notices and made a fortune.

'After that came *A Night to Remember*. We had a twenty-one-week schedule on that of which over two weeks involved night work. We used the Ruislip swimming baths for the scenes of the people in the water. We went there for the first night's shooting and it was very cold. I chucked about ten or twelve people into the icy water at around 10 p.m. and they nearly died. In fact, I thought one or two of them *were* going to die. Christ, I thought, I've gone too far! But I never had to direct anyone in those scenes; they all knew exactly what it was all about – they didn't have to pretend they were struggling in icy water, they *were* struggling in icy water. It was grindingly hard work – sheer agony to get every single, bloody shot.

'For some scenes we used an old ship that was about to be broken up. It had got straight, flat sides exactly like the *Titanic* though it wasn't as big. I sent my cutter out to do those shots – it was the only time I ever used a second-unit director, but I knew I could trust him and he turned out to be a good director later. The problem was that you had to establish contact between people on the top deck and the people in the water – you had to see them both together because it was a picture that everybody knew was going to be a fake. You would have an audience that would be saying that this is all cardboard so somehow or other, to create the best illusion, you had to incorporate all the vital elements in the same frame. So we had a lifeboat come down and go smack into the water and that way we gave support to the bits that had to be faked. We did all the model shots at the big, open air tank at Pinewood. We had quite a big model over forty feet long as well as some smaller duplicates. It was a motor boat, in fact, with a shell built over it. And we had lots of little rowing boats with clockwork motors that moved the oars. We spent £90,000 on the special effects which, in those days [1958], was a lot.

'After the success of those two pictures they told me I could do anything I liked, which sounded fine, but everything *I* suggested the executives didn't like and everything *they* suggested *I* didn't like. One of the things they put up was *The Singer, Not the Song*. And the first thing I said was that it would be a marvellous subject for a brilliant Spanish director called Luis Buñuel, who they hadn't heard of, but I said I didn't want to do it. A year went by and I was still doing nothing so when the subject came up again I gave in. Apart from being about Catholicism – I'm not a Catholic and I have no desire whatever to put stuff on the screen that is prejudicial to other people's ideas – there was also a tremendous element of homosexuality in the story, which was very tricky stuff at the time. So I was in a bit of a pickle over this but they gave me practically all the money I wanted and the only thing they insisted on was that Dirk Bogarde be in it. I got on extremely well with him and he turned out to be a much deeper person than I thought, which was good, and he was also a very fast-thinking man. He could also act, which is more than most of them on the screen can do, because he has a stage background. So, one way or the other, there were a lot of advantages in doing it but it was not a very easy picture for me to make.

'When it came out it got the most crushing notices that I've ever had for anything I've done. Why it angered the critics so much I don't know. I just didn't understand their reaction and I still don't. I've looked at those notices since then – they absolutely broke my heart. I'd made a very difficult, very controversial picture. I'd had to steer around all kinds of dangerous areas and I thought I'd succeeded. To rub salt in the wound, after all those terrible notices we had just about the grandest première ever seen at the Odeon Theatre in Leicester Square. It was a charity première and everything and I had to face all those people. Christ, it was awful! I was dying!

'One thing that makes you think, looking back on it now, was that every critic mentioned and made fun of the fact that Dirk Bogarde was wearing black leather trousers. The reason why he wore them was that

A scene from The Singer, Not the Song *— a film that Baker would prefer to forget (John Mills is the priest, Dirk Bogarde is the body, complete with leather pants)*

in the first place we decided, Dirk and I, that he was the villain and he was going to dress in black from head to foot all the way through the picture, and since it was thought appropriate to have a leather jacket, why not leather trousers as well? Now before this I'd had Hardy Kruger go through a whole film in black leather trousers because he was a German pilot and that was all he had to wear, so how the hell was I expected to know that the critics were going to go absolutely insane with glee about the fact that Dirk Bogarde was swanning around in a pair of black leather trousers.

'For some reason it has become something of a cult picture now. I don't quite know why but it's always the first picture I'm asked about.

'I got into horror films by accident. Hammer rang me out of a clear blue sky and asked me if I would like to do a science fiction picture. It was *Quatermass and the Pit*. So I read the script and of course it was a damned good one. I'd never seen the original *Quatermass* when it was shown on TV. The reasons behind the success of the picture are simple – Nigel Kneale is such an extremely good scriptwriter. He won't do more, you see, because he will only publish what's good. He won't publish rubbish. He probably writes an enormous amount of stuff that no one ever sees.

'We also had a very good cast – James Donald, Andrew Keir and Barbara Shelley – she is *very* good, and one of the loves of my life. We were very lucky again because we were supposed to make it in one studio and they rather snootily said: "Oh, we're sorry, we haven't got the space now, you'll have to go somewhere else." So we got tucked in at MGM, and we were about the only picture on the floor there at the time so it was absolutely wonderful. We had the whole studio behind us. They were a wonderful crew there, they fell over themselves to help. And it was a good film, I think. I enjoyed making it and it was one of those films that was thoroughly satisfying to be involved with. It was such a happy exercise that I kept working with Hammer.

'I get on very well with the Hammer people. We're almost too friendly now. Michael Carreras and I are very close friends. I don't really enjoy making horror pictures as such. I don't consider *Quatermass and the Pit* as a horror picture, and certainly *The Anniversary* (which was a Hammer film that I directed that starred Bette Davis) wasn't, though a lot of people said it was. The first straight horror picture I did was *The Vampire* Lovers. A film about lesbian vampires was a logical development really. I mean they had done everything with vampires that could possibly be done and they just had to think of something else. Some day, somebody will come up with Lassie the Vampire out of sheer desperation. But it was fun to make. It was a goodish script, though it was rather repetitious – the second half was almost the same as the first half. But it was based on a rather old story which I happened to be very familiar with. At the beginning someone rang me up and told me what the film was going to be about and I said: "Surely this is *Carmilla*?" Do you know it, they asked. "Of course I know it," I said, "I've got the book right here. I've had it since I was fourteen." So I read it again and before I knew it I was involved with the picture.

'Once again we had a very good cast, with people like Peter Cushing. Peter was great. It was the first time I had worked with him. But from the beginning I was determined not to make an exploitation movie about lesbian vampires – I wasn't going to be "funny" about the subject. It came off rather better than people expected simply because the characters were simply treated as lesbians and that was it. You've got to take these films seriously while you're making them. You've got to make it seem real. You can joke on the set and send up the scene, or you can get the nerves out of actors by camping it up but you must never let that go too far. Of course one of the great things to do with almost any actor is to say: "I've just been reading this scene – this couple of lines you've got here, and my God, they are bloody *dreadful*. I don't know what you're going to do with them." And they'll invariably say: "Well, don't worry, dear boy. Leave it to me, I'll see what I can do." You challenge them that way and they come up with something marvellous. But basically you must believe in what you are doing. It's no good just sailing through it.

Andrew Keir (left) as Professor Quatermass in Quatermass and the Pit *(also known as* Five Million Years to Earth*)*

I've had one or two actors who have just sailed through a picture and they look pretty silly afterwards. They look like the only ones in the picture who don't know what's going on.

'*The Scars of Dracula* – I was in Paris last year and I met a couple of young fellows there who asked me about that. I told them I didn't think much of it. "What?" they said, "It's one of our favourites! Christopher Lee was so marvellous!" And I said, yes, he was, but he always is. I'm taking that for granted but I really think a great deal of that picture was awful. As for the violence in it: well – that's all part of my policy that if it's required by the story you've got to do it properly. In the sequence which shows what had happened to all the women and children in the church after the bats had got to them, the men, when they return from burning down Dracula's castle, had to be absolutely stricken by what they find. Therefore they had to have something to be stricken about. If I hadn't shown the audience something rather gruesome at that point they would have wondered what the men were going on about. All these things have to lock together. From my point of view there's no such thing as being *too* horrible. But I wouldn't go for what I call degeneracy or sickness – I mean bestial perversion and that kind of stuff, which I regard as obscene. I do believe there is such a thing as obscenity though a lot of people say there isn't. But I don't mind eroticism and I don't mind pornography – as someone once said: "Nobody ever got killed by a tit." But there are a lot of things that I wouldn't do. I've turned down a number of scripts simply because they've contained things that I wouldn't want to put on the screen.

'*Scars of Dracula* was the only thing I've done with Chris and we got on extremely well, I thought. He's a fusser, of course. Everything has to be right. Both Chris and Peter Cushing are real perfectionists though they are totally different. But I think Chris is marvellous the way he plays the part of Dracula. He's announced that he doesn't want to do it again and I don't blame him, but he certainly did it well. His whole interpretation of the character was his own right down to the smallest detail. He played Dracula like no one ever did before, or will ever do again, and that's a great contribution – that's an actor's contribution.

'I did have a few things in that movie that I was pleased with. One thing that I am keen about in horror films is that there should be a kind of supernatural element – an unexplained element. In that film Dracula never opened or shut a door. This is something I never expect the audience to notice, but whenever he went in or out of a room the door opened and shut automatically behind him. And I don't think I ever had him sit down or stand up – he was always standing, and whenever he walked he walked at a tremendous rate. In the last picture, *Legend of the Seven Golden Vampires*, there was a scene where Dracula is in his coffin and

A scene from The Vampire Lovers

At work on the filming of The Vampire Lovers

the lid has to slide off and he has to rise up and come out of it. I had the lid slide off and I had the actor, John Forbes Robertson, on a plank and he was raised up automatically. You never see him get out of the coffin, he just appears beside the other man in the scene as if he'd floated down. You cannot have a character like Dracula getting up, hitching up his cloak, and stepping out of his coffin. That would just destroy the mood immediately.

'Another thing I liked in *Scars of Dracula* was the scene where I had Dracula crawling upside-down along the wall. I could not understand why nobody had ever done that before. I mean, it was difficult to do, I grant you, and I never really got it right because the set wasn't big enough and did look a bit cheap. But at least I did it – I got it on the screen and I was very pleased with it. Because it's a great moment in the book when the fellow looks out the window and there is Dracula crawling down the wall! It's a super effect but I had trouble with his cloak falling all around him and that sort of thing. It needed a much more complicated trick effect than I actually managed.

'*Dr Jekyll and Sister Hyde* – there you had a case where none of us realized how good Ralph Bates and Martine Beswick looked together. It was uncanny. And it was Jimmy Carreras who cast the girl, oddly enough, against the wishes of the producers, Albert Fennell and Brian Clemens. There was a controversy going on over three or four different girls though I didn't have much of an opinion about it one way or the other. Anyway, in the end Hammer put its foot down and said you're going to have Martine Beswick, and she turned out to be an absolute crackerjack. I regret that I didn't make more out of the eroticism in the situation, and it needed above all things a confrontation scene between the man and the woman. But Brian Clemens was determined to be consistent with his logic and as they only had one body between them you couldn't have a two-shot scene. We did a mirror scene at one point that went part of the way towards capturing the effect I wanted.

'*Asylum* did very well and I thought it was a good picture, quite frankly. But there was very little wrong with Bloch's script, only one or two lines that had to be changed. We also changed the running order of the stories, which Bloch wasn't happy about, I know. But it was one of the producers, Max Rosenburg, who insisted on making the change. He came to the picture quite fresh, he hadn't seen any of it until it was finished, then he said he liked it but he thought we should switch the order of the stories around. He said if you don't hit them in the first two reels you can forget it. I don't know whether this is true or not. People make pictures for all sorts of different people – they don't necessarily make them for audiences. In a lot of cases they make them for the distributors, and when you know that the booking man at the distributors is going to

Ralph Bates as Dr Jekyll

Martine Beswick as his alter-ego Sister Hyde (from Dr Jekyll and Sister Hyde*)*

see about six pictures that same day, that he knows nothing about your picture, you've got to catch his attention during the first two reels. With *Asylum* it was definitely a case of playing up to the distributor rather than the audience, which was crazy because I think the audience would have preferred the stories the other way around. Anyway, it was a very successful picture and it got a prize in Paris and a lot of compliments all round. But my God, it was cheap! We made it for less than £150,000 despite the good cast, and we shot it in twenty-four days. Bloody ridiculous! If they don't make money on a picture that costs peanuts then they'll never make money.

'After I did *Asylum* I did a film which had half-a-dozen different titles to begin with. It was originally called "Fengriffin" but now it's called *And Now the Screaming Starts*. It's a ghost story but it didn't, in my opinion, get the credit it deserved. It had magnificent sets, though they were actually very cheap, and another good cast, including Stephanie Beacham, but it was a kind of ghost/fairy story that got mucked up somehow. It should have been a much more erotic picture; and it could have been quite easily. Basically it was about a girl who has nightmares and keeps seeing things in this huge, country house. She's just arrived as the bride of this young man in a sort of arranged marriage, and he turns out to be a really charming young man – and from that point on he falls out of the story which I think is wrong. He should have turned out to be very sinister or impotent, which would have given the girl a reason for having these funny fantasies about her wedding night. It turned out to be a muddled picture but some of it is beautiful to see. It was beautifully photographed by Denys Coop, who is a really top-class photographer, and so quick.

'After that I did another one for Amicus called *Vault of Horror* which was meant to be a follow-up to *Tales from the Crypt*, but it wasn't any good – it was a bore. We had a good cast but the script was really rubbish. That good cast was absolutely wasted and the producer, Milton Subotsky, says so himself. But it's so rare that you get everything right on a picture – often it's luck. Everything slots in together and you have a success. Sometimes you can tell from the moment you see the script that a picture is going to be something special. For instance, when I read the script of *Morning Departure* I knew it was going to be an outstanding film and I would have paid money to have directed it.

'I'm not happy about being a "horror director". I did a few horror pictures of varying shape and size and I was automatically typed as a horror director which isn't right. I don't want to be, and I don't like it.'

Freddie Francis, like Roy Ward Baker, has come to horror films rather

Francis explains a scene to Veronica Carlson, one of the stars of The Ghoul

late in his film career. The first film he worked on, as a clapper boy and camera loader, was *The Marriage of Corbal* in 1936. Later he became a camera operator and worked on such films as *Night Beat* (1947), *The Small Back Room* (1948), *The Tales of Hoffman* (1951), *Beat the Devil* (1953), *Moulin Rouge* (1953). He was the second-unit and effects photographer on *Moby Dick* in 1956 and that same year worked on his first film as a lighting cameraman – *A Hill in Korea*. As a cameraman he achieved quite a distinguished reputation for his photography on films like *Room at the Top* (1958), *Saturday Night and Sunday Morning* (1960), *The Innocents* (1961), and *Sons and Lovers* (1960), for which he gained an Oscar. His first film as director was *Two and Two Make Six* (1961), and his later films include *Paranoiac* (1962) *Dr Terror's House of Horrors* (1964), *The Skull* (1965), *Dracula Has Risen from the Grave* (1968), *Tales from the Crypt* (1972), and *Legend of the Werewolf* (1975).

'I got a lot of fun out of being a cameraman,' said Francis, 'but obviously directing is more interesting. One thing wrong with being a cameraman in Britain is that from the financial point of view you have to keep working all the time and you often have to work with people whose work, frankly, doesn't excite you. When I got the opportunity to direct I decided to try it and if I wasn't excited with what I did, well, that would be my own problem and no one else's. But basically I love making films. If someone asked me now to photograph a film I still would. I photographed a film for Karel Reisz, [*Night Must Fall* (1964)] after I had directed about six pictures. If someone like Karel or Jack Clayton, whom I like working with, asked me to photograph a film for them I would have no hesitation.

'John Huston and I got on very well together, but I started off with him as a camera operator and it was very difficult for me to do anything else while working with him. He didn't want me to become a cameraman, he just wanted me to stay operating for him for the rest of my life. It was quite by chance I became involved with him. He was about to make *Moulin Rouge* and suddenly he didn't have a cameraman and Ozzie Morris stepped in. Because I'd been working with Ozzie I became the operator. The whole thing clicked and I stayed with John after that until *Moby Dick*. After that I became a cameraman in my own right but Ozzie stayed with John for several pictures after that.

'Working on *Beat the Devil* was fun. The situation was that Bogart owned the rights to it and Huston had agreed to direct it in a weak moment. Right up to the last moment I'm pretty sure that John didn't want to do it. He tried all sorts of ways to get out of it but he couldn't and suddenly there we all were – out in Italy committed to do a film for which there was virtually no script. I don't think anybody knew what sort of a film it was going to be until Robert Morley arrived – and Robert Morley being Robert Morley, he decided it was going to be a comedy, and then everyone else decided it was going to be a comedy. Truman Capote was there to rewrite the script and I think we were shooting the film faster than he was rewriting it. It could have been a disaster but I don't think it was entirely. It was certainly great fun to make. Peter Lorre was great to work with, he had a great sense of humour; though I didn't particularly like Humphrey Bogart. I'm sure, when it was released, people were expecting another *Maltese Falcon* which they didn't get. A lot of people hated it, but a lot liked it and it's become something of a cult film now.

'On *Moby Dick* I shot all the model stuff and I photographed some live whaling out in Madeira. They still did whaling there with the old methods. We were chasing whales in an open boat. After that I came back to London and for about fifteen to sixteen months I was shooting all the special effects on the tank at Elstree studios. We used several model whales for the tank shots – the largest one was about twenty feet long. For the scenes with Ahab on Moby Dick's back we used a model whale with a model Ahab strapped to it. There was also a big section of one that we had on the stage – a full-sized section, that Gregory Peck was strapped to for the close-ups. We had someone from the USA, Gus Lohman, supervising the effects and he was very good.

'*The Innocents*, which I photographed for Jack Clayton, has been described by some people as a horror film, but I wouldn't say that to Jack. It was always enjoyable to work for him because I'd known him for

Jack Clayton and Deborah Kerr take a break during the filming of The Innocents *(Freddie Francis was the cinematographer on the picture)*

a long time, even before he started directing. There was always an understanding between us that if he directed a film I would photograph it. I only did two pictures for him and I was involved with them from their inception. After *Room at the Top* turned out to be very successful I had quite a lot of freedom, and I was able to influence the style of *The Innocents*. We worked out all sorts of things before the picture started, including special filters. I still think it was the best photography I've ever done – as much as I like *Sons and Lovers* I think *The Innocents* was better, but you rarely get an Academy Award for a film that isn't successful no matter how good your work is on it.

'I'm sure Jack was terribly disappointed with the reaction that *The Innocents* received. He, unfortunately, gets terribly tied up in his films. Everybody, I'm sure, involved with it thought it was a great picture and I'm not completely sure what went wrong but I think it was because it was based on Henry James. When you read James you've got to think about it and make up your own mind – and the great thing about James is that you must never *really* make up your mind, you must always be not quite sure. The film lacked this ambiguity and I think, basically, that was the reason it wasn't a success. I somehow think that in a film, and this may sound a bit pretentious, a director has got to make up the audience's mind for them – a director has got to *know* what's going on. There was that, plus the fact we had Deborah Kerr, a brilliant actress but always absolutely charming and no one could ever think she was slightly bonkers, so in the film all the suspicion fell on the children – whereas having read *The Turn of the Screw* one doesn't know whether it is the governess who is a bit strange or the children.

'I'm not sure what effect winning the Academy Award had on my career. It happened around the time I turned to directing and whether it was a help to me in that area it's difficult to say. At the time two people asked me to direct for them but I don't really think either of them asked me just as a result of the Oscar. The producer of the first film I directed, *Two and Two Make Six*, asked me because I had photographed a film for him in the past and we had got on well together. At the same time Harry Saltzman asked me to direct a film for him because I think *he* thought he owed me a favour – he and Tony Richardson had forced me on to Karel Reisz when he was doing *Saturday Night and Sunday Morning* more or less because they were worried about Karel, it being his first feature, and they put me in to hold his hand, though it was completely unnecessary because Karel certainly didn't need any help. Anyway, Harry never made this film so that was that.

'As to why I've become typecast as a horror director, the answer is simple. The reason is not, I think, a positive one. Several cameramen have turned to directing but have never forgotten they are cameramen and consequently they have made pictures without any heart or soul. I find that they are always referred to as cameramen, no matter how many pictures they've directed. So when I turned to directing I decided I had to do something that would make people think of me as a director rather than as a cameraman. And after my first film, which wasn't very successful, I then got involved with Hammer – although I got involved with Tony Hinds rather than Hammer, and he is now a dear friend of mine. I like him very much and I like business associations with people I like, and it was also a very happy atmosphere at Bray, we had great fun down there. And because I wanted to do a lot of pictures very quickly as a director, and because I was enjoying myself so much at Bray I could rarely refuse to do a picture, I just kept on making these pictures for Hammer. Some of them were out-and-out horror films; but some could be classified as thrillers, but because they're Hammer films they're horror films, and suddenly I woke up one morning and found out that I'd done so many films for Hammer I was classified as a horror film director. I'd got myself in a rut which I find it very difficult to get out of.

'I had a chip on my shoulder about this for some time but about a year ago I was debating this with my wife, who is a great critic of mine and understands the business, and we suddenly looked around and found, although I didn't like these films and was almost ashamed to mention them to some of my friends, people were coming from all over the world to interview me and I had become something of a cult figure. So we decided that here we were in a business that's almost on its last gasp but I'm always working, so let's not be stupid about this, let's not go and starve in a garret while I wait for the right film to come along. I'm making these pictures and whatever pictures they are, I decided, I love doing them because I love making pictures, so why not enjoy them? And funnily enough, on the last picture I made, which was for my son [Kevin Francis – see Chapter 14], I approached it completely differently – I decided I wasn't going to worry about it being a horror film, I was just going to enjoy it – which I did. So I'm just starting a second career really.

'Although I became known as a horror director while I was at Hammer I hadn't really done any Gothic horrors apart from *The Evil of Frankenstein* and *Dracula is Rising from the Grave*. I must say that I approached the latter as more of a love story than as a horror film. I was more interested in the love affair between the boy and the girl than with Dracula, he was just a fly in the ointment. Unfortunately a lot of that was cut out by Hammer and I never had a chance to put it back again. The thing with Hammer, as far as the scripts were concerned, was that one was given a pretty free hand on the floor. But one really didn't have much time to do anything on the editing side – the films went through a mincing machine and it was almost just a case of cutting out the clapper boards and putting the film together. But I liked working at Bray, not particularly because of the studio itself, but because of the whole Hammer organiza-

Francis (top left) at work on The Evil of Frankenstein *with Peter Cushing on the right*

tion. I was working with people like Tony Hinds and Jimmy Sangster and we had great fun. I believe movies have to be fun to make because once I undertake to do a movie they own me body and soul for that period and it becomes my whole life; so if you don't have fun while you're making the movie you don't have any fun at all. I haven't made any more films for Hammer since Tony Hinds retired – that was *Dracula is Rising from the Grave.*

'*Dr Terror's House of Horrors* was the first of the anthology type of films that I've done for Amicus. Of these *Tales from the Crypt* has been the most successful. It was a tremendous success, a blockbuster in terms of what it took in comparison to its cost, and I'm delighted that it was but I don't know why. It just happened to come at the right time, if there is a right time for these sort of things, because you can always see a horror film. I suppose that type of film, with four or five different stories, is like a cocktail really – sometimes a particular cocktail mixture is better than others because the mixture has blended differently and something happens. But I really don't know why *Tales of the Crypt* was such a success – I was just amazed at the time. *Dr Terror* was very successful too, and it's still going around. One of the producers lives off that film, he put up part of the money and eventually he bought out all the other partners. But my approach to these films is that no one is really going to believe

On the set of Paranoiac *– Francis is second from the left; to his right is Oliver Reed*

that these sort of things happen – that, for example, Barbara Murray is really cutting up Richard Greene [in *Tales from the Crypt*] into small pieces – so I believe that though people may find it horrid for a while, they find it horrid in a *giggly* sort of way. Whether this is true or not I don't know. I may be fooling myself.

'I still think there are an awful lot of bad horror films, cheap and nasty ones, being made. I turn down the really bad ones when they're offered to me but I flatter myself that I can make better horror films than the scripts of the films I get. I think my films transcend the scripts, and I don't mean that in any conceited way. That is the opinion of the critics. But with these sort of films the only way one can make them is to use the script as a sort of guide. I work on the script a lot before we start shooting but often you find that the mood of the film is changing as you shoot it and you can often make capital out of this by giving the film some new facets which it didn't have before. All the scripts I've had I've treated in this way. There may come a time when somebody will say no – this is the script and I want it done as written – but in that case I would have to be jolly sure that I liked the script before I started, as opposed to what I do now, which is to just like the general idea before I start.'

One film that Francis wishes he never became involved with was a German horror film called *Gebissen Wird Nur Nachts – Happening Der Vampire* (also known as *The Vampire Happening*) which he made in 1971. 'That was definitely a mistake,' he said. 'It all sounded quite good fun when it came about – the producer was a young German millionaire, a playboy, and it was a sort of home movie. His wife was in it too. She was an actress and I'm sure she's fine with the proper material but she certainly wasn't right for this. Actually the way I made it I thought it could be very funny because I was promised that I could dub an English version with English actors but they were too mean to spend the money for that. They dubbed the English version in Hamburg picking up all sorts of odd American servicemen off the streets.'

Of the films that he has directed, Freddie Francis's two personal favourites are ones that haven't received a good distribution in either the USA or Britain. They are *Mumsy, Nanny, Sunny and Girly* and *Tales That Witness Madness* (1969 and 1972). 'There is always a problem when you give distributors a film,' he said. 'This happened with my *Mumsy, Nanny* film. It didn't fit into any category so they didn't want to know about it. The distributors are all geared up to handle horror films or comedies, or musicals etcetera, but when they get something that doesn't fall into one of their accepted categories they don't know what to do with it. With *Mumsy* they first tried to treat it as an outright horror film then they changed the title to just *Girly* as if it was a sex picture, which is certainly wasn't. I looked upon it as a black comedy. Slightly more black than comedy. But I would defend it against anything or anyone as a piece of *cinema*. I saw it again recently and it's still one of the films that I'm tremendously proud of. *Tales That Witness Madness* hasn't been released in England and is suffering the same sort of thing that affected *Mumsy*. It was based on short stories by J. Fairbank. The author and I collaborated on the script, and the producer and I absolutely loved it, but it was financed by Paramount and when they saw it they didn't like it because it wasn't a horror film. To which I replied, "I'm sorry about that but it was never supposed to be a horror film as you would have seen when you read the script." And they replied that they had never *read* the script. They had put the money up because they thought I was going to make another *Tales From the Crypt*. So having made this film, which I thought was a very fine one, I then had to do some re-shooting and inject blood and gore into it, but it could never really become an out-and-out horror film. It was really about the question of what is truth and how truth is what you want to believe. That was the sort of link between the stories. It was about four people who are in an asylum and they were all involved in what could have been murders or not. The fellow who ran the asylum, played by Donald Pleasance, completely believed and, in fact, saw their fantasies. I liked them because they were Roald Dahl-type stories. I would love more than anything to buy *Tales* and *Mumsy* and put them out as a double bill, because I think they were both representative of my type of black humour and if they were sold properly they would be tremendously successful films. But in the meantime I think Paramount is wondering what they can do with this strange film they've got.'

Francis is still vaguely optimistic about breaking out of the horror rut. 'This is a strange business. When I was a camera operator I never worried about becoming a cameraman because I knew something would happen and it did. It was the same with becoming a director. But as long as you are enjoying life . . .'

14　Producing Horror: Milton Subotsky and Kevin Francis

Milton Subotsky, an American, though now based in England, is the production head of Amicus Productions Ltd, the company he formed with partner Max Rosenburg. Amicus has specialized in producing quick, cheap horror films (though among the list of their titles one will find such things as Pinter's *The Birthday Party,* and *Danger Route,* a spy thriller) and have had a great deal of success with their anthology films – *Dr Terror's House of Horrors, Torture Garden, Tales from the Crypt, Asylum,* among the best known.

'I've always wanted to make pictures since I was a kid,' said Subotsky. 'I've always been crazy about films. But when I got out of high school I went to college at nights and studied chemical engineering because my parents weren't happy about the idea of me going into the film industry – they thought it was terrible and immoral. But then I got a job with a company that was making documentary and educational films. I started by carrying the cameraman's camera and then I did some editing. One day they got a bid to do a government film on a subject I knew something about so I wrote the script, and that was how I got into script writing. This was in New York City in 1938, when I was seventeen years old.

'During the war I worked on army technical training films for the Signal Corps. One of the films was called "Loading and Unloading Telephone Poles from Flatcars in Sidings" – I'll never forget that title. Apart from working on the training films I spent my last eight months in the army editing the camp newspaper. After the war I worked in New York for a columnist called Billy Rose. He had a column called "Pitching Horseshoes" and he had four writers helping him, of which I was one. He did a lot of work on the column himself but needed people giving him original ideas for stories. Then I joined a film company that was selling films to television and the best experience I had there was re-editing old feature films. We had a lot of these and I realized that the television companies would have a lot of half-hour slots to fill, so I took all our features and I edited them down to twenty-six minutes on the 16mm print. And I learnt so much about script construction out of doing that on film after film. I'd just sit in this room and screen the films myself – I had nobody helping me – and I found you could take tremendous chunks

out of pictures and it didn't make any difference, providing you took any reference of what happened during that chunk out as well. And I can't think of one instance where my twenty-six-minute version wasn't better than the original. I think that was what made me go on to making multi-story films where you're telling four or five stories in the length of a normal feature. Stories are always more interesting when you've cut out all the extraneous things.

'While I was with this TV company a group of Harvard students came to us with a film they had made which I liked. They showed it to my boss but he wasn't interested in it. It was called *A Touch of the Times* and was about somebody who suddenly stops work and decides to fly a kite, and pretty soon the kite craze catches on and everyone is out flying kites and nobody works any more. It was a lovely little film and I told them I'd give them the money to finish it providing we could find a distributor. And one of the distributors I went to see was Max Rosenburg, he had a company called Classic Pictures, and he said yes. Later he lost interest in it but he said he'd like to work with me and wanted to know if I had any other ideas. I had been preparing a series called Junior Science, a children's programme, and he said, how much money would you need to make the first thirteen episodes and I said $25,000 because we were going to do it very cheaply. I planned to use my own relatives in it. He said okay and we never even signed a contract, he just gave me the $25,000. And on the basis of the first thirteen episodes he sold thirty-nine for $240,000, so we then had to make another twenty-six and, of course, wound up with a big profit on it. From then on we were in partnership.

'The first feature we made was after I saw a review of *Rock Around the Clock* in *Variety* magazine. I ran into Max's office and said we've got to make the second rock-and-roll picture. I had never heard rock-and-roll music so I started to listen to it on the radio and then I wrote a script in four days. I found out who the big groups were and we booked them – Max provided the finance. We were on the floor shooting that picture within three weeks. We shot it in nine days, edited and dubbed it in about another two weeks, and the picture was on the screen almost immediately after *Rock Around the Clock*. It was called *Rock, Rock, Rock*.

'I got into horror films because I like fantasy. I like fairy tales, satires, anything imaginative or fantastic. Nearly all the films we've made have been films of imagination, not just horror films. We've done science fiction too, we did the *Dr Who* films and *The Mind of Mr Soames*. We've always done films that were non-realistic.

'I came to England in 1959. I'd written a story called *City of the Dead* which was adapted as a script by George Baxt, and the film was going to be a co-production between American money and an English company. So I came to England to supervise it and found that Baxt had only written a sixty-minute script – he thought it was only going to be a second feature. Well, it was going to cost £45,000 and for that sort of money it had to be at least a co-feature, so I wrote another twenty minutes of script which linked very well with the rest of the picture. I actually think it's one of our better films and it's still playing on late-night shows on TV. Anyway I liked England from the very start. I felt more at home here than I did in New York. And once we made *Dr Terror's House of Horrors*, which was our first big success in England, we started getting more pictures to do here. So I settled here – my wife is British and so are my children.

'Amicus isn't really in competition with Hammer. I don't think we are in the same field, frankly. We make a different kind of film but both ours and theirs are unfortunately covered by the word *horror*. Ours, I think, are more fantastic films. What I'm interested in is not what they're interested in – I mean, they make films that are shocking and have a lot of blood and gore, and sometimes I envy their bad taste but I just can't do that sort of thing. Their films have punch but I find that, for me, their stories are boring. I mean, you could take big chunks out of any Hammer film and it wouldn't make any difference. You could take six reels out and just leave reels one and two, and nine and ten, and you've got a picture. All the rest are just extra murders and extra gore. But they have made films that I've thought have been quite good. The one that they

Donald Sutherland prepares to do the 'right thing' for his vampire wife in Dr Terror's House of Horror, *one of the several anthology films produced by Amicus*

lost money on I thought was their best – that was *The Kiss of the Vampire* which Don Sharp directed. That had a mythic quality about it.

'But we try to make films that are imaginative and relate to an audience in a different way. We never have any blood and gore in our films. You never see it, it's always suggested. I mean, if we have someone kill somebody he'll just stab them once – in a Hammer film you'll see the slit throat and the blood pouring out and all of that. What I'm out to do is make story points. In a case like that the story point *is* that someone has killed somebody, the story point isn't *how* someone kills somebody. The details of the murder don't add anything to a story. It's the same with sex. We've never done a sex scene on the screen simply because it's boring. I mean, what are you going to show? It's always the same, every time. If you want to make a point that people are going to be making love to each other all you have to do is show them going to bed. You don't have to show all the details because then your story is standing absolutely still while you're doing it.

'I like to keep an audience guessing – keep them puzzled right up to the very end of the film. In a way our films are puzzle films and we're playing a game with the audience in which they're trying to guess the answer and outsmart us. There aren't many ways you can shock an audience anyway. I've watched so many horror films when I was a kid and I noticed that the audiences only yelled at two things – one is when there is a slow build-up and then suddenly something happens, like in the beginning of *Great Expectations* when the kid is grabbed. And the best example of that type of thing I've ever seen – the audience literally screamed and jumped out of their seats – was in a picture called *The Ship That Died of Shame*. There's a scene in that in which somebody hears a shot, goes into a house and slowly goes up the stairs; and just as he gets to the top a hand falls down in front of him. I saw this in Greenwich Village with a sophisticated audience and they really just screamed. The other thing is when you have a shock effect without any build-up at all, one that comes as a complete surprise.

'I love doing these shock scenes and I think audiences enjoy them. We did one in the first story in *Asylum* when that hand comes out of the freezer and grabs Richard Todd. And also in the first story in *Tales from the Crypt* when the murderer's hands come through the window at Joan Collins. I think that stuff is great. Anything that involves an audience and gets them either screaming, laughing or anything is marvellous. But you can't do that sort of thing too often in one film. Two or three times, perhaps. Hitchcock only did it twice in *Psycho*, when the girl gets killed in the shower and when the detective gets stabbed going up the stairs, but that's all you need.

'Hammer aren't really into suspense – they're doing action films which is a different thing altogether. And we're not interested in doing versions of either *Frankenstein* or *Dracula*. I can't really take them seriously. We've done three vampire stories in our multi-story pictures and we've treated them all as comedies because I just can't take vampires seriously. I get script after script for vampire films but I'm always looking for something different. I always want to do something unusual but Hammer make the same film over and over again – they have two or three varieties of the same film. But I don't want to touch all the same old horror themes because they're so banal. I often get a script on my desk and I can give the writer the name of twenty stories that have the same theme but he hasn't read enough to know that what he sent me wasn't original. I can tell on page one whether the idea is worth pursuing or not.

'The script is the most important thing in film making – the script and the editing. The direction is not that important. I think the cult of the director came into being because the critics have to attach some name to a film and so they think the director is the man who makes the film, but he's not. I don't really think it's all that important who directs a picture. That's one of the reasons we've given so many people their first picture to direct. I think we've given more directors their first chance than any other company. One of the reasons you work with a novice is that you think that maybe he can give you something more interesting than some-one who's stuck in the mud. But I also like to give new people their first opportunity to direct because if they make it big later on you can say, well, *I* gave him his first break. The other thing is that I don't think any new director can do great harm to a picture providing you've got a good script. If you've got a bad script the best director in the world is not going to make a good film out of it.

'I don't have much involvement with the actual shooting of our films. I work on the casting but I never bother the director while he's working

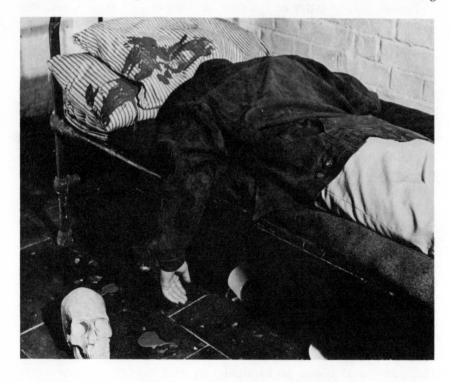

A character in Torture Garden *loses his head*

because it's *his* job. I look at the rushes every day from the point of view of editing and if I feel that he didn't cover a scene well enough I would ask him to take the extra shot that I would need. But you can't tell a director how to direct a film – you let them alone. You can always take a director off a film if things go completely wrong but that's a terribly enormous thing to do. But directing a picture isn't that hard to do once you know how to place your camera and so on. Working with actors is harder and some directors work better with actors than others.

'Editing is the thing that really interests me. You can make or break a film in the cutting room – you can do anything you like with it. Take *The Skull*, for instance, which Freddie Francis directed. We really made the picture in the cutting room. Originally it was only a little eight-page Robert Bloch story and when I read it I saw that we could do the last four reels without any dialogue. One of the things I like about horror films is that you can make them very cinematic and have long, long sections without a word, just music and effects. So I wrote the script for *The Skull* with that in mind. All the ideas on how to shoot it were Freddie's – he did marvellous things, such as shooting through the skull's eyes, he got on roller skates for that and operated the camera himself, shooting through a large mock-up of the skull. But when we got it in the cutting room and assembled it we found there was no story. The plot, for some reason, didn't work. So we began to put it together in a different way and the whole last part of it, from the time Cushing gets the skull, is now made up of little bits and pieces of film that were shot for a different reason. Most of Cushing's reaction shots were made up of these. We actually reconstructed the whole last four reels out of teeny trims and bits and pieces of film. Nobody knows the wonders that can be worked in the cutting room!

'*Psychopath* is a similar example of what you can do with editing. Robert Bloch sent me an unpublished original story and then we assigned him to script it. We finished the picture, edited it and we showed it to people and they all guessed the murderer's identity. So what we did was that every time Patrick Wymark opens his mouth in the next to last scene we cut away from him and overlaid his dialogue, and every time someone replied we cut away from them and overlaid their dialogue – we changed the whole last scene with post-synched dialogue and that way we changed the murderer! We did the same sort of thing in *Torture Garden* with the last story. That was the one about Poe that starred Jack Palance. In the scene with Palance when he discovers Poe in that room, every time that Palance starts talking we cut away from him and changed all the dialogue. What happened was that Freddie Francis changed the ending on the floor without telling me. Not that our original ending was that good but Freddie's version left us with no motivation for the whole place burning up. We had to do something before Palance went back to the States so that he could post-synch it, so I wrote a whole new ending in the cutting room, basing it on the footage we had.

'Freddie Francis is a brilliant director pictorially. He is one of the world's great cameramen, he sets up the most beautiful and intricate shots, and his pictures are so good to look at, but I don't think he has a very good story sense.

'Our series of multi-story films came about because I had always thought the British film *Dead of Night* was the greatest horror film ever, and I wanted to do something like it. For the first one, *Dr Terror's House of Horrors* I wrote five horror stories and connected them with a framework story. That's always the hard part – linking the stories together. There isn't much you can do with that and we always find that we cut those sections shorter and shorter because we find them boring when we get them to the cutting stage. But I prefer to do short stories instead of one long picture and I hope that people keep wanting to see them so that we can keep making them.

'It was my idea to base *Tales from the Crypt* on the old E.C. horror comics. I'd wanted to do that for a long time, but it was very hard to get the rights because Bill Gaines, who owns the rights to them, is very touchy to deal with. I mean he even vetted the script and made suggestions for changes and so on. I'm hoping that he will let us do *More Tales from the Crypt*, we're waiting to hear what he says about it. *Vault of Horror* was also based on E.C. Comics. I don't know what went wrong with that one. Maybe I chose the wrong stories. You can never tell until a picture is finished whether it's good or not. Sometimes you're so close to a film you don't know whether it's good or bad. Sometimes we'll call in people while we're editing and say, what do you think of this? Maybe we were too funny in *Vault of Horror* because we were really kidding it. It was probably too tame. In that I bent over backwards not to be gory or shocking and I think I went too far.

'It's funny, but when *The House That Dripped Blood* was finished the censor gave it an "A" and the distributors in Britain said they wouldn't take it unless it was an "X" ["X" is the maximum rating in Britain]. I don't know why. I had told the distributors in advance that it was going to be an "A" because it would have brought in a whole new audience – young people who weren't allowed to see "X" films would have been allowed to see it. But the distributors went to the censor and asked him for an "X" and he said alright. But strangely enough, he gave *The Beast Must Die* an "AA" when the distributor asked for an "X"; he said no. So the distributors asked me to add some gory footage so the picture would warrant an "X". I said to the censor, "They're going to force me to put in more gore than the story needs – they're going to force me to put in stuff I don't *want* to put in." And he said he couldn't honestly label it an "X" because an audience expects something when they go to see an "X" film. So I took one shot where a guy had been killed by the werewolf, and what we had done originally was to cut immediately to a reaction shot, but I changed it so that in the middle of the reaction shot we cut back to the guy lying dead. That was all I added and the censor said, "That's not enough." And I said, "Please don't force me to make it more gory than it should be." He said, "Okay, I'll give it an 'X' but this is the very last time."

'I think it's silly that the distributors should want an "X" when they could get a bigger audience with an "A". I'd love to make a "U" horror

Ingrid Pitt shows her fangs and (below) Jon Pertwee reacts accordingly. Both scenes are from the final segment of The House That Dripped Blood

film that children could go and see. I've got stacks of horror anthologies for children but I don't think the distributors would go for it. I mean, it's much more scary hearing a ghost howl and *not* seeing it than actually seeing the thing.

'We've never really had any trouble with the censor wanting us to cut things out of our films. Very often, though, he has made us re-think something. In *Danger Route*, when they torture the girl by burning her feet, we had originally showed that explicitly and he said no, that's too nasty. So we cut away to the people watching and the scene seemed much more horrible than it was, because when you imagine what is happening to her it seems worse. So very often a censor's suggestion artistically improves a scene.

'One scene that the censor did cut was in *Tales from the Crypt* where Richard Greene was lying in the coffin.' Greene had spent several hours lying in a coffin that was too small for him and covered in animal offal, which had begun to stink under the hot lights. The script had called for his wife in the film, played by Barbara Murray, to hack at him with a large sword in an attempt to kill him (he had been brought back to life by a magic spell but the embalming fluid in his veins was causing him some discomfort) and the animal offal was to simulate his exposed innards – the special effects men had rigged it with air tubes so that everything moved about. 'But he did allow a shot of Greene's dismembered hand moving about under his chin,' said Subotsky. 'That hand cost £400 and we've used it in three pictures. It was built by Ted Samuels at the Shepperton special effects department. It was a very delicate mechanism – it worked beautifully but it kept breaking down. It looked great except in close-ups. There was one shot that we didn't want to use in *House of Horrors* when it was in the car with Christopher Lee; the hand was in the foreground and you could see the seam, but we had no other choice.

'We've been criticized for using big-name stars in our anthology films, but we don't hire them just for their names but because they are really good people. We have done some stories with unknown actors and I find that the same stories would have been carried better with stronger, more identifiable personalities in them. In *From Beyond the Grave* we had a segment with Donald Pleasance and with Angela Pleasance playing his daughter and it was perfect – with other actors it wouldn't have worked as well.

'But I do wish there were more horror stars available. I haven't used Christopher Lee recently because his agents are now asking an enormous amount of money for him and he's become too expensive. Cushing, on the other hand, is good value. I think his agent is very smart – he asks for an amount which is reasonable – if he asked more I don't think people would use him, but he asks the maximum reasonable amount. And Cushing is very good – he can do anything. In our films we always cast him against his usual type. He loves it because it gives him a chance to do something different. But I would love to have more people to choose from who are considered as horror names.'

Subotsky's latest production to date isn't a horror film, but a film based on a novel by Edgar Rice Burroughs – *The Land That Time Forgot*. Full of mechanical dinosaurs and other special effects, it is about a mixed group of British and German seamen, plus one girl, who discover a lost continent near Antarctica. 'It was an amazing film to make in England,' said Subotsky. 'I think there is a new interest in this type of film. *Sinbad's Golden Voyage* did very well. I love that kind of film – the sort of films that children like. I'd like to make a musical too, anything that has fun and imagination.

'I don't know what's going to happen to horror films now because there is so much of that sort of thing on television. I think we're going to have to start making them directly for TV – whether we will make TV series or individual films I don't know yet. Remember that Amicus films play in the same cinemas that films like *The Godfather* and *The Sting* play in – we're in competition with these films – so we have to make a film for the audience that will go and see *The Godfather* and *The Sting* and I don't think the normal type of horror film is something they'll go and see any more. So in future we're going to have to do something different –

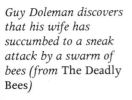

Guy Doleman discovers that his wife has succumbed to a sneak attack by a swarm of bees (from The Deadly Bees)

and better. I've got one horror film in the script stage called *The Last Horror Film* and it's going to be a honey if I ever get it off the ground. I've got Clive James to do the dialogue and I think he'll do a brilliant job which will put the picture in a different category. It's not quite a comedy, it's about the closing of Shepperton studios really. We set it in a film studio about to be closed and it's the last day of the last picture and suddenly everyone starts getting murdered. And each person gets murdered by one of the famous monsters out of the costume department – Frankenstein, Dracula and so on. I love using a film studio as a film studio in a picture.

'You want to know how Hammer started making horror films? Well, after we did *Rock, Rock, Rock* I wrote this script of *Frankenstein* and stuck very closely to Mary Shelley's novel. I wanted to do an absolutely authentic *Frankenstein* and in colour too because that was a new idea at the time. So we took it to the head of Seven Arts and of course you get typed in this business, so he said: "What do you know about horror films? You make musicals." And he said he'd send it to his friend Jimmy Carreras in London. So we got a fee and percentage of the profits from *The Curse of Frankenstein* even though they didn't film my script – they changed it completely. But from then on Hammer went into the horror business, due to that success.'

(Said Michael Carreras: 'I'm fairly certain Mr Subotsky had nothing to do with it but if he wants to take the credit I'm perfectly happy to let him.')

Hammer, AIP and Amicus now have a new competitor – Tyburn Films. Tyburn has only been in existence for a short time and to date has produced three films – *Persecution, The Ghoul,* and *Legend of the Werewolf.* The force behind Tyburn is a young man named Kevin Francis, the son of director Freddie Francis, though the two seem totally opposite in temperament and personality – Freddie Francis, quiet and thoughtful, his son, brash and bristling with energy. At the moment they form a perhaps uneasy partnership with Kevin producing the films and Freddie directing them. 'The reason Freddie is working for the company,' said Kevin Francis, 'is because of sound commercial judgment on my part. He's not got a dog behind him horror-wise, apart from that German thing, and nobody even *knows* whether that is a dog or what it is. He's a good director.' Even so, Freddie Francis doesn't find it any easier working for his son rather than for Hammer or Amicus; instead it seems to be rather more difficult. 'But in fairness to him,' said Freddie, 'I realize that he, like any other producer – *especially* he, because his films are privately financed – is the guy who has to go and sell the film. So I appreciate the fact that if he asks me to do something I must pay attention to what he says. This doesn't mean I will do *anything* he tells me but I think one has to bear this in mind. It's very self-indulgent not to listen to producers.'

'As long as the director is shooting it my way he's okay,' said Kevin. 'I put it this way – we're making films with our own money, and the day a director proves to me he can go out and sell them for as much or more than I can, *then* he can do exactly what he likes, but as long as I have to go out and sell them then we do it *my* way. I don't mean shot for shot, that's stupid, I'm talking about doing it in terms of ideas, and in what direction the film as a whole is going. But just as I will say to a writer that a certain line will get the bird, so will I say to a director a cliché shot will get the bird just as easy. I spend a lot of the time on the set during shooting; and when I'm not there I'm in the office within screaming distance. When I stick my oar in it's when I *know* that something is not right. It's gut instinct, that's all, and that can be as wrong as it can be right. But if I'm asked for an opinion I'll give it – I'm the greatest opinion-giver in the world. I'm also a great believer in meetings. We have a production meeting every week, we have a script meeting every week and lots of chats with the artists. That way I don't have to get involved sorting out problems because I stop them from happening beforehand. I make sure that we're all thinking the same before we start and therefore the problems, if they arise, are all insignificant – unless somebody drops dead, but there's nothing you can do about that.

'I got into the film industry totally by accident. My father never had any influence over me professionally in any shape or form. I mean, he could have been a chimney sweep instead of a director – it had that amount of bearing on my present occupation. I got a pretty sound training by very weird and wonderful ways and means, and by working in a company [Hammer] where you did everything, otherwise you didn't stay working for the company. The first time that Freddie and I worked together was on *Dracula Has Risen from the Grave*. I was assistant director, and Terence Fisher was supposed to have directed it, but he fell under a bus or something; and Freddie was called in at the last moment. But we've gone our separate ways and I've just gone mine a little faster.'

When asked in what way Tyburn's films differed from those of Hammer and the other companies, he said: 'I think they're better. That's exactly what you'd expect me to say, isn't it? But that's all I can say. I do think they're better, but it's up to the public to prove me right or wrong. Our first film, *Persecution*, is totally different as far as the story is concerned – it's a modern-day Gothic horror story. When I say horror – there's no blood in it, no vampires or monsters in the attic, it's a story about a mother and her son, a very weird, bizarre relationship, but it is a horror film by definition. Forty per cent of all stories ever written are

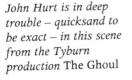

Peter Cushing with producer Kevin Francis on the set of The Ghoul

horror stories. *The Ghoul* is set in the 1920s, a period that hasn't been ventured into before by the makers of horror films. *The Ghoul* is the one classic horror story that has never been filmed, though there was a comedy based on it in the 1930s. I had this synopsis sent to me and I liked it right up to page one. I liked the title and I liked the characters in it but that was all. So we spent three months knocking it into shape and I think we ended up with a fine film. *Legend of the Werewolf* – well, it has always struck me that nobody has ever done a werewolf film properly. Universal had a go but their version is creaky now in terms of the technique they had. You see, I believe that no matter how good the film is, no matter how scintillating the dialogue is or how good the action is, you've got millions of people sitting there waiting for this bloke to turn into a werewolf. So we spent a lot of time and money developing a new photographic technique that can do this absolutely marvellously. Basically what we're doing is making a jolly good horror yarn with some good people in it and we're doing what the people want to see better than anybody has ever done it before.

'Our films are also different from the other companies' because we spend more money on them. I think the "other" company has not been worth considering for five years in terms of horror films for the people I hope to cater for – which are people who have the same tastes as me. They've become cheap, rip-off exploitation films which they never were

John Hurt is in deep trouble – quicksand to be exact – in this scene from the Tyburn production The Ghoul

in the good old days. Don't mention the name "Hammer" because it upsets me. I think Hammer is now like any other film company. They're just trying to raise money to make films, and I think over the past few years they've been the wrong kind of films. I don't think they've got the right people there any more – I *know* they haven't, because the man who had artistic control at Hammer is now working for me [Anthony Hinds, alias John Elder, has written scripts for Tyburn]. And I don't think they've got the showmanship that they had when James Carreras was at the helm. He was a sight to behold, he was just unbelievable. He could go and set up six pictures over a two-hour lunch. I think Bette Davis made the best comment about Hammer while she was making a picture for them: "It's just like working for Warner Brothers in the old days." The pictures had to be turned out, and turned out at a certain price, but they injected a bit of quality into them. They made pictures incredibly cheaply but they didn't *look* cheap. They do now but they didn't before.

'I *am* a horror film fan and I always have been. We used to have this game when we were kids – we weren't particularly flush, financially, and on top of that most of the horror films were "X" certificate – so there were ten or eleven of us who used to go together and we'd pool our money and the tallest would go and buy one ticket, go inside then let us all in through the fire exit. The oldest trick in the book, I'm sure. I'm sure that's why they finally closed that cinema down, the old Finchley Road Odeon, because more people got in that way than those who paid. Because I'm a fan I alter scripts now because I think I've got the public's point of view. I can read a line and I know whether someone in the front row is going to give it the bird when someone says it on the screen. I can see us as kids now heaving stuff at the screen every time somebody came out with some load of unadulterated rubbish.

'Personally, I love making horror films; but basically I'm a commercial animal and if nobody wanted to pay to go and see horror films – well, as James Carreras once said: "If people liked Strauss waltzes we'd be in the Strauss waltz business." I'm very lucky at the moment, and in the foreseeable future, because I am able to do something I enjoy doing and which is commercially viable. I would be happy if Tyburn made nothing but horror films but I'll read any type of script. If someone brings me in a script about two people in love in Regent's Park I'll read it – but while there is still a demand for horror films we'll keep making them.

'The thing about horror films is that it's possible to make a passable one reasonably cheaply, and no matter how much the box office suffers through falling attendances, that horror film will at least recoup its cost, providing you make it cheaply enough. I personally don't think that's a good policy, which is why we are spending more money on ours. I know it's very fashionable to make multi-story horror films and get Laurence

Olivier to walk past the camera twice and then advertise it as ''Starring Sir Laurence Olivier''. What is more difficult to do is to get that kind of actor to star in the whole film. We try to get people like Ron Moody, Trevor Howard and Hugh Griffith into our films. It's basically not difficult to get big names into anthology films for a couple of days – it's very easy, you just ring them up and say if you've got a couple of days with nothing to do here's a couple of thousand quid if you'll come and be in my film – but it's very difficult to get someone with a name to be in the whole film. But as far as I'm concerned, if these films are well-made there's no reason why anyone shouldn't be as proud to be in them as anything else.

'Actually I'm not too keen on the anthology type of horror films anyway. Amicus set out with this great new idea and were very selective at first about what they did but now they churn them out fifteen to the dozen. This whole idea of four stories and a link is now as old hat as anything. I think they've had it – and having said that I'm sure the next one they release will take about £3,000,000 and prove me wrong. But I think they've had it for the time being at least. The surprise twist at the end of these films is also getting a bit tired; in about four of them so far all the characters have turned out to be dead in the end – well, you can only do that once. With these films it was similar to Hammer's attitude to Dracula. They earned good money with their first *Dracula*, fairly good money with *Dracula, Prince of Darkness* and took an absolute fortune with *Dracula Has Risen from the Grave*. So they said, sod it, let's make one a year because the market will stand it. Well, the market *won't* stand it. If people want to watch the same thing every night they can watch it on television for nothing. Now everyone has seen Dracula so many times they're no longer shocked or surprised by him – everyone knows he's wearing a set of false teeth and red contact lenses but in 1957 everybody was horrified. Of course the Dracula films also depend upon sex. I think Freddie brought a lot of that into *Dracula is Rising from the Grave* – not sex, but sensuousness. Mind you, there was a lot in the original one but I think people were too naïve to notice. But whatever a Dracula film does to audiences the last few haven't been doing it.

'But I would like to make a proper Dracula film. I don't say that you could film the book but you could make something that wasn't a nasty exploitation film. Actually I've always thought the Bela Lugosi one was rather weak, though I think the first Hammer Dracula was super. Their second one had its moments but it was definitely beginning to go downhill. The third one, the one that Freddie did, continued the downhill trend story-wise, it bore no resemblance to the novel, but it was well-made technically. Then Hammer found out that they could make just as much money by just having Christopher Lee in them and the films themselves really started to go downhill. Dregs of the dregs, really. And when they started doing the modern-day versions I thought, oh well, the end has come.

'I'd love to use Chris Lee in our version of *Dracula* if we do it. All the kids used to walk around talking about Elvis Presley and Tommy Steele and so on but a little band of us used to say, sod that – we were Christopher Lee and Peter Cushing fans to a man. I would love to do a film with both Peter and Chris and I think this Dracula vehicle, which we keep working and reworking, trying to get it right, would be the perfect opportunity. I would especially like to bring Peter back as Van Helsing, because, after all's said and done, we all get older and I think Peter could now play Van Helsing as written – as a strange, funny old character. Of course Chris has said he's given up Dracula but he's always saying that. I'll believe it if, in forty years' time, he drops dead and hasn't made a Dracula film between now and then.

'I think the Frankenstein idea is absolutely finished, because every time you write a new Frankenstein script you find out that someone has done the operation for real. And Universal has made a classic version for television, which was released theatrically in England, and I think that will finish off Frankenstein once and for all. I've only seen a couple of reels of it and I thought it was terrible but that's beside the point.

'We've been developing, over the last few months, a Golem script but, I mean, who really wants to see man of clay trotting about? And if we make it someone will probably say we're anti-Semitic or something. And basically it's just the Frankenstein plot dressed up differently. Who cares whether you've got a monster made out of bits and pieces or one walking around because some guy has sprinkled magic powder in a tomb like in the Mummy films. Mummy films had it ages ago. There is no variation you can make with a mummy film. The first one that Universal made was okay and Hammer's first one was okay but the rest? Rubbish! It all comes down to this bloke coming out of a tomb covered in bandages. There's nothing very horrible about that after you've seen it once. As for the series of murders type of films, such as *Dr Phibes* – well, I've only seen one of them and that was *Theatre of Blood*. I thought it was jolly good and very funny – I hope you were supposed to laugh at it because I did. But again, once you've done one, that's it.

'Something I would like to do is a film like *The Cat and the Canary*, but you need a leading man in that who is a good comic, like Bob Hope. It was one of the scariest films I've ever seen yet it had some marvellous funny stuff in it. It's the *Old Dark House* type of thing – injecting humour into a horror setting. But if you are going to do that I honestly believe that the rest of the film has got to be better than the average horror film so that the whole thing doesn't become a joke.

*All in the family –
producer Kevin Francis
discusses a problem
with the director
Freddie Francis, his
father*

'I don't think we'd ever consider doing a film like *The Exorcist*. That's all a bit too nasty. I haven't seen the film but I've read the book and that was nasty enough. A horror film should be like a Grimm's fairy tale and I don't think *The Exorcist* is a fairy story. Now I'm not a censorship bod so if people are going to turn out *Exorcists*, especially if they're going to earn that sort of money, good luck to them, but it's not our game. Here I am calmly turning down a fortune, but I believe that there are fortunes to be made out of doing other things and I prefer to do other things. We have blood and gore in our films though. We use the corny old excuse that actresses give when they strip off – we're making the film as we think that the film needs to be made artistically. If the script says a scene is gory then we have gore, if the script says no gore then we don't have any. It's as simple as that, but we don't have a policy on gore – lack of or surfeit of.

'We're not doing out of our way to publicize ourselves at the moment. We hope that Tyburn products will promote Tyburn. We hope that people will go and see a Tyburn film as many moons ago they used to go and see a Hammer film. We're already getting a good coverage in the press and we're respectable now in the trade press.'

One unexpected piece of publicity that Tyburn received was during the making of *The Legend of the Werewolf* when one of the wolves being used in the film escaped from Pinewood studio and enjoyed several hours of freedom before it was caught and shot (a wolf-lover later wrote to the company and threatened to put a curse on them). 'I loved the publicity,' said Francis, 'but I was sorry the whole thing happened. The only reason the animal had to be killed was because the stupid journalists stampeded all over the place and kept frightening the poor thing. If we'd been left alone, as we asked, we would have been able to tranquillize it and get it back in its cage. But the thing had to be killed and that was unfortunate, otherwise it could have started killing people and that would have been even more unfortunate. I would have liked that amount of publicity about something pleasant.

'The name Tyburn came about simply because I wanted a film company and a friend of mine said, "Now I've got a company that I formed to do something with and I never used it, so if you want it, you can have it for what it cost me." So I said, "What's it called?" And he said, "Tyburn Film Productions Ltd." So I said, "Alright, I'll have it." I quite liked the sound of the name. Jimmy Carreras used to say – I mean Sir James Carreras used to say, and he said it to me once when we were talking about one thing or another – he always had an ear for somebody trying to hustle – "It's as simple as this," he said, "Forget the ego trip. Forget Kevin Francis Productions and any of that rubbish. Get yourself a name, a noticeable name but not a stupid one, and in everything you do, mention that name. Make sure everybody in the company uses the name whenever they're doing something, and if anybody doesn't – fire them. Then make a lot of films quickly and you'll have a viable proposition." And he was right. So we nicked his advice and here we are.'

15 The Horror Fans

People are attracted to horror films for many different reasons – intellectuals enjoy sifting through and analysing them in an endless search for hidden symbols; there are those who are interested in the occult and take the films seriously; others find escape in the fantasy element of horror films; some just like watching cinematic blood and gore, and there are those who simply enjoy being frightened. This last is probably the most common reason – the vicarious thrill one receives from the better type of horror film is similar to the enjoyment one used to receive as a child when pretending that there was something too horrible to contemplate hiding in the darkness of the back garden. The ability to *enjoy* being frightened is surely one of the things, along with a sense of humour, that makes man a race apart.

Another explanation for the strong fascination that horror films exert on people is that they embody many powerful cultural myths and obsessions. Blood, death and the fear of the unknown are three of the most common themes in horror films – Frankenstein's monster, zombies, mummies, vampires, all are walking dead, and Dracula, with his mixture of blood, sex and power over death is a particularly strong totem. But it's probably the fear of the unknown that is the most powerful force in horror films and, as various people have noted in the preceding chapters, the better films are those that leave a lot unexplained and avoid showing too much. A good example is *The Haunting* (Robert Wise, 1963) – its unseen 'something' that goes crashing and banging along the corridor of the haunted house is much more terrifying than if the presence had been visually manifested. Horror films really serve as packages in which we can gather the fears and impulses that disturb us most and, by doing so, defuse them to a certain extent or at least pretend we don't really care by having a good laugh at them.

Intellectuals have long enjoyed rummaging through the paraphernalia of the horror film to see what new variations in meaning they could discover, and some of their results have been amusing. Robert Bloch agrees: 'I think Parker Tyler was the first guy to go into this whole film symbolism thing in print. His contribution was to equate the Frankenstein monster with the phallus, a stiff, rigid figure that rises up and stalks about

– which I think is a little far-fetched. It's like the idiot who claimed that King Kong was a representation of the blacks and that this was what Willis O'Brien had in mind when he made the film. But I do think that the basic appeal of the Frankenstein Monster *was* symbolic, and Boris Karloff agreed with me. *Frankenstein* caught on with youngsters, and continued to appeal to youngsters, because the monster was actually an unconscious identification symbol of themselves – the adolescent of the early 1930s felt himself to be bumbling, awkward, ungainly, inarticulate, unable to communicate with adults on an equal level, a victim of persecution by authority, at odds with his father – in this case Dr Frankenstein – the parallels are all there and quite obvious. And finally when the monster was forced into rebellion there was a certain catharsis on the part of the then much-regimented audience with the monster getting back at all the various authority figures that have placed him in this intolerable position. Very definitely in the 1930s adolescents felt downtrodden, and in the Depression they became outcasts because they couldn't get jobs. They were terrible rivals with the adult world and were treated as such; but the Frankenstein monster gave them the perfect figure to identify with, and they did.

'The Dracula figure, in the 1930s, represented the foreigner – the then feared and hated menace who nevertheless exerted a considerable attraction. Again you have to view this against the context of the times. In the 1930s a very small percentage of the American population had ever been to Europe and those who had were most likely to have been members of the armed forces in the First World War. We still had the notion in films and in drama that the foreigner was not to be trusted. The American hero was a sort of rugged Gable or Cooper type – down to earth, fairly inarticulate, while the foreigner, even as exemplified by Valentino, was a menace. Valentino, like Dracula, was a man whose sexual approach was direct, who was a slimy, sophisticated type who wore evening clothes, which was very unmanly, and who kissed hands, which was even worse! The moral was that anyone who kissed your hand was likely to bite your neck. But at the same time there was this attraction – he was an oily, sinister type, the foreign seducer – but there was this suppressed female attraction towards him, and this had a great deal to do with the success of *Dracula*.'

Clubs, societies and magazines devoted to the horror film and its stars abound. The more illustrious of the various organizations include the Count Dracula Society in America and its British counterpart, the Dracula Society. The latter has only been in existence since 1973 but has already been instrumental in getting Bram Stoker some posthumous recognition in Ireland, the country of his birth, and has arranged tours to Transylvania where the members can visit the locales used by Stoker, such as the Borgo Pass, and other interesting sites including the house where Vlad Dracula was born in 1430 and the Castle of Poenari which he erected in about 1460. The society already has over two hundred members from all walks of life (Christopher Lee, Peter Cushing and Vincent Price are honorary members). It describes itself as 'devoted to the lore of the vampire and his kindred' and is at great pains to emphasize that it does not conduct 'ceremonies' though rather strange people keep ringing up and showing interest in ceremonies. The magazines vary between the excellent *Cinefantastique*, edited by Frederick S. Clarke (which is devoted to the whole range of fantasy films, not just horror), and Forrest J. Ackerman's *Famous Monsters of Filmland* which is aimed at a much younger readership. 'I guess I did something unique in human history a few years ago,' said Ackerman. 'I don't like to write in a vacuum, and in my magazine I always encourage the readers to send in their photos. I like to see all these youngsters, and sometimes oldsters, but one day I decided I would actually like to go out and meet them. So I announced in the magazine that I would be available for a visit and asked them to let me know where they were and how I could contact them. I set out an itinerary and let most of them know where I was going to be on such and such a date, and I suggested each boy or girl in one town should phone all their friends and get as many as they could over for the occasion. So in a period of about five weeks my wife and I drove 8,700 miles – and I don't even *like* to drive – zig-zagging all over the USA, from Hollywood to Denver, Detroit, the Bronx, Chicago – all the way from one lonely boy with forty-nine sheep on a farm to a large black and white group in Philadelphia. It was a very rewarding experience for me to meet, face to face, all these bright-eyed and bushy-tailed youngsters who were exercising their talents as writers and artists – moulding things, making models, collecting – it was sort of like I never left home. Everytime I stopped at a new boy or girl's address I would inevitably be led into a room with all sorts of familiar things – posters of Kong, Frankenstein, Dracula, models, and copies of my magazine.

'I had also wondered about the parents and what sort of reception I might get, but it was always a kingly reception. All the parents of the fans that I met were very enthusiastic about it all. I remember one particular mother and father took me aside and sort of thanked me – they said they had been afraid that their child wasn't even going to crack the cover of a comic book and that he showed no interest in the written word at all, then he was first attracted by all the crazy faces in my magazine and he began to look at the words. Before long he was off to the library and reading Bradbury and Heinlein, and so on.

'I would have infinitely preferred in my life to be writing up to whatever my literary capabilities are by attempting to entertain and perhaps

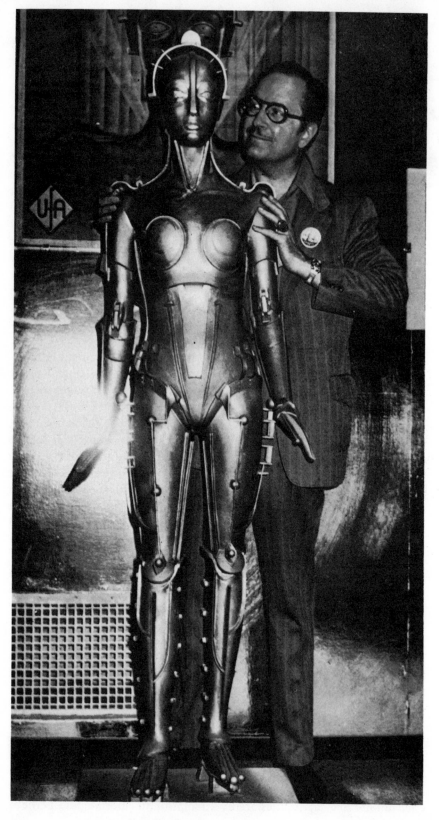

*Forrest Ackerman
meets an old friend – a
reconstruction of the
robot from* Metropolis
(from Famous Monsters
no. 111)

educate adults; but I seem to have been cast in this role as the Pied Piper of Monsterdom, with all the little kiddies following after me. But it's rewarding. Sixteen years after the magazine began obviously a lot of boys and girls who were eight years old once are now twenty-four and are beginning to make their mark upon the movie world. We had a very amusing film recently released called *Schlock* that was done by one of the original readers of *Famous Monsters*. He gathered together $60,000 and made himself an eighty-minute spoof on monster movies that has really clicked. This is happening over and over. There was one called *Equinox*, an animation monster movie which got a commercial release, and the latest one is *Dark Star*, made for an incredibly miniscule budget, but the special effects equal those of *2001*. I look to the kids who have been raised on my magazine as the Great White Hope of the movie industry – they will go back to first principles. I find that they admire the work of James Whale and Tod Browning and though, with the prosthetics and appliances available today, you can do incredible things like *The Planet of the Apes*, they like to go back and use the methods of, say, someone like Jack Pierce, the great master of make-up. They take longer but they feel that they get a more satisfactory result.'

Ackerman himself is probably the world's most devoted, and famous, horror fan. Fifty-eight years old now, he has been an avid collector of monster memorabilia since he was nine years old. His collection now resides within a large, twenty-five room house in Hollywood Hills that once belonged to film star Jon Hall. The collection had grown too large for Ackerman's previous house which had only thirteen rooms – even the kitchen and bathroom had begun to be filled with books and other items.

He believes his early years were largely shaped by his grandfather, architect George H. Wyman. 'He also loved science fiction,' said Ackerman, 'the supernatural, and movies. On some Saturdays we would manage to hit as many as seven movies if we timed it right. I saw my first Lon Chaney film when I was seven, and now I have one of his make-up kits in my collection.' Ackerman is also a well-known figure in the science fiction world and once served as Ray Bradbury's literary agent (he is still the agent for A. E. Van Vogt and for L. Ron Hubbard, the founder of Scientology) as well as being the editor of many science fiction anthologies.

'I have three great regrets in my life,' he said. 'I never met Conrad Veidt, Claude Rains or Lon Chaney Snr, but otherwise I think I have been very fortunate. I at least saw Colin Clive both alive and on his death-bed, I know Elsa Lanchester, I was with Boris Karloff on ten different occasions, I knew Bela Lugosi for the last three years of his life, I've met John Carradine, Peter Lorre, Lon Chaney Jnr, Glenn Strange and I know

The back of the robot, revealed by Ackerman in his magazine Famous Monsters

Vincent Price.' Actually Ackerman rather resembles Vincent Price and there were plans to use him in the third Dr Phibes film, which was never made, as Price's double in one sequence.

Ackerman's magazine, *Famous Monsters*, which has a paid circulation of 150,000 (and it's still growing) features mainly stills from horror films accompanied by a rather simplistic text filled with the most appalling puns. A recent issue (October, 1974) contained an article on *The Exorcist* – apparently, while the adults have worked themselves into a frenzy over the film, to FM's young readers it's just another monster film – and a series of photographs of Ackerman touring the exhibits of the Cinemathèque Française. Among the photographs is one of the *back* of the famous robot from *Metropolis*. 'I saw *Metropolis* when I was ten, in 1926,' said Ackerman, 'and I fell in love with the robot then. In later years I began to realize that I'd never seen its back.' Ackerman admits to placing a 'chaste and reverent kiss on her cold, metallic lips.'

'I'm sure a lot of people think I'm a damn fool,' he said, 'But all I know is that everyone who visits my house and collection goes away happier.' Ackerman has really achieved a kind of Peter Pan wish-fulfilment – he's managed to remain a little boy, and make a living at it.

Horror films, of course, also attract the genuine weirdos – people whose contact with reality is tenuous at the best of times. Ackerman, who acts as a focal point for horror film addicts, has come in contact with a few of them since he started his magazine. 'One fascinating example was a woman, who used to write to me, obsessed with Bela Lugosi. My wife had the theory that when I met the woman she was going to turn out to be deformed in some way, but she was actually a gorgeous girl with a figure that didn't quit. You'd think she'd have the choice of any guy she wanted, yet she was just constantly dreaming of Bela Lugosi, and this man had been dead for eighteen years! She's changed her name to Lugosi and spends all her time seeing his movies and pumping people for information about him. I've got some poetry that he wrote in his own handwriting, in Hungarian, way back in 1907, I think. I had it photo-copied and sent it to her and she went out of her mind over that. She called up the Hungarian consulate and they finally got some little old lady from a goulash joint who could translate it for her and this just thrilled her from head to toes. She built up this whole romantic fantasy about it – here was Bela Lugosi, a handsome young man of seventeen, sitting in his little garret and pouring out his heart in poetry to *her*, the one he desires most but who is forever denied him. This girl actually told me that, though she knows it would be illegal, immoral and certainly fattening, if it was conceivably possible she would like to seduce Bela Lugosi Jnr so she could bear a child and have her own little bundle of Bela Lugosi's flesh and blood! It's understandable with Christopher Lee, who is, after all, alive, tall, vital and virile, and the fact that he has a beautiful wife doesn't deter a lot of the women of this world. At *Famous Monsters* I have intercepted letters to him from young girls who say, in effect: "Look, Mr Lee, your wife has got to be generous. After all, she's had you for many years and I'm ready, willing and able to get on the next plane and camp on your doorstep so surely she could spare you for one week of love with me." But to have a passion for a man who has been dead for eighteen years – to keep him alive and burning in your womanly bosom when there's no earthly hope of ever meeting him – that is weird.'

The actors who play vampires definitely bear the brunt of unwanted female attention. Robert Quarry, who resembles a rather more compact Christopher Lee and who has played Count Yorga in two cheap but entertaining vampire films, quickly discovered the problems that such a role creates. 'I've been getting very funny mail and I've had my number taken out of the phone book as I've been getting obscene phone calls. I mean strange things really happen. I always figured that if people made obscene phone calls, it would be at a decent time, say 2.30 in the afternoon, but they always call at 8 a.m. or midnight, or just as you're sitting down for dinner, and who wants to listen to ''Oh Count Yorga'' and then the sound of heavy breathing over the phone. I'll say, ''Listen, call at 1 p.m. tomorrow afternoon when I haven't got anything to do and when there's nothing on TV. I'll get a drink and we'll lap it up a little.'' '

Horror directors, as well as stars, are sought after by the horror fans. 'Some who come to interview me,' said Freddie Francis, 'get very disappointed when I've got nothing to say about horror, witchcraft and all this nonsense. I find they take it so seriously while I find it hard to accept it with a straight face. I have to *sort* of accept it because it's my bread and butter now, but they really do take these films so seriously. They seem to understand the legends of horror, the myths etc, far more than they understand films, unfortunately. I'd much rather that someone admired a film of mine because they thought the set-ups were fine, and that the characterization was good and the atmosphere effective rather than the fact that someone cuts somebody's throat in the correct ritualistic manner.' As well as fans coming to see him Francis also receives a steady stream of letters from the horror fans. 'It used to be a lot but I must say that I'm very bad at answering them so I don't get so many now.' Christopher Lee, on the other hand, receives over 18,000 letters a year but at least he can call upon the assistance of his staff to handle them.

'I read them,' said Lee, 'and I work on the answers with my secretary and public relations people. When I first got fan mail I used to answer it personally but, of course, that's become impossible over the years. We get thirty to forty letters a day and it just mounts and mounts. They're mostly just straightforward, very pleasant, appreciative letters saying: ''I like your films and the parts you play.'' I get letters from all over the world, though mainly from the USA and Britain. A few dislocated psyches come my way, some of which are repeatable and some of which aren't. An amusing letter came from Ghana once in which the writer said my activities were unspeakable, but he didn't say my *professional* activities. Another one was from a group of people in Rumania who said, ''We have formed a club in your honour and'' – they had obviously taken tremendous trouble to learn the right words in English and, indeed, they picked on a word which, in its literal meaning, is absolutely correct – they said, ''We have decided, after careful thought and consideration, that you are, without any doubt, the most terrible actor in the world.'' A great compliment.'

Epilogue

The major event within the horror film field in recent years has undoubtedly been the release of *The Exorcist* – the first horror movie to gross $20 million (the figure has now passed the 60-million mark). It is a film that has also created an enormous amount of controversy, and critical opinion about it has been sharply divided. Readers will have noted that the reactions of most of those questioned about the film in this volume were adverse, and a few people – professionals in the horror film business – refused even to go and see it. Not surprisingly, the varying opinions have often reflected a generation gap. Writing in *Cinefantastique*, a magazine which features mainly younger contributors, Harry Ringel said of the film:

The Exorcist has done for the horror film what *2001* did for science fiction: legitimized it in the eyes of thousands who previously considered horror movies nothing more than a giggle. Like *2001*, *The Exorcist* has wormed its way into people's lifestyles by using the rules of the *genre*, not despite them; both are also *Zeitgeist* films, which promise a social experience as well as an artistic one. However *The Exorcist*, unlike *2001*, will never need a cult; *everyone* is going to see.

Whereas in the more staid *Film Comment* a reviewer wrote:

The Exorcist is not the first bad movie to be a hit, but it is a new kind of blockbuster; it represents a new extreme in the cinema of cruelty. What is it that makes people pay to be abused? It isn't just a case of publicity hype. The crowds know what they're going to see, and the freak show doesn't disappoint them. Are their emotions so deadened that they need sledgehammer blows to make them respond? Or are they titillated by the spectacle of a child degraded, tortured and defiled? The film offers perverse sexual kicks that make ordinary porno movies look wholesome.

I must admit that I consider *The Exorcist* to be a very fine film, as well as a rather horrifying one (already it has become fashionable to claim that one was bored by it), though I can't say I was aware of all those 'perverse sexual kicks' that so upset the writer in *Film Comment*. Director William

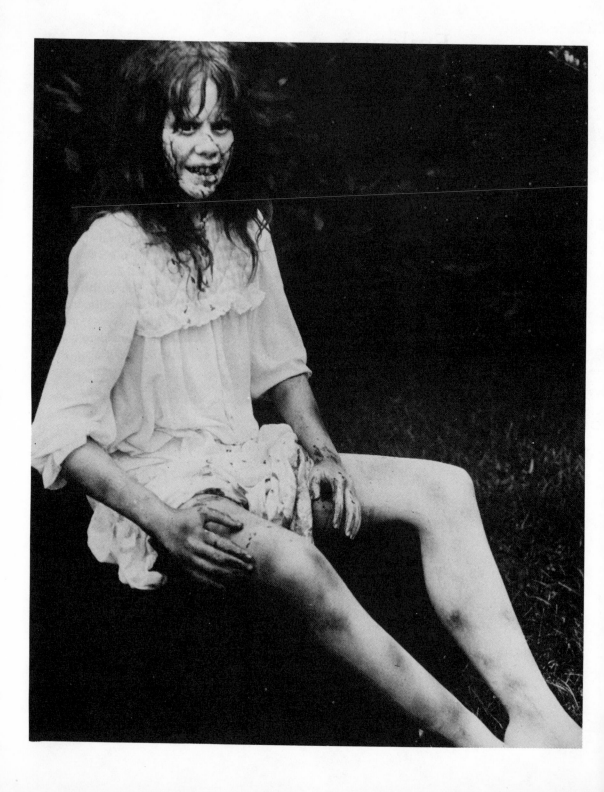

Friedkin set out to make a film that shocked and horrified and, in my
opinion, he succeeded most impressively.

One of the most important things about *The Exorcist* is that it has
revitalized the horror film. Audiences had become too accustomed to the
traditional horror film with its over-familiar paraphernalia. It no longer
offered any surprises – instead, potentially disturbing themes were
defused by being placed in a horror film setting. Demonic possession, the
subject of *The Exorcist*, was by no means new to horror films, but it was
the *way* that Friedkin treated it that made the difference. Purists may
object, of course, to the horror film being removed from the comfortable
fairy-tale setting where it has resided for so long and given a new set of
teeth – but they should keep in mind that such safe old films as *Dracula*
and *Frankenstein* were originally designed to shock too. For instance,
when Universal first began considering the possibility of filming *Dracula*
a number of the studio's readers protested after examining Stoker's
novel. One reported that the book was 'without doubt one of the most
gruesome stories that has ever been written . . . For a picture it is out of
the question.' A second reader said : 'Were this story put on the screen,
it would be an insult to every one of its audience. We all like to see ugly
things . . . (For instance the big appeal of *The Phantom of the Opera*). But
when it passes a certain point, the attraction dies and we suffer a feeling
of repulsion and nausea. This story certainly passes beyond the point of
what the average person can stand or cares to stand.' And a third commented : 'It is *not* picture material from the standpoint of the box office
nor of ethics of the industry. It would be a thing which no child and for
that matter no adult of delicate nervous temperament should see, a thing
beside which *The Cabinet of Dr Caligari* would seem like a pleasant fire-
side reverie.' It all sounds very familiar, and of course the studio ignored
their advice.

As I write this in the middle of 1975 it is interesting to speculate on the
future of horror films as a separate cinematic *genre*. At this point the horror
film seems to be diversifying in a way it has never done before. There
have been lavish television adaptations of *Frankenstein* (partly scripted
by Christopher Isherwood, no less), *Dracula, Turn of the Screw*, and *Dr
Jekyll and Mr Hyde* (done as a musical) starring such people as Michael
Sarrazin, James Mason, Jack Palance, Lynn Redgrave, Kirk Douglas and
Simon Ward. There have been the Warhol/Morrissey interpretations of
Frankenstein and *Dracula*; ex-Beatle Ringo Starr has made *Son of Dracula*;
Mel Brooks has paid homage to James Whale (and Rowland V. Lee too,
though Brooks seems unaware of that) with his *Young Frankenstein*
spoof; there is a rock-opera version of *Phantom of the Opera* called
Phantom of the Paradise, and now a film adaptation of the successful
camp parody of old horror films, *The Rocky Horror Show*. In America, it

seems, one can no longer point to a single group of people and say that they are responsible for the majority of horror films. Roger Corman, Jack Arnold, William Castle have all moved into other areas – the nearest to a *genre* figure these days is Dan Curtis whose work has mainly been in television. In recent years the centre of Anglo-American horror film production has been in Britain, and it is there that one will still find directors and producers who are active solely in the field of horror (whether they want to be or not). But even Hammer seems to be moving more and more into other areas, and the big Amicus movie of 1975 was *The Land That Time Forgot*, a lost-world-and-dinosaurs type of film (it will probably put dinosaur films back a million years but that's beside the point). Only Kevin Francis and his Tyburn company seem optimistic about producing a series of horror films in the traditional manner.

The horror stars themselves also seem to be a vanishing breed. Of the survivors – Christopher Lee, Vincent Price and Peter Cushing – both Price and Cushing are in their sixties, and Lee is obviously succeeding in his ambition to escape his horror image. There is no new generation of horror stars waiting in the wings to replace them, which is probably just as well – as one thing I hope this book has illustrated is the frustration and bitterness that can be caused by typecasting. But while there may eventually no longer be such a thing as 'the horror people', horror films themselves, in one form or another, seem likely to survive.

Appendix: More Horror People

ATWILL, LIONEL

A noted stage actor who later became a regular in horror films of the 1930s and 1940s. Most famous horror role was the mad sculptor in *Mystery of the Wax Museum* (Michael Curtiz, 1932), which was later remade as *The House of Wax* in 1953 (Andre de Toth) with Vincent Price in the same part. Atwill was born in Croydon, England, in 1885. After a successful career on the London stage he departed for the USA in 1915 and went on tour with the famous Lily Langtry. Appeared on the American stage with most of the leading ladies of the time – such as Nazimova, Katharine Kornell and Helen Hayes. Began acting in films before the end of the silent era and was soon typecast as a villain. He later said: 'Screen villainy is like everything else – just a commercial business. When you have reached my age there are only two things you can do – stock characters, like the heroine's father – or villains.'[90] His horror films include *Dr X* (Michael Curtiz, 1932), *Vampire Bat* (Frank Strayer, 1933), *Mark of the Vampire* (Tod Browning, 1935), *The Gorilla* (Alan Dwan, 1939), *Son of Frankenstein* (Rowland V. Lee, 1939) – Atwill played the police captain with the artificial arm – which provided him with the opportunity of performing a number of hilarious sight gags, many of which were repeated by Kenneth Mars, playing the same character, in the recent Mel Brooks film *Young Frankenstein, Man-Made Monster* (also known as *The Electric Man*, directed by George Waggner in 1941), *Ghost of Frankenstein* (Erle C. Kenton, 1942), *Frankenstein Meets the Wolfman* (Roy W. Neill, 1944), *House of Frankenstein* and *House of Dracula* (both Erle C. Kenton, 1945). He died in 1946, after contracting pneumonia, aged 61.

BATES, RALPH

Played a younger version of Baron Frankenstein in Hammer's *The Horror of Frankenstein* (Jimmy Sangster, 1970). Born in 1940, educated at Dublin University and later won a drama scholarship to Yale. Did a lot of television work in Britain, often in villainous roles, and was spotted in one of these by Jimmy Sangster. First film role was as Dracula's young acolyte in *Taste the Blood of Dracula* (Peter Sasdy, 1969). Other Hammer films include *Dr Jekyll and Sister Hyde* (Roy Ward Baker, 1971) and *Lust for a Vampire* (Jimmy Sangster, 1970); he starred in Tyburn's first film *Persecution* (called *Sheba* in the USA and directed by Don Chaffey in 1974). But the idea of being typecast in horror films worries him: 'That's always a problem and one that all actors have to face. If I'm doing this in ten or twenty years I'll be delighted – as long as I'm doing something else in between.'[91] Roy Ward Baker, who directed him in *Dr Jekyll and Sister Hyde*, said: 'Ralph is very good but he hasn't yet found the thing that is right for him. When he does he'll be absolutely superb. He's a wonderful mime – his hero is Buster Keaton – and someday something will click with him and he'll be really great.'

BAVA, MARIO

Flashy but sometimes very impressive Italian director who has specialized in horror films. Born in 1914 in San Remo, he was originally a lighting cameraman and has remained closely involved with the photography in his films. His horror films include (English titles) *The Mask of the Demon* (1960, also known as *Black Sunday* and *Revenge of the Vampire*), which is now a cult film, the excellent *Black Sabbath* (1963), *The Evil Eye* (1962), *Night is the Phantom* (1963), *Blood and Lace* (1964) and *Curse of the Dead* (1966).

BESWICK, MARTINE

A striking British actress who has appeared in a number of Hammer films, notably *Dr Jekyll and Sister Hyde* (1971). Born in 1941, in Jamaica, she came to Britain in 1953. First worked as a model then trained as an actress. First film appearance was in *Saturday Night Out* (Rupert Hartford Davis, 1963). Roles in two James Bond films followed. First Hammer film was *Slave Girls* (Michael Carreras, 1966).

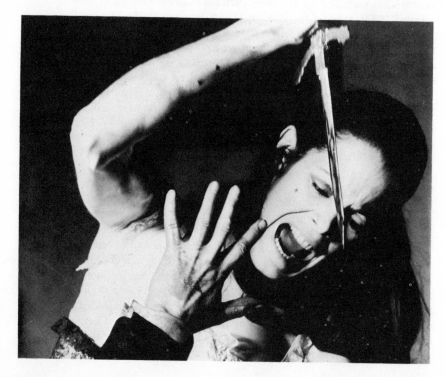

Martine Beswick as female Jack the Ripper in Dr Jekyll and Sister Hyde

BLAIR, LINDA
Just 12 years old when she made the film, her performance as Regan, the girl possessed in *The Exorcist*, caused more comment and controversy than Karloff's did in *Frankenstein* back in 1931. Born in 1960, in Connecticut, she hadn't acted before being chosen for the part by director William Friedkin,

William Friedkin, director of **The Exorcist,** *with its star Linda Blair*

though she had appeared as an extra in a couple of films and had worked as a model. According to Friedkin, she hasn't been affected by the role, despite rumours to the contrary. 'She is probably less disturbed by any of these events than anyone in the audience,' he said. 'She couldn't be in a better frame of mind or better health. Neither she nor I ever considered that anyone would draw that conclusion from the fact that she gave a great performance in the movie.'[92] Nonetheless, it will be interesting to see how *The Exorcist* will affect her future career. To date, her one film appearance since *The Exorcist* was in that flying soap opera *Airport 1975*.

CARLSON, VERONICA
British actress who has appeared in a number of Hammer horror films. Born in Yorkshire, 1945. First film appearance was a walk-on part in the Morecambe and Wise comedy *The Magnificent Two* (Cliff Owen, 1967). Other small parts followed in *Smashing Time* (Desmond Davis, 1967) and *The Best House in London* (Philip Saville, 1968) but a change of agents that same year resulted in bigger roles. Tall, blonde, with voluptuous good looks, she was very

effective as Dracula's virginal and unwilling victim in *Dracula Has Risen from the Grave* (Freddie Francis, 1968). Other horror films include *Frankenstein Must Be Destroyed* (Terence Fisher, 1969), *The Horror of Frankenstein* (Jimmy Sangster, 1970), and *The Ghoul* (Freddie Francis, 1974).

CARRADINE, JOHN

Tall, thin American actor of great ability who has probably appeared in more bad horror films than anyone alive. Born in 1906 in New York he made his stage debut at the age of nineteen with a small part in a New Orleans production of *Camille* and two years later was appearing on Broadway. Was also interested in painting and it was as a scenic artist that he got his start in Hollywood, working for Cecil B. DeMille. This led to a number of acting roles in DeMille's films, such as *The Sign of the Cross* and *The Crusades* (1935 and 1936 respectively). The peak of his career in films occurred in the late 1930s with much-praised performances in *Stagecoach* and *The Hurricane* (both John Ford, 1936) and *Captains Courageous* (Victor Fleming, 1937). The 1940s, however, saw the beginning of his appearances in horror films – such as *King of the Zombies* (Jean Yarborough, 1946), *The Voodoo Man* (William Beaudine, 1944), *House of Dracula* and *House of Frankenstein* (in both of these 1945 films he played Count Dracula and his performance is highly regarded by many horror fans) and *The Mummy's Ghost* (Reginald Le Borg, 1945). In the 1950s he appeared in that star-studded disaster of a horror film *The Black Sleep* (Reginald Le Borg, 1956) and his other horror films include such monstrosities as *Billy the Kid vs Dracula* (William Beaudine, 1965), *Blood of Dracula's Castle* (Al Adamson, 1969) and *Terror in the Wax Museum* (George Fenady, 1973). Marvellously sent up bad horror films, and himself, in a hilarious segment of Woody Allen's *Everything You Always Wanted to Know About Sex* in 1972.

CLIVE, COLIN

British actor who played Dr Frankenstein in the two Frankenstein films directed by James Whale – *Frankenstein* (1931) and *The Bride of Frankenstein* (1935). Billed as the star in *Frankenstein*, but it was Karloff who became most associated with the name (in Hammer's later series Cushing's Frankenstein remained the dominant character, not the Monster). He was born Colin Clive Greig in St Malo, Northern France, in 1900. The son of a British Army colonel, and a descendant of Lord Clive of India, he planned a military career at first, but a fall from a horse, which injured his knee, forced him to choose another profession. He turned to the theatre and made his debut in 1919 at the Garrick theatre in London. His acting career was nothing out of the ordinary until he was chosen by James Whale and R. C. Sherriff to replace Laurence Olivier (who had other commitments) in the London West End opening of Sherriff's First World War play *Journey's End*. 'Nobody had heard of him,' wrote Sherriff in his autobiography, 'He didn't appear in *Spotlight* [the British stage actors' directory] but had recently had a small part in *Showboat*. But he was asked to come in for a reading and the moment I saw him I knew he was our man. Whale also knew. Clive was highly strung and temperamental, and one day, after a bad rehearsal, he went to Whale and offered to give up the part.'[93] He didn't, of course, and the subsequent success of the play changed his life, as well as the lives of Whale and Sherriff. Clive repeated his stage role in the film version of the play made in Hollywood in 1929 but made it clear at the time that he didn't enjoy film making. He claimed that he considered films to be 'unreal', rarely visited the cinema himself, was disconcerted by the lack of continuity in filming and maintained that nothing would induce him to make another film after *Journey's End*. Naturally he *was* induced, by money, and soon after making that statement accepted a role in a British film. Whale persuaded him to return to Hollywood to appear in *Frankenstein* in 1931 and he continued to make films until his death six years later. Apart from the two Frankenstein films he appeared in another famous horror film – *Mad Love*, Karl Freund's 1934 remake of *The Hands of Orlac*. He died in a Hollywood hospital on 25 June 1937. Cause of death was listed as intestinal and pulmonary ailments. He was thirty-seven.

CURTIS, DAN
American television producer and director who specializes in horror subjects. Originally produced a daytime television horror soap-opera (a TV first!) called *House of Dark Shadows* which concerned the activities of a vampire called Barnabas Collins. In 1970 a film version of the series was released starring Jonathan Frid. Apart from a sequel in 1971 – *Night of Dark Shadows* – the remainder of Curtis's work has been in television. He has made a number of successful made-for-TV horror films, several of them based on scripts by Richard Matheson. One of the most acclaimed of these was *The Night Stalker* (1972) which was about a vampire loose in modern-day Las Vegas. It has since been turned into a regular series called *Kolchak: The Night Stalker*. Curtis has since produced and directed *The Night Strangler* (1973), *Scream of the Wolf* (1974), *Dracula* (1974 – released outside of America as a feature film) and *The Turn of the Screw* (1974). As a director Curtis fluctuates a great deal in quality – his films usually contain some fine atmospheric moments of horror but he tends to go in for too many gimmicky, and distracting, camera movements.

DANIELL, HENRY
Familiar supporting actor in many Hollywood films from 1920 to 1962 who specialized in villainous roles. Tall, dignified and suave with an unmistakable voice, he was born in London in 1894 and began acting at the age of eighteen. First went to the USA to appear with Ethel Barrymore in *Déclassée* and later played other roles with her. His portrayal of Lord Iver Cream in S. N. Behrman's *Serena Blandish* in 1929 was especially acclaimed. Boris Karloff, who worked with him on *The Bodysnatcher* (Robert Wise, 1945) said: 'He was a pro, a real honest-to-goodness pro. There was no rubbish with him. No faking.'[94] His films include *Last of the Lone Wolf* (Richard Boleslavsky, 1930), *Hotel Berlin* (Peter Godfrey, 1945), *The Egyptian* (Michael Curtiz, 1954) and *The Four Skulls of Jonathan Drake* (Edward Kahn, 1959). He died in 1963 aged sixty-nine.

FLOREY, ROBERT

An important influence on Universal's first horror cycle – he was one of the scriptwriters who worked on Whale's *Frankenstein*. Born in Paris in 1900, for a time he lived at the back of Georges Méliès' theatre, which provided him with the opportunity to observe the famous film pioneer at work. Florey was obsessed with the cinema from an early age, and at seventeen began writing film reviews for a Geneva newspaper. Then worked in the Swiss film industry as an assistant director, writer and actor. Went to the USA just before his twenty-first birthday on a writing assignment for the French magazine *Cinémagazine*. He arrived in Hollywood unable to speak English but was immediately hired as a technical adviser by a studio shooting a French costume melodrama. Within a short time he had become a gag writer and the following year was made director of foreign publicity for Douglas Fairbanks Snr. Then became an assistant director. He was given his first opportunity to direct when the director of *That Model from Paris* fell ill. That same year (1926) he directed his first complete feature film, *One Night of Love*. At the same time he began to make experimental fantasy films that were heavily influenced by the German films of the period. Moved on to directing talkies and directed the Marx Brothers' first film, *Cocoanuts*. In 1931 he worked on the screenplay for *Frankenstein* and planned to direct it himself, but his two test reels, with Bela Lugosi as the Monster, were rejected and the assignment went to Whale. Florey later regarded Whale's film as a travesty of his original conception. Florey's contributions to the film include the old mill setting and the mix-up of brains by Frankenstein's assistant (a rather pointless plot device as all the Monster's subsequent actions stemmed from his fear and confusion – not from any basically evil streak). There is a growing opinion that Florey's version would have been superior to Whale's but there really isn't much evidence to support this. *Murders in the Rue Morgue,* which he was given to direct as a consolation prize for missing out on *Frankenstein,* is an efficient, sometimes impressive, horror film (he shot it in only three days) but it lacks all those fine, audacious touches that make Whale's horror films so memorable. Florey went on to direct films for Warner Brothers and then Paramount, but the only other horror films he directed were *The Face Behind the Mask* in 1939, a rarely seen film that starred Peter Lorre, and the interesting *The Beast With Five Fingers* in 1946 that also starred Peter Lorre (Florey claimed that the film was savagely cut by Jack Warner). Florey was one of the first Hollywood directors to appreciate the potential of television and later enjoyed a successful career working in that medium.

FRIEDKIN, WILLIAM

Director of *The Exorcist*. Born in 1940, he began his career working in the mailroom of a Chicago TV station but within two years was directing live TV shows. That led to making documentaries, which in turn led to feature films. His films include *The Night They Raided Minskys* (1968), a quirky comedy about vaudeville, *The Birthday Party* (1968), based on the play by Harold Pinter, and *The Boys in the Band* (1969), a rather careful adaptation of a play about homosexuals by Mart Crowley. His first big commercial success came with *The French Connection* (1971), a fast-paced, though confusing, New York police thriller. Despite having directed what someone described as 'the Rolls Royce of horror films', he doesn't consider *The Exorcist* to be a horror film. In an interview published in *Cinéfantastique* he said: 'I've never made a horror film. *The Exorcist* is not a horror film. I would call *Frankenstein*, *Freaks*, *Phantom of the Opera* and *The Wolfman* horror films. There is a horror *genre* I'm conscious of, but I'm less interested in it than in the Hammer stuff that goes on today. I've never made one of those. I'd like to someday.' Of *The Exorcist* he said: 'Strange as it may sound, I tried not to make a film about Satan. *The Exorcist* is more about the mystery of faith, the mystery of goodness. What it is to me is a realistic film about unexplainable things. I personally have no strong conviction about Satan or a personified devil. I have no strong conviction against that either, but I didn't want to make a film that pushed that.'[95]

FRYE, DWIGHT
Created a now-cliché horror role – that of the mad doctor's misshapen servant and helper. He played Fritz in *Frankenstein* (1931), the hunchback who got the brains mixed up, and Karl, Dr Pretorius's helper, in *Bride of Frankenstein* (1935). He was born in Denver, Colorado, in 1899 and became interested in acting at an early age. Against the wishes of his parents he joined the local Denver theatre company. Later went to New York and developed a relatively successful vaudeville act. Was spotted by a Broadway producer and good roles followed in a number of Broadway plays. Went to Hollywood in 1930 and was chosen to appear, by director Tod Browning, as Renfield in *Dracula*. His memorable mad scenes in the film led him to become typed as a horror actor, though he did appear in the 1931 version of *The Maltese Falcon* (Roy del Ruth, 1931). His other horror films include *Vampire Bat* (Frank Strayer, 1933) and *Dead Men Walk* (Sam Newfield, 1943). He died in 1945.

FUEST, ROBERT
Wrote and directed the two Dr Phibes films – *The Abominable Dr Phibes* (1971) and *Dr Phibes Rises Again* (1972) – which starred Vincent Price and were inventively amusing. Fuest was born in London in 1927 and entered television in 1957. Until 1962 he was a designer with ABC TV (London). His interest in visual design has been evident in all the feature films he has directed. First directed TV commercials, then progressed to TV series, including eight episodes of the quirky, and popular, *Avengers*. First film was *Wuthering Heights* for AIP in 1970. He then managed to interest AIP in the Phibes films – they were to become a long-running series but AIP abandoned these plans when the second one failed at the box office. Fuest also wrote and directed the interesting science fiction film *Final Programme* (1973) based on the work of Michael Moorcock.

GILLING, JOHN
Has something of a reputation among horror fans mainly because of two films he directed for Hammer – *Plague of the Zombies* and *The Reptile* (both 1966).

Like Terence Fisher, Val Guest and other British directors of that generation, he is competent but not particularly outstanding. In other words, a safe commercial director who is not likely to upset his employers by injecting unwanted individualistic touches into his work. Born in 1912, Gilling entered the film industry in 1933 as an assistant director. He has since written the screenplays for a large number of British films, as well as directing several himself. Many of these have been horror films. He scripted *House of Darkness* (Oswald Mitchell) in 1947, which was apparently inspired by the British horror classic *Dead of Night* (1945, Michael Balcon produced; Cavalcanti, Charles Crichton, Basil Dearden, and Robert Hamer directed). In 1952 he directed Bela Lugosi in the terrible but fascinating *Mother Riley Meets the Vampire*. Directed *Flesh and the Fiends* in 1960 and that same year made his first film for Hammer – *The Shadow of the Cat*, which was somewhat tedious. Other horror films include *The Mummy's Shroud* (1966) and *Trog* (1970) (he wrote the script for the latter).

GOUGH, MICHAEL

A fine actor whose film career has been mainly restricted to below average horror films. Born in Malaya in 1917 and trained at the Old Vic school along with such people as Laurence Olivier, Vivien Leigh and Edith Evans. Made his stage debut at the Old Vic in 1936. Has had a distinguished stage career – successes include *The Prime of Miss Jean Brodie*, and has appeared in a number of British television plays. His films include *Dracula* (Terence Fisher, 1956), *Horrors of the Black Museum* (Arthur Crabtree, 1958), *Konga* (John Lemont, 1961), *Black Zoo* (Robert Gordon, 1963) and the hilarious *Horror Hospital* (Antony Balch, 1973). Also made an uncredited appearance in *The Legend of Hell House* (John Hough, 1973). Has been described as 'a melancholy man resigned to working in horror films'.

GUEST, VAL

Director of the classic *The Quatermass Experiment* (1954, also known as *The Creeping Unknown*). Born in London in 1911, and after working as a journalist and screenwriter in America, including a period spent on the *Hollywood Reporter*, he returned to England as a screenwriter on the Marcel Varnel comedies of the 1930s. He also collaborated on the scripts for many of the Will Hay comedies. He began directing in the late 1940s. His first film for Hammer was *Life With the Lyons* in 1953. Other early Hammer films include *The Lyons in Paris* (1954) and *Break in the Circle* (1954). His first horror film was *The Quatermass Experiment*. Then came *Quatermass II* (1955, also known as *The Enemy from Space*) and *The Abominable Snowman* (1957). His non-horror Hammer films include *Yesterday's Enemy* (1959), *Hell is a City* (1959), *The Full Treatment* (1960) and *When Dinosaurs Ruled the Earth* (1969). Also produced and directed the successful science fiction film *The Day the Earth Caught Fire* in 1961, and his latest film to date is the sex-comedy *Confessions of a Window Cleaner* (1974). He is a competent, unspectacular commercial director with a natural inclination towards comedy; but capable of producing a workmanlike picture in any genre. *The Day the Earth Caught Fire* is the film that has earned him the most praise but his best film is undoubtedly *The Quatermass Experiment*, and also one of the best of all British horror films, though a great deal of the credit must go to Nigel Kneale's script.

HATTON, RONDO

American actor who suffered from severe facial and bodily deformity as a result of a disease called acromegaly. This led him to be cast as a villainous type in such films as *House of Horrors* (Jean Yarborough, 1946), *Spider Woman Strikes Back* (Arthur Lubin, 1946), and *The Brute Man* (Jean Yarborough, 1946).

HULL, HENRY

American character actor born in 1890 whose one claim to horror fame lies in his role of the wolfman in *The Werewolf of London*, a creaky but still interesting film directed by Stuart Walker in 1935. But it was Lon Chaney Jnr who later became identified with the role, probably to Hull's great relief.

KENTON, ERLE C.

Director of the superb *Island of Lost Souls* (1932) (which was based on H. G. Wells's *The Island of Dr Moreau*) and several other less impressive horror films. He was originally a school-teacher before deciding to become an animal exhibitor – he worked with dog, pony and other animal shows for a number of years – then entered vaudeville as a comedian. It was as a comedian that he entered the film industry, working on the Keystone Cops series of films. He later turned to directing and made short comedies for every major studio in Hollywood before becoming a feature film director. His other horror films include *The Ghost of Frankenstein* (1942), *House of Frankenstein* (1944) and *House of Dracula* (1945). The latter two films are interesting curiosities in which Dracula, the Wolf Man and the Frankenstein Monster defy the laws of chance and all turn up in the same area. *House of Dracula* was the better of the two with plenty of Gothic atmosphere and some impressive moments that helped one ignore the absurd plot.

LAUGHTON, CHARLES

His extravagant, bravura style of acting, which made his portrayals of Nero, Henry VIII and Captain Bligh so memorable, was perfectly suited for his two famous horror roles – that of the evil, whip-cracking Dr Moreau in *Island of Lost Souls* (Erle C. Kenton, 1932) and the pathetic Quasimodo in *The Hunchback of Notre Dame* (William Dieterle, 1939). He was born in Scarborough, England, in 1889, served in the army during the First World War, then worked in the family hotel until he was twenty-six. During this time he took part in amateur theatricals before persuading his father to provide him with a £3-a-week allowance to enable him to study at the Royal Academy of Dramatic Arts in London. After leaving RADA he obtained various small stage roles and succeeded in getting the title role in Arnold Bennett's *Mr Prohack* in 1927. It was then that he met actress Elsa Lanchester and they married in

Charles Laughton as the evil Dr Moreau surrounded by his understandably annoyed victims in Island of Lost Souls

Elsa Lanchester, Laughton's wife, as the female Monster in The Bride of Frankenstein

1929. His first film experience was in 1928, when Elsa was filming three short plays that H. G. Wells had written for her and Laughton took part in them for fun. His first feature film appearance was a small one in Britain's last major silent film – *Piccadilly*. A successful play called *Payment Deferred* led to the Laughtons doing a tour of the USA and while there he began to receive film offers. His first Hollywood film was Whale's *The Old Dark House* (1932). Other early films include *The Island of Lost Souls* and *Sign of the Cross* (both 1932). His wife, Elsa, also entered the horror hall of fame when, in 1935, she appeared in *The Bride of Frankenstein* as both Mary Shelley and the female monster created as a mate for Karloff's creature. Laughton's portrayal of Quasimodo in *The Hunchback of Notre Dame* was as memorable as Chaney's original, and in 1954 he directed *Night of the Hunter*, an excellent film about two children pursued through a dream-like landscape by the man who has murdered their mother, which was spoilt only by its overly sentimental ending. Laughton's last film role was in *Advise and Consent* (Otto Preminger) in 1962. He died of cancer that same year.

LEE, ROWLAND V.

Director of *Son of Frankenstein* (1939), the third and last film in which Karloff played the Monster. Lee was born in Ohio in 1891 and was a stage actor before joining the film industry. He worked for the Thomas Ince Company until the First World War, during which he fought in France, then resumed his acting career for a year after the war before turning to directing. One of his earliest films was *Cupid's Brand* in 1921. His films include *The Mysterious Dr Fu Manchu* (1929), *The Return of Dr Fu Manchu* (1936) and *Tower of London* (1939). His non-horror films include *Paramount on Parade* (1930), *The Three Musketeers* (1935), *Service DeLuxe* (1938), in which Vincent Price made his film debut, and *Captain Kidd* (1945). Gave up directing in 1945 because: 'The fun had gone out of the picture business entirely. People were coming into the business who had been making safety pins.'[96] Came out of retirement in 1959 to script and produce *The Big Fisherman*.

LORRE, PETER

One of the screen's most popular villains – his bulging eyes and sibilant voice were known, and imitated, all over the world. Born in 1904, in a remote part of Hungary, he ran away from home at the age of seventeen to become an actor. He found work difficult to obtain during the first three years of his career and was often obliged to sleep on park benches. But in 1924 he managed to get a small job in a Breslau theatre run by Leo Mitler who later became a film director in Berlin and Hollywood. Things improved for Lorre after that and from Breslau he went to Berlin where his performance in a German production of Galsworthy's *Society* led to an offer of work in Vienna, which, in turn, led to the People's Theatre in Berlin. It was here that Fritz Lang saw him for the first time – Lorre was playing the part of a sex fiend in a play called *The Recruits of Inglostadt*. Late in 1930 Lang offered him the role of a child murderer in his film *Moerder unter Uns* (also known as '*M*'). During the day Lorre worked on Lang's picture while at night he was a comedian in

The always impressive Peter Lorre in a publicity still from Mad Love

Valentin Katayev's *Squaring the Circle*. When 'M' was released it brought Lorre international fame and as a result he was immediately signed up by UFA, the famous German film company, and subsequently appeared in two of their films. Other film and stage offers followed in Germany, but with the rise of Hitler Lorre decided to leave the country. He first went to Vienna and then on to Paris in 1933 where he lived in a cheap boarding house that also included Billy Wilder among its refugee guests. In 1934, he arrived, without money or a knowledge of English, in England; but soon had the good fortune to be introduced to Alfred Hitchcock who offered him a part in *The Man Who Knew Too Much*. Soon after the film's completion he married Cecilia Lvovsky, his co-star whom he had known in Berlin. The following year he went to Hollywood to appear in Karl Freund's *Mad Love*, then returned to England to make another Hitchcock film – *The Secret Agent*. In 1936 he was given a long term contract by 20th Century Fox in Hollywood and his first film for them was *Crack-Up* (Malcolm St Clair, 1936), a mediocre spy thriller. Two more pictures, just as forgettable, followed in 1937 and in that same year he began the Mr Moto series in which he starred as the Japanese detective. Lorre made *nine* of the Moto films within the space of a single year (they were directed by Norman Foster and James Tinling). He didn't enjoy them but they were successful and he made a great deal of money out of the series. Artistically, his career became more satisfying in 1941 when he appeared in John Huston's classic version of *The Maltese Falcon* as the effeminate rival of criminal mastermind Sydney Greenstreet. This resulted in a contract with Warner Brothers and more good roles – such as in *Casablanca* (Michael Curtiz, 1943) and *Arsenic and Old Lace* (Frank Capra, 1944) in which he gave a marvellous performance as Raymond Massey's drunken assistant. His last film for Warner's before his contract expired was *The Beast With Five Fingers* (Robert Florey, 1946). Lorre's Hollywood career deteriorated in the late 1940s and he decided to return to Europe. While touring refugee camps in 1949 he received the inspiration to make *The Lost One*, a film based on a story by Egon Jacobson. Two years later he wrote, directed, co-produced and starred in the film, which was shot on location in Germany (the story is of a psychopath who murders several women before the war and is discovered afterwards to be working as a doctor in a refugee camp). *The Lost One* is a black film that effectively reflects the shattered, shocked and pessimistic atmosphere of post-war Europe. Lorre directed with skill but its gloomy subject-matter ensured that it wasn't a financial success at a time when film audiences were hungering for escape. Unfortunately, the making of it cost Lorre more than money – during the shooting his friend and co-producer Arnold Pressburger fell ill and died, and shortly after it was completed Lorre himself became very ill. He survived, but the illness left him with a weight increase of 100 lbs and he never really regained his health. In 1953 he resumed his acting career with an appearance in Huston's eccentric *Beat the Devil*. During the remainder of the 1950s he appeared in a number of Hollywood films, none of them particularly good (with one or two exceptions), usually as 'comic relief'. But along with the other ageing horror stars he was swept up by AIP for their new cycle of horror films in the early 1960s. He appeared in *Tales of Terror* (1962), *Comedy of Terrors* (1963) and *The Raven* (1963) and gave fine comic performances in all three. He died of a stroke in 1964. In private life Lorre was an erudite man with a keen interest in the arts, particularly the theatre. He was also known for his sharp and very dry sense of humour. As an actor, especially when at his peak in the 1930s and 1940s, he was a true artist with a range that went from slapstick to real villainy: he was certainly more than just the collection of familiar mannerisms for which he is now best remembered. One regrets that Hollywood did not make better use of his talents.

MARCH, FREDRIC

A versatile stage and screen actor included in this list because of one role –
in the 1932 version of *Dr Jekyll and Mr Hyde* (directed by Rouben Mamoulian),
for which he won an Academy Award. Despite being handicapped by an
excessive amount of make-up and some awkward-looking front teeth when

*Fredric March as Mr
Hyde in the 1932
version of* Dr Jekyll
and Mr Hyde

appearing as Hyde, March succeeded in giving a memorable, and often subtle,
performance. Particularly impressive were his scenes with the terrified
prostitute, played by Miriam Hopkins, when he chillingly conveyed the
depths of Hyde's sadism. March's other roles in the fantasy field include
Death Takes a Holiday (Mitchell Leisen, 1934), in which he played Death, and
I Married a Witch (René Clair, 1942). He died in 1975 at the age of seventy-
eight.

MAYNE, FERDY

German actor born in 1916 who has appeared frequently in British films and
has played Count Dracula at least twice – in Polanski's *Dance of the
Vampires* and in the rarely seen *Vampire Happening* (Freddie Francis, 1971).
Ivan Butler, in his book *Horror in the Cinema*, described Mayne as 'the best
vampire count ever,' though fans of Christopher Lee will probably disagree.

MILLAND, RAY

One-time Hollywood leading man reduced to horror roles in his later career
(though he has since moved on to character roles in films such as *Love Story*
and *Gold*). Born Reginald Truscott-Jones in Wales in 1905 (though sometimes

his birthdate is given as 1908), the son of a steel mill superintendent. Went to King's College at Cardiff and was then accepted into the Household Cavalry. In his years with the regiment he became its second best boxing champion and an expert marksman. During a period of financial trouble he decided to take up acting. His first role was in the British film *The Plaything* (Castleton Knight, 1929). His first big role was in *The Flying Scotsman* (Castleton Knight, 1929) and he was spotted by an MGM talent scout. The studio gave him a fifteen-month contract but his first stay in the USA was a short one – 'I couldn't act a damn,' he said later. After a short period back in England he returned to Hollywood and this time he was signed up by Paramount, and from then on his career improved rapidly. His horror/fantasy

Ray Milland in The Man With the X-Ray Eyes

films include the excellent *The Uninvited* (Lewis Allen, 1943), *Alias Nick Beal* (John Farrow, 1949), in which he played an agent of the devil, *The Premature Burial* (Roger Corman, 1962), *Panic in the Year Zero* (1962), a harrowing post-Third World War thriller which he also directed, *The Man With the X-Ray Eyes* (1963), probably Corman's best film, *Terror in the Wax Museum* (George Fenady, 1973), *The Thing With Two Heads* (Lee Frost, 1972) and *House in Nightmare Park* (Peter Sykes, 1973).

OGLE, CHARLES
The first screen Frankenstein Monster, in the Thomas Edison version of
Frankenstein made in 1910. Little is known about him, but his publicist
described Ogle's performance as follows: 'A giant in stature, Mr Ogle attracts
instant attention whenever he appears on the screen and from that moment
never fails to hold it.' He created his own make-up for the role and, judging
by a surviving still, it was nearer to the original conception of the Monster
than was Karloff's, though naturally not as impressive.

PITT, INGRID
Polish actress who has starred in several horror films since arriving in
Britain in 1969. Born in Poland in 1944 and grew up in East Berlin where she
studied to be an obstetrician. She switched to acting when she failed her
medical exams and later became a member of the Berlin Ensemble theatre.
One day, as she was walking by the River Spree, guards opened fire on a man
trying to escape. Thinking they were firing at her she jumped into the river
and was pulled out by an American Army officer – on the other side. Far
from happy in her new situation she made out as best she could and has since
worked as a model, bull fighter, stunt girl and novelist (she has had two
novels published in Germany). Had a number of small parts in American films
and on television but her first big role was in *Where Eagles Dare* (Brian G.
Hutton) in 1969. Went to Britain when offered a five-year contract by AIP and
has appeared in several Hammer films. Horror films include *The Vampire
Lovers* (Roy Ward Baker, 1970), *Countess Dracula* (Pater Sasdy, 1970), *The
House That Dripped Blood* (Peter Duffell, 1970) and *The Wicker Man* (Robin
Hardy, 1973).

POLANSKI, ROMAN
Director of the superb *Repulsion* (1965), *Dance of the Vampires* (1967) and
Rosemary's Baby (1968). Various aspects of horror pervade all his films but
his three more direct forays into the field are all masterpieces of their kind.
Born in 1933 to a Polish couple living in Paris, his own life has often been
filled with horror and tragedy – both his parents were arrested in Poland and
held in a concentration camp during the war, during which time his mother
died (Polanski himself was protected and hidden by friends). He was reunited
with his father after the war but left home soon afterwards when his father
remarried. His need to escape into a different world was to be expected and
he became a passionate film- and theatre-lover. He began acting at the age of
fourteen and at twenty-one he enrolled in the National Film Academy at Lodz.
During his time there he made the award-winning short *Two Men and a
Wardrobe* as a graduation project. His first feature film, made in 1962, was
Knife in the Water, which earned him an international reputation. In 1965 he
made *Repulsion* in Britain, a brilliant and disturbing examination of the breakdown of a girl's mind and the subjective horrors she creates. In 1967 he made
the very funny, but affectionate, spoof on vampire films – *Dance of the
Vampires*, which was unfortunately cut for its US release and retitled: *The*

Fearless Vampire Killers or Pardon Me But Your Teeth Are in My Neck. In 1968
he directed *Rosemary's Baby*, an excellent film adaptation of Ira Levin's novel
about a woman who discovers she is carrying the devil's child. But the
following year tragedy struck again for Polanski when his pregnant wife,
actress Sharon Tate, and four of her friends, were brutally murdered at
Polanski's California home (see Chapter 8). 'There is no more violence in my
films,' he has said, 'than there is in life.'[97]

PROWSE, DAVID
Former British weightlifting champion who has played the Frankenstein
Monster in two of Hammer's films. Born in Bristol, 1941, he started weightlifting at the age of sixteen and became British champion for the first time
when he was twenty-one. He retained the title the following two years.
Entered show business when he played Death in the play *Don't Let Summer
Come* (Death was required to pick up one of the actors and carry him off the
stage). TV commercials followed, then a small part in *Casino Royale* (1967). First
played the Monster in *The Horror of Frankenstein* in 1970 but not very
successfully – the Monster resembled a bland, bald muscleman, not
surprisingly. Prowse apparently didn't receive much assistance from director

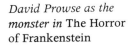

*David Prowse as the
monster in* The Horror
of Frankenstein

Jimmy Sangster. 'I arrived on the set,' said Prowse, 'and he [Sangster] asked
me if I had any idea of how I was going to play the monster. I told him I was
expecting direction from him. I showed him how I played the monster for the
kids at home, just shuffling across the floor mumbling "I am the monster,"
and he said, "That's perfect! Just what I wanted."'[98] Prowse was rather
more effective in his second appearance as the Monster in *Frankenstein and
the Monster from Hell* (Terence Fisher, 1972). Has also appeared in Hammer's
Vampire Circus (Robert Young, 1971) and played Patrick Magee's bodyguard
in *A Clockwork Orange* (Stanley Kubrick, 1971).

QUARRY, ROBERT
Alias Count Yorga the vampire, Christopher Lee's greatest rival. Born in 1928
in America he attended the famous Actor's Lab in Hollywood. Made his film
debut at the age of fifteen in Hitchcock's *Shadow of a Doubt* in 1943. Signed up
by Universal that same year for their juvenile actors' training school, which
he hated. Escaped into stage acting and played a wide variety of roles,
including Shakespeare, during the following two decades. Career almost came
to an end in the early 1960s when he contracted cancer, but after a two-year
struggle he overcame the disease and returned to work. Toured America in
1966 with a production of *Who's Afraid of Virginia Woolf?* Close friend of
Paul Newman and Joanne Woodward and has appeared in a couple of their
films, such as *WUSA* (Stuart Rosenberg) in 1970. During the making of that
film he became involved with *Count Yorga – Vampire* when some friends of his
decided to make a low-budget horror film. It was shot at weekends and the
resulting film, directed by Bob Kelljan (who had never directed a feature film
before), became a surprise financial success after being sold to AIP. Actually
Count Yorga, despite an obviously cheap budget, is quite an effective little
horror film that cleverly blends shock with tongue-in-cheek humour, and
Quarry gives a good performance as a present-day vampire who regards his
mortal adversaries with a certain wry amusement. It is far superior to
Hammer's more recent Dracula films, especially those also set in modern
times. Even better, for a change, is the sequel, *The Return of Count Yorga*,
made by the same team with a slightly bigger budget in 1971. But after making
a vampire film of his own, *Khorda*, Quarry has decided to hang up his fangs,
though he will continue to appear in horror films. 'I love the fun of making
horror films,'[99] he has said. Co-starred with Vincent Price in *Dr Phibes Rises
Again* (1972 Robert Fuest).

RAINS, CLAUDE
Marvellous character actor who gave two famous horror performances during
his long and varied film career – as the mad scientist Griffin in Whale's
The Invisible Man (1933) and as the pathetic, tortured Erik in Arthur Lubin's
1943 version of *The Phantom of the Opera*. He was born William Claude Rains
in 1889 in London. The family was a poor one, and, handicapped by both a
lisp and a cockney accent, he started in the theatre by working as a prop-
builder and prompter. By eighteen he was a stage manager and determined to
become an actor. He made his debut at the age of twenty-two, and the

following year toured Australia and the US as both actor and stage manager with the company of *Bluebird*. During the First World War he served in France, was gassed, and made Captain before the war ended. He returned to the theatre and also taught at RADA (one of his students was John Gielgud) before going to the USA and starring on Broadway as Samuel Pepys in *And So to Bed*. He became discouraged with acting in 1932 and retired – but soon returned to acting when the farm he had bought was destroyed in a storm. The next year he was chosen by James Whale, whom he had known in England, to play the lead in *The Invisible Man*, which led to a contract with Universal. His film career became so successful that he didn't feel inclined to return to the stage until late in his career. Despite his two horror roles he was never typecast in the *genre* and the only other horror film he appeared in was *The Wolf Man* (George Waggner, 1941) in which he played Lon Chaney Jnr's father. One of his last film roles was in *Lawrence of Arabia* (David Lean, 1962). He died in 1963.

RATHBONE, BASIL

Tall, suave character actor who was a popular villain in many Hollywood films from the 1930s onwards. He was one of the several old stars whom AIP used in the 1960s horror cycle. He was born in 1892, in Johannesburg, and educated at an English public school. His first stage appearance was in 1911 as Hortensio in *The Taming of the Shrew* at Ipswich, England. Served in the British army during the First World War and won the Military Cross. After the war he returned to the English stage and remained there until 1923 when he went to America and enjoyed a great deal of success on Broadway. Made his first film in 1925 and became established as a villain in the 1930s in such films as *Captain Blood* and *Robin Hood* (he was out-fenced by Errol Flynn in both films). Played Richard III in *Tower of London* in 1938, which starred Karloff and Vincent Price, but his first real horror role was in *Son of Frankenstein* (1939) in which he played the title role. Also in 1939 he made the first of a long series of Sherlock Holmes films and soon became closely identified with the character, something he didn't appreciate very much (Rathbone considered himself to be a serious actor and thought the Holmes films were rather beneath him). His last films were *Tales of Terror* (1962) and *Comedy of Terrors* (1963), but he remained active on the stage almost up until his death in 1966.

REED, OLIVER

British actor born in 1938 (the nephew of the famous director Sir Carol Reed). Now has an international reputation but started out in the film industry as a Hammer regular. One of his first films was *Two Faces of Dr Jekyll* (Terence Fisher, 1959) in which he had a brief scene as a drunk. He apparently made an impression because Hammer then starred him as the wolfman in *The Curse of the Werewolf* in 1960. His other Hammer horror films include *The Damned* (Joseph Losey, 1961) and *Paranoiac* (Freddie Francis, 1962), probably his best Hammer film. He also appeared in a number of non-horror Hammer films that are best forgotten.

REEVES, MICHAEL

A cult director on the basis of three films – *Revenge of the Blood Beast,* (1965), *The Sorcerers* (1966) and *Witchfinder General* (1967). Born in 1944, part-American, but educated in Britain. After leaving school he attempted to break into the film industry by going to Los Angeles and asking director Don Siegel, whom he much admired, for a job. In true Hollywood fantasy tradition Siegel admired his nerve and *did* give him one – though it was only temporary. Reeves then returned to England and became an errand boy for producer Irving Allen. He worked as an assistant director on a number of commercials, then went to Rome and became assistant director on *Castle of the Living Dead* (Warren Kieffer) in 1964. This led to the producer offering Reeves the assignment of directing a whole film – a very cheap one called *Revenge of the Blood Beast*. Reeves was only twenty-one at the time. Back in England, he adapted, with Tom Baker, a novel called *The Sorcerers* by John Burke. After persuading Boris Karloff to star in it he was able to interest Tigon Films in providing the finance. The resulting film was, on one level, a fascinating study of voyeurism (two old people take over the body of a youth in such a way that they can control his actions and also experience all his sensations). It also made money and Reeves went on to make, in 1967, *Witchfinder General*, a slick, fast-moving melodrama about the horrific activities of Matthew Hopkins, a witch hunter during the reign of Cromwell. One of Reeves's biggest triumphs in the film was in drawing from Vincent Price a really chilling performance. Reeves planned to direct Price's next film, *The Oblong Box*, but died in early 1969. Cause of death was an overdose of barbiturates. He was still only twenty-five.

RIPPER, MICHAEL

A very familiar face in Hammer films during the last two decades. Born in England, 1913, and began drama school at the age of sixteen. First worked as a stage actor, then entered films in 1934. Worked for George Smith Enterprises at Walton Studios for a number of years as both actor and assistant director. Gave up film work and returned to the stage for several years. Became a Hammer regular in the 1950s when the company was based at Bray Studios: 'It was great,' said Ripper, 'absolutely great. It was a fine studio – everything worked smoothly, even the food was good.' As for being typecast in horror films, he said: 'It's better to be known as a "horror actor" than not be known at all. An actor is earning his living the same as everybody else. Very often a man is forced to take a job that he doesn't particularly like. If it pays, you take it.'[100] Films he has appeared in include *The Mummy* (1959), *Brides of Dracula* (1960), *The Reptile* (1965), *The Secret of Blood Island* (1964), and *Dracula Has Risen from the Grave* (1968). He also makes regular appearances on British television.

ROMERO, GEORGE

Director of the phenomenally successful horror film *Night of the Living Dead*. Born in 1940, Romero was the head of a small Pittsburgh commercial film company – The Latent Image, Inc., – that made, together with another small film company (Hardman Associates) a cheap, black-and-white horror film over a period of several months in 1967. Filming was done on weekends and at nights, whenever there was any spare time available from their usual work of making commercials and promotional films. 'Our friends in distribution circles told us to make something exploitive,' said Romero, 'because it's safer. So we decided to do a horror film, and when we did it we said, we're not just going to do a horror film, we're going to really go out with it and make it gutsy.'[101] Gutsy it certainly was. This unrelenting, downbeat film about a horde of revived, and cannibalistic, corpses who lay siege to a house, is an extremely effective piece of horror cinema. Released as just another exploitation film it surprised everyone, especially its director, by becoming an almost instant cult film, reaping both money and critical praise (it was finally released in Britain in 1970 but the excess of gore had been too much for the censor, who left the film looking more hacked about than some of the corpses it featured). Romero, unfortunately, hasn't been able to repeat his success to date. He made two non-horror films after *Night of the Living Dead*, then returned to the horror format with *The Crazies* (1972), which was about an escaped government virus that turns people insane. Technically it was more polished than *Night of the Living Dead*, but failed to catch on with audiences in the same way.

SANGSTER, JIMMY
One of the important influences behind Hammer Films in the 1950s and 1960s. Wrote the scripts for many of the early Hammer classics, such as *The Curse of Frankenstein* (1956), *Dracula* (1957) and *The Mummy* (1959). He began his film career as a clapper boy with Hammer and by the time he was nineteen he was the youngest assistant director in the British film industry. Two years later he was the youngest production assistant and in 1955 he became Michael Carreras's personal assistant. It was at this time that he began script-writing. *X-the Unknown* in 1956 was his first screenplay. Since then he has been very prolific, writing scripts for other companies as well as Hammer. In 1970 he began producing and directing his own scripts, and the first of these was *The Horror of Frankenstein* (not a particularly successful venture). Other Hammer films he has directed include *Lust for a Vampire* (1970) and *Fear in the Night* (1971), judging from these one can only say that Sangster would be better advised to concentrate on script-writing. Of his work, he said: 'My first twelve to fifteen pictures were monster pictures. I changed the format myself and started writing "fear" pictures – such as *Taste of Fear* (1960), *Paranoiac* (1962), and two Bette Davis films – *The Nanny* (1965) and *The Anniversary* (1967). Two or three years ago my writing altered and I started writing novels – all very lightweight and funny. I would rather write lightweight than heavyweight material.' He also said that: 'The only hobby I have is the film business. I love it.'[102]

SASDY, PETER
Director of a number of the 'new look' Hammer films in the early 1970s. Born in Hungary, studied at the University of Budapest and graduated as a

stage producer and drama critic. For a time he worked as a newspaper reporter in the same office where Alexander Korda once worked. He produced
a number of plays at the National Theatre in Budapest and made a highly
acclaimed film about gypsies. After the failure of the uprising in 1956 he left
Hungary and went to Britain. Arrived aged twenty-two and spent the next
nine months working in a coffee bar while he learned English. He then wrote
a novel about his experiences during the Hungarian revolution which was
published in 1957. This led to a place at Bristol University where he studied
drama. A television training course with the BBC followed and during the next
decade he worked continuously on British TV where his work attracted the
attention of critics. In 1969 he directed his first feature film – *Taste the Blood
of Dracula*. Then came *Countess Dracula* (1970), *Hands of the Ripper* (1971),
Doomwatch (1972) and *Nothing But the Night* (1973). All his films have been
extremely stylish in the visual sense but so far he has always been let down
by his scripts. He is someone who has a great potential that will not be
exploited until he is provided with more challenging material. At the moment
he is obviously getting greater satisfaction out of his television work.

SCHRECK, MAX
The first screen Dracula, though he was called Nosferatu in F. W. Murnau's
1922 version of the Stoker novel. The film has dated, of course, but
Schreck's vampire – thin and spiderlike with an evil leer and long curving
claws – still has the power to chill the blood. Schreck was born in Berlin in
1897 and received his stage training at the Berlin Staats Theatre. His career
consisted of work in both the theatre and films – he made over fifty of the
latter, spanning the silent and sound eras. He wasn't typecast by *Nosferatu*
and continued to play a variety of roles after its release. He died in Munich
in 1936.

SHARP, DON
At first glance just another one of those competent but basically
unadventurous directors that are so common in the British film industry,
but on closer inspection his films reveal a certain vitality and control
that is missing from similar hack-work. He is another director who would
seem to be capable of greater things if he could only break out of the
exploitation grind (his latest film to date, *Hennessy*, is a step in the right
direction). Sharp was born in Australia and came to Britain shortly after the
Second World War; he first worked as an actor before taking up script-
writing and producing. One of the first films he worked on was *Conflict
of Wings* (1954), which was based on his own novel. The first film he directed
was *The Stolen Airliner* in 1955. His horror films include the much-praised
Kiss of the Vampire (1962), *Witchcraft* (1964), *The Curse of the Fly* (1965) and
the incredible *Psychomania* (1971), a tongue-in-cheek tale about a Hell's
Angel who makes a pact with the devil and spectacularly returns to life –
roaring out of his grave on his motorbike! Sharp also directed the first two
of the Christopher Lee Fu Manchu films, and his two efforts were brilliant
examples of the art of achieving something out of very little.

SIODMAK, KURT
Wrote the screenplays for a number of horror and s.f. films – also directed
some of them, and was the author of the often-filmed novel *Donovan's Brain*.
He was born in Germany in 1900 and worked as a screenwriter in the German
film industry – his credits include the classic *Der Tunnel*. Left Germany in the
mid-1930s and went to America. First Hollywood screenplay was for
Non-Stop New York in 1937. Horror and fantasy screenplays include *The
Invisible Man Returns* (Joe May, 1939), *The Invisible Woman* (A. Edward
Sutherland, 1941), *The Ape* (William Nigh, 1940), *Frankenstein Meets the
Wolfman* (Roy W. Neill, 1943), *I Walked With a Zombie* (Jacques Tourneur,
1943), *Son of Dracula* (Robert Siodmak, 1942), *House of Frankenstein* (Erle C.
Kenton, 1944), *Lady and the Monster* (George Sherman, 1945), *The Beast With
Five Fingers* (Robert Florey, 1946) and *Creature With the Atom Brain* (Edward
L. Cahn, 1955). Films he has directed include: *Bride of the Gorilla* (1951), *The
Magnetic Monster* (1953) and *Curucu, Beast of the Amazon* (1956).

STEELE, BARBARA
The 'Queen of Horror' to many horror fans, Italians particularly. Born in
Britain in 1938, she was the last female starlet to be signed up for Rank's
acting school. Her first film appearance was in Wolf Rilla's *Bachelor of
Hearts* in 1958. Rank later sold her contract to 20th Century Fox in Hollywood
and she went to live there for two years – and later claimed that she spent
most of the time sitting on the beach waiting for a call from the studio that
never came. During an actor's strike she seized the opportunity to go and
work in Italy where she made the first of her horror films – Mario Bava's
The Mask of the Demon in 1960 (see note on Bava for alternative titles). She
returned to Hollywood in 1961 and appeared in Corman's *The Pit and the
Pendulum*. Other horror films include *The Terror of Dr Hichcock* (Robert
Hampton alias Riccard Freda, 1962), *The Spectre* (Riccard Freda, 1964) and
The Revenge of the Blood Beast (Michael Reeves, 1965). She has appeared in
several non-horror films, such as *Fellini's 8½*, and resents the fact that she's
been tagged as a horror actress. 'But,' she said, 'the horrors are the only
films one hears about, which is a drag. I always used to think they'd end up
only in Sicily. It's not so. They end up at the Marble Arch Odeon in London
while the things you did for love and nothing end up in late-night showings
at the Tokyo Film Festival.'[103] She has retired from films but still appears on
US television. She is married to script-writer James Poe – no relation!

STRANGE, GLENN
American stunt man and actor who appeared in a number of horror films in
the 1940s and also played the Frankenstein Monster in three films: *House of
Frankenstein* (1944), *House of Dracula* (1945) and *Abbott and Costello Meet
Frankenstein* (Charles Barton, 1948). Was chosen to play the Monster by
make-up expert Jack Pierce and was coached in the movements by Karloff
himself. Other horror films he appeared in were *The Mad Monster* (Sam
Newfield, 1941), *The Black Raven* (Sam Newfield, 1942) and *The Monster
Maker* (Sam Newfield, 1943). Was supposed to play the Gillman in *The

Creature from the Black Lagoon but turned it down (he was once picked to play Tarzan back in the early 1930s but then Johnny Weissmuller came along). Familiar to television viewers for many years as Sam the bar-tender in the long-running Gunsmoke TV series. Died in 1973.

THESIGER, ERNEST

Best remembered by horror fans as the fey, eccentric Dr Pretorius in *Bride of Frankenstein*. Born Ernest Frederic Graham Thesiger in London, 1879, the grandson of the first Baron Chelmsford. Began his career as a painter but became a stage actor in 1909. Remained almost constantly on the British stage from that year until his death in 1961 at the age of eighty-one (his last play was *The Last Joke* with Sir John Gielgud and Sir Ralph Richardson). He managed to fit in a large number of film roles during his long career, including *The Old Dark House* (1932), *Caesar and Cleopatra* (Gabriel Pascal, 1946) and *The Man in the White Suit* (Sandy Mackendrick, 1951).

TRACY, SPENCER

One of Hollywood's most respected actors who, like Fredric March, took on one famous horror role and managed to leave it safely behind him afterwards. And, like March, his one horror performance was in a version of *Dr Jekyll and Mr Hyde* – the 1941 production directed by Victor Fleming. Fleming's version was more genteel than the 1932 one, lacking its vitality, but Tracy's performance, unhindered by heavy make-up or false teeth, was almost as memorable as March's. (Tracy was born in Wisconsin in 1900 and died in 1967.)

VEIDT, CONRAD

A tall, saturnine actor who was the Christopher Lee of an earlier film era. Born in Germany in 1893, he spent his early years on the stage – a pupil of Max Reinhardt. Originally typecast as a romantic hero but from his first film appearance onwards – he played a fanatical Hindu in a film called *The Indian Monument* – he was typed as a villain. The classic German films he appeared in include *The Student of Prague* (Henrik Galeen, 1926), *The Cabinet of Dr Caligari* (Robert Wiene, 1919), in which he played Cesare the somnambulist, a forerunner of Karloff's Monster, *The Hands of Orlac* (Robert Wiene, 1924), *Waxworks* (Paul Leni, 1924) and *Love's Mockery* (F. W. Murnau, 1920). His first Hollywood film was *The Beloved Rogue* in which he played King Louis XI, but Veidt didn't like working in America and returned to Germany, though he did continue to make the occasional Hollywood film. In 1932 he went to Britain to play the villain in *Rome Express* (Walter Forde, 1932) – he gave an excellent performance and had one of the best lines in the picture: his accomplice, after learning that Veidt had just murdered a man, cried: 'You must have been mad!' To which Veidt coolly replied: 'No, just annoyed.' Veidt made all his pictures in Britain from 1932 to 1940, but went back to Hollywood that year and stayed there until his death. His last British film was *The Thief of Baghdad* (Ludwig Bergen, Tim Whelan, Michael Powell, 1940) – it was started in Britain but transferred to Hollywood because of the war – in which he played the evil vizier. Veidt spent the remainder of his career playing villainous Nazi officers in numerous war films, something he didn't enjoy but which he did with his usual style and flair. He played such a role in one of his last films – *Casablanca* (Michael Curtiz, 1943). He died in 1943 aged fifty.

WRAY, FAY

American actress born in 1907 who will always be remembered for her role in *King Kong* as the giant ape's love object. She also appeared in a number of other horror films in the early 1930s, including *Doctor X* (Michael Curtiz, 1932), *The Most Dangerous Game* (Merian C. Cooper, 1932), *The Vampire Bat* (Frank Strayer, 1933) and *The Mystery of the Wax Museum* (Michael Curtiz, 1933).

WARHOL, ANDY

The famous pop artist and 'underground' film-maker, who has made two rather individualistic horror films to date – *Flesh for Frankenstein* (US title: *Warhol's Frankenstein*) and *Blood for Dracula*, both made in Italy in 1972. Actually both films were written and directed by Paul Morrissey and he, rather than Warhol is the person responsible for their style and content. Both films star Udo Keir in the central roles, are attractively photographed and full of improvised dialogue in the usual Morrissey/Warhol manner. Both also contain a large amount of explicit gore, particularly *Frankenstein* which was released in 3-D. They are very amusing on a certain level but are unlikely to satisfy the average horror fan (*Flesh for Frankenstein*, incidentally, didn't make it into Britain without the censor performing some extensive carving himself).

References

1. *Films in Review*, November 1973.
2. 'Tonight' show, 8 October 1969.
3. *Photoplay*, November 1930.
4. *Photoplay*, February 1928.
5. *Photoplay*, November 1930.
6. Ibid.
7. *Photoplay*, February 1928.
8. *Photoplay*, November 1930.
9. *Photoplay*, February 1928.
10. Ibid.
11. *Films in Review*, November 1973.
12. *Photoplay*, November 1930.
13. 'Tonight' show, 8 October 1969.
14. *Films in Review*, November 1973.
15. *Photon 20*, 1971.
16. 'Tonight' show, 8 October 1969.
17. *Films in Review*, November 1973.
18. *TV Times*, November 1957.
19. Forrest J. Ackerman, editor *Boris Karloff – The Frankenscience Monster*.
20. Arthur Lennig, *The Count*.
21. *Films in Review*, August 1964.
22. Universal publicity release, 1933.
23. Newspaper clipping – source unknown.
24. *Classic Film Collector*, winter 1970.
25. Ibid.
26. Newspaper clipping – source unknown.
27. Peter Underwood, *The Horror Man*.
28. Ibid.
29. Denis Gifford, *Karloff, The Man, The Monster, The Movies*.
30. Newspaper clipping – source unknown.
31. Denis Gifford, *Karloff, The Man, The Monster, The Movies*.
32. Ibid.
33. Peter Underwood, *The Horror Man*.
34. Newspaper clipping.
35. Newspaper clipping.
36. Peter Underwood, *The Horror Man*.
37. Peter J. Jarman, *The House at the End of the World*.
38. *Famous Monsters of Filmland*, November 1967.
39. Peter J. Jarman, *The House at the End of the World*.
40. Forrest J. Ackerman, editor *Boris Karloff – The Frankenscience Monster*.
41. Ibid.
42. *Motion Picture Classic*, March 1928.
43. Ibid.
44. *Photoplay*, February 1928.
45. *Photon 23*.
46. *New York Post*, 1936, exact date unknown.
47. Ibid.
48. *Photon 25*.
49. *Cinefantastique*, summer 1973.

50. Ibid.
51. Ibid.
52. The Velvet Light Trap, 10.
53. *Films in Review*, January 1963.
54. *Photon 22*.
55. *Films and Filming*, October 1959.
56. *Films and Filming*, July 1964.
57. *Take One*, vol 3, number 9.
58. *Radio Times*, 15 June 1972.
59. Hammer publicity release.
60. *Time Out*, issue no. 87.
61. *Kinematograph Weekly*, March 1970.
62. Ibid.
63. *Films Illustrated*, May 1974.
64. *Take One*, vol 2, number 12.
65. Paul Willemen, *Roger Corman*.
66. *Sight & Sound*, autumn 1970.
67. *Film Comment*, fall 1971
68. *Sight & Sound*, winter 63/64.
69. Denis Gifford, *Karloff, The Man, The Monsters, The Movies*.
70. *Take One*, vol 2, no. 12.
71. *Films and Filming*, June 1972.
72. Ibid.
73. *Take One*, vol 4, number 2.
74. *Kinematograph Weekly*, 1970.
75. *Little Shoppe of Horrors*, number 3.
76. *Exciting Cinema*, Vol 2, number 1.
77. *Cinefantastique*, summer 1972.
78. *Little Shoppe of Horrors*, number 3.
79. *Films in London*, November 1969.
80. *Cinefantastique*, vol 4, number 1.
81. *Supernatural*, number 1.
82. *Cinefantastique*, fall 1973.
83. *Supernatural*, Number 1.
84. Ibid.
85. Ibid.
86. Ibid.
87. *Films Illustrated*, November 1972.
88. *The Times*, 12 December 1972.
89. *Cinefantastique*, fall 1973.

Appendix
90. Newspaper clipping, source unknown.
91. Hammer publicity release.
92. *Cinefantastique*, vol 3, number 3.
93. R. C. Sherriff, *No Leading Lady*.
94. Forrest J. Ackerman, editor *Boris Karloff – The Frankenscience Monster*.
95. *Cinefantastique*, vol 3, number 4.
96. *Films in Review*, December 1974.
97. Publicity release.
98. *ABC Film Review* Sept 1971.
99. *Cinefantastique*, summer 1972.
100. *Photon 22*.
101. *Cinefantastique*, summer 1972.
102. *Today's Cinema*, December, 1971.
103. *Premiere*, December 1970.

Index

INDEX OF NAMES

Figures in *italics* refer to illustrations

Ackerman, Forrest J., 24–6, 35, 37–8, 40, 41, 55, 158, 181, 255, *256*, 257–9
Adams, Julie, *6*, 89, *93*
Adamson, Al, 24, 268
Agee, James, 73
Aldrich, Alfred, 43
Alland, Bill, 92
Allen, Irving, 284
Allen, Irwin, 151, 152
Allen, Lewis, 279
Allen, Woody, 268
Ambler, Eric, 213
American International Productions, 2, 3, 125 *passim*, 154, 198, 244, 271, 277, 280, 282
American Releasing Corporation, 125, 130
Amicus Productions Ltd., 7, 109, 205, 224, 233, 235, *236*, 243, 249, 264
Arkoff, Samuel Z., 6, 125, 127, 135
Arch, Lillian, 33
Arnold, Edward, 208
Arnold, Jack, 6, *86*, 87 *passim*, 195, 264
Arness, James, 87
Asher, Jack, 109, 188
Asher, Jane, 101, *130*, *158*
Asher, William, 153
Ashton, Roy, 109, *191*
Atwill, Lionel, 5, 50, 265
Auer, John H., 183
Avalon, Frankie, 153, *157*

Baclanova, Olga, 65
Baker, Roy Ward, 7, 108, 170, 192, 206, 212 *passim*, 265, 266, 280
Baker, Tom, 284
Balch, Antony, 272
Balcon, Sir Michael, 112, 272
Barrett, Edith, 149
Barrymore, Ethel, 269
Barrymore, Lionel, 66–7, 211
Barton, Charles, 287
Bates, Ralph, 108, 222, *223*, 265–6
Bava, Mario, 54, 266, 287

Baxt, George, 235
Beacham, Stephanie, 224
Beaudine, William, 36, 268
Beaumont, Charles, 128, 195
Beck, Helen, 183–4, 186–7
Beckett, Samuel, 135
Behrman, S. N., 269
Bennett, Arnold, 273
Bennett, Compton, 85
Berg, Jon, 57
Bergen, Ludwig, 288
Bernard, James, 110, 118
Bernds, Edward L., 152
Beswick, Martine, 222, *223*, 266, *266*
Blair, Linda, 98, *262*, 267, *267*
Blatty, William, 99, 143
Bloch, Robert, 3, 7, 28, 35, 57, 179, 200 *passim*, 239, 253
Bodeen, DeWitt, 74, 77–8, 81, 83
Boese, Carl, 59
Bogarde, Dirk, 216–17, *217*
Bogart, Humphrey, 226
Bogdanovich, Peter, 35, 54, *55*, 133–4
Boleslavsky, Richard, 269
Booth, Edwin, 149
Borg, Reginald le, 23, 38, 54, 153, 268
Borland, Carol, 35
Brabin, Charles, 49
Bradbury, Ray, 88, 91, 255, 257
Brahm, John, 151
Britten, Sir Benjamin, 110
Brooks, Jean, 75, 80
Brooks, Mel, 50, 70–1, 263, 265
Browne, Coral, 149
Browning, Ricou, 93
Browning, Tod, 2, 5, 15, 16, 17, 35, 59 *passim*, 73, 257, 265, 271
Buñuel, Luis, 216
Burke, John, 284
Burroughs, Edgar Rice, 243
Bushell, Anthony, 184
Butler, David, 54
Butler, Ivan, 115

Cabanne, Christy, 44
Cagney, James, 23

Cahn, Edward, 287
Calvert, Phyllis, 84, 85
Capote, Truman, 226
Capra, Frank, 52, 277
Carlson, Richard, 89
Carlson, Veronica, *225*, 267–8
Carradine, John, *39*, 40, 257, 268
Carreras, Enrique, 101
Carreras, Sir James, 6, 101, 102–3, 112, 113, 117, 120–4, 187, 222, 244, 248, 252
Carreras, Michael, 2, 6, 101, 102, *102*, 103, 106, 107, 109, 110, 116, 117, *117*, 118, 166, 218, 244, 266, 285
Carstairs, John Paddy, 107
Carter, Ann, 75
Castle, William, 6, 33, 35, *136*, 137 *passim*, 152, 205, 264
Cavalcanti, 272
Chaffey, Don, 108, 265
Chaney, John, 9, 10
Chaney, Lon, Senior, 2, 4, 5, 7, *8*, 9 *passim*, 30, 43–4, 46, 49, 58, 60, 63, *63*, 64, 159, 168, 175–6, 257, 283
Chaney, Lon, Junior, 2, 5, 9 *passim*, 33, *39*, 40, 257, 273, 283
Chaplin, Sir Charles, 143, 181
Charlemagne Productions Ltd., 174
Chase, Stanley, 199
Christonson, Benjamin, 64
Cinefantastique, 255
Clair, René, 278
Clarens, Carlos, 67
Clark, Colbert, 33
Clark, Jim, 157
Clark, Mae, *45*
Clarke, Frederick S., 255
Classic Pictures, 234
Clayton, Harry, 186
Clayton, Jack, 226–7, *227*
Clemens, Brian, 222
Clive, Colin, 47, 48, *68*, *70*, 103, 257, 268–9
Cohn, Harry, 44, 52, 138
Collins, Joan, 237
Colman, Herbert, 202
Colman, Ronald, 152
Columbia Pictures, 44, 52, 103, 138, 139, 151
Conway, Tom, *74*
Coop, Denys, 224
Cooper, Gary, 23
Cooper, Merian C., 289
Coppola, Francis Ford, 133
Corman, Roger, 3, 5, 6, 24, 54, 129 *passim*, 152, 153, *154*, 195, 198, 264, 279
Count Dracula Society, 25, 254
Court, Hazel, *130*
Coward, Sir Noël, 3, 183

Crabtree, Arthur, 272
Crawford, Joan, 205
Creighton, Cleva, 9, 10
Crichton, Charles, 272
Crowley, Mart, 270
Curtis, Dan, 195, 198, 264, 269
Curtis, Tony, 24
Curtiz, Michael, 24, 149, 150, 265, 269, 277, 289
Cushing, Peter, 5, 7, 71, 103, *104*, 108, 118, 147, 162, 164, 174, 178–9, *180*, 181 *passim*, 218, 220, *229*, 239, 242–3, *246*, 250, 255, 264, 268

Dahl, Roald, 232
Dale, Alan, 29
Daniell, Henry, *82*, 269
Davis, Bette, 149, 218, 248, 285
Davis, Desmond, 267
Davis, Rupert Hartford, 266
De Ruiz, Nick, 13
Dean, Julia, 81, *81*
Dearden, Basil, 272
Dehn, Paul, 100
De Mille, Cecil B., 53, 151, 268
Derleth, August, 201
Dieterle, William, 33, 273
Dillon, John Francis, 49
Doleman, Guy, *243*
Donald, James, 215
Donlevy, Brian, 188
Douglas, Kirk, 80, 263
Dracula, Prince Vlad Tepes, 178, 255
Dracula Society, 254
Driscoll, Sonya, 183
Duffell, Peter, 280
Dwan, Alan, 265

Earles, Harry, *17*, *63*, 65, *65*, 66
Edwards, J. Gordon, 29
Elder, John, 248
Evans, Dame Edith, 272
Exclusive Films, 101

Fairbank, J., 232
Fairbanks, Douglas, 43, 59, 270
Famous Monsters of Filmland, 255, 257, *258*, 259
Faragoh, Francis Edward, 69
Farrow, Mia, 140, *141*
Farrow, John, 279
Fenady, George, 268, 279
Fennell, Albert, 222
Ferrer, Jose, 150
Fields, W. C., 33
Fisher, Terence, 5, 6, 103, 105, 106, 108, 109, 110, *111*, 112–16, 131, 166, 188, 192, 195, 268, 272, 282
Flaherty, Robert, 90–1

Fleming, Victor, 268, 288
Florey, Robert, 30, 32, 61, 69, 270, 277, 287
Flynn, Errol, 149, 165, 182, 283
Forbes-Robertson, John, 109, 171, 222
Fonda, Peter, 133, 134
Ford, John, 62, 268
Forde, Walter, 288
Fort, Garrett, 69
Foster, Norman, 277
Fox, Wallace, 36
Francis, Freddie, 7, 107, 169, 192, 224 passim, 238–9, 244, *251*, 260, 268, 278, 283
Francis, Kevin, 7, 229, 244 passim, *251*, 264
Franco, Jesus, 172
Frankham, David, 132
Franklin, Pamela, *198*, 199
Fregonese, Hugo, 85
Freund, Karl, 5, 23, 49, 59 passim, 73, 269, 277
Frid, Jonathan, 269
Friedkin, William, 4, 99, 142, 261, 263, 267, *267*, 270–1
Friedlander, Louis, 50
Fritsch, Gunther von, 81, 82
Frost, Lee, 279
Frye, Dwight, 271
Fuest, Robert, 155, 271, 282
Fuller, Samuel, 150
Fulton, John P., 72
Funicello, Annette, 153

Gaines, Bill, 240
Gainsborough Films, 213
Galeen, Henrik, 59, 288
Galsworthy, John, 275
Garnett, Tay, 187
George Smith Enterprises, 284
Gibson, Alan, 107, 108, 170
Gielgud, Sir John, 283, 288
Gilling, John, 37, 106, 107, 271–2
Godfrey, Peter, 269
Gordon, Robert, 272
Gough, Michael, 272
Goulding, Alfred, 183
Grant, Cary, 204
Grant, Mary, 149
Gray, Charles, 198
Grayson, Godfrey, 102
Greene, Richard, 231, 242
Greenstreet, Sydney, 159, 277
Griffith, D. W., 62
Griffith, Hugh, 249
Guest, Val, 5, 100, 105, 107, 108, 272–3
Guidice, Filippo del, 164
Gwynne, Fred, 50

Hall, Jon, 257
Haller, Daniel, 132–3
Halpern, Victor, 32
Hamer, Robert, 272
Hamilton, Guy, 161, 174
Hammer Films, 2, 3, 5, 54, 100 passim, 166, 168 passim, 174, 175, 178, 187, 188, 196, 198, 217, 218, 222, 228, 229, 235, 236, 237, 244, 245, 248, 249, 250, 251, 264, 265, 266, 267, 268, 271, 272, 280, 282, 283, 284, 285
Hammer (Hinds), Will, 101
Hampton, Robert (Riccard Freda), 287
Hardman Associates, 285
Hardy, Robin, 280
Harris, Julie, 58
Hart, William S., 12, 181
Hathaway, Henry, 150
Hatton, Rondo, 273
Hawks, Howard, 44, 49, 87
Hay, Will, 272
Hayers, Sydney, 195
Hayes, Helen, 265
Hayward, Louis, 182
Hayward, Susan, 82
Hedison, Al, 152
Hellman, Monte, 133, 135
Helmore, Evelyn, 53
Herman, Albert, 33
Herrman, Bernard, 202
Hessler, Gordon, 155
Heston, Charlton, 151, 152
Hibbins, Nina, 105, 106
Hickman, Dwayne, *157*
Hickox, Douglas, 157
Hill, George W., 15
Hillyer, Lambert, 36, 52
Hinds, Anthony, 6, 100, 101, 102, 103, 112–13, 116, 118, 166, 228, 230, 248
Hitchcock, Alfred, 107, 137, 143, 201, 202, 204, 237, 276, 277, 282
Hitchcock, Bill, 72
Hobson, Valerie, *4*
Holden, William, 184
Holt, Seth, 107, 117
Hope, Bob, 23, 250
Hopkins, Matthew, 284
Hopkins, Miriam, 278
Hopper, Dennis, 133
Horsley, David, 72
Hough, John, 195, 272
Houghton, Don, 123
Howard, Trevor, 249
Hubbard, L. Ron, 257
Hughes, Howard, 68
Hugo, Victor, 12
Hull, Henry, 22, 273
Hurt, John, *247*

Huston, John, 187, 226, 277
Huston, Walter, 208
Hutton, Brian G.. 280
Huxley, Aldous, 78, 145

Ireland, John, 130
Isherwood, Christopher, 263

Jacobson, Egon, 277
James, Clive, 244
James, Henry, 227
Jannings, Emil, 60
Julian, Rupert, 14
Juran, Nathan, 23, 130

Kahn, Edward, 269
Karloff, Boris, *1*, 4, *4*, 5, 23, 24, 27
    passim, 62, 66, 69, 70, 71, 75, *82*, 100,
    103, 128, 132, 147, 149, 153, 158,
    159, 175, 176, 181, 211, 254, 257,
    268, 269, 275, 280, 283, 284, 287
Katayev, Valentin, 276
Katzman, Sam, 36
Kaufman, Millard, 153
Keaton, Buster, 181, 210, 266
Keir, Andrew, 217, *219*
Keir, Udo, 171
Kelljan, Bob, 282
Kemp, Valli, 148
Kennedy, Burt, 172
Kenton, Erle C., 23, 33, 36, 53, 73, 265,
    273, 287
Kerr, Deborah, 85, 227, *227*
Kerrigan, J. Warren, 11
Keys, Anthony Nelson, 174, *212*
Kieffer, Warren, 284
King, Henry, 150
Kneale, Nigel, 100, 217, 273
Knight, Castleton, 279
Knight, Shirley, 205
Knox, Dr Robert, 190
Koch, Howard W., 54
Koerner, Charles, 76, 83, 84
Korda, Sir Alexander, 109, 286
Korda, Zoltan, 166
Kornell, Katherine, 265
Kramer, Stanley, 24, 80
Krauss, Werner, 60
Kruger, Hardy, 217
Kubrick, Stanley, 99, 282
Kun, Béla, 28

Ladd, Alan, 187
Laemmle, Carl, 59, 62, 63
Laemmle, Carl, Junior, 30, 71
Lancaster, Burt, 77
Lanchester, Elsa, *70*, 71, 257, 273, *274*,
    275
Landau, Richard, 100

Landers, Lew, 54
Landon, Michael, *126*
Lang, Fritz, 59, 60, 151, 196, 275
Langdon, Vern, 56
Langtry, Lily, 265
Laughton, Charles, 20, 69, 273, *274*, 275
Leach, E. R., 131
Leakey, Phil, 100
Lean, David, 283
Lee, Christopher, 4–5, 6, 30, 103, *104*,
    105, 106, 108, 114, 118, 122, 159
    passim, 182, 192–3, 198, 208, 220,
    242, 249, 250, 255, 259, 260, 264,
    278, 282, 286, 288
Lee, Rowland V., 36, 50, 52, 73, 149,
    263, 265, 275
Leigh, Janet, 202
Leigh, Vivien, 272
Leisen, Mitchell, 278
Lejeune, C. A., 103, 105
Lemont, John, 272
Leni, Paul, 288
Lennig, Arthur, 28
Lester, Richard, 173
Levin, Henry, 165
Lewton, Val, 5, 53, 73 *passim*, 88
Lininger, Hope, 38
Locan, Clarence A., 15, 18
Lohman, Gus, 226
Lom, Herbert, *107*
Lorre, Peter, *1*, 53, 55, 62, 128, *128*,
    132, 153, 159, 209, 226, 257, 270,
    275, *276*, 277
Losey, Joseph, 283
Lovecraft, H. P., 153, 201
Lubin, Arthur, 273, 282
Lubitsch, Ernst, 36
Lugosi, Bela, 4, 5, 27 *passim*, 62, 64, 66,
    67, 106, 113, 137, 147, 159, 249, 257,
    259, 270, 272
Lvovsky, Cecilia, 276

MacDonald, John, 166
Mackendrick, Sandy, 288
MacNee, Patrick, 164
Magee, Patrick, *206*, 282
Mamoulian, Rouben, 278
Manciewicz, Joseph L., 150
Mann, Anthony, 151
Marceau, Marcel, 143
March, Fredric, 278, *278*, 288
Marin, Edward L., 33
Marlowe, Don, 36–7
Mars, Kenneth, 265
Marshall, Herbert, 148
Martin, Eugene, 192
Marx Brothers, 152, 270
Mason, James, 263
Massey, Raymond, 52–3, 69, 277

Matheson, Richard, 7, 89, 99, 128, 129, 132, 148, 152, 153, 195 *passim*, 209, 269
May, Joe, 149, 287
Mayer, L. B., 66
Mayne, Ferdy, 278
McCambridge, Mercedes, 98
McDowall, Roddy, *198*, 199
McGowan, Jack, 142
McLeod, Norman, 2, 53, 151
Menzies, William Cameron, 32
Mercury Theatre Workshop, 149
Meredith, Burgess, *19*
Metro-Goldwyn-Mayer, 62, 64, 66, 67, 77, 78, 83, 84, 85, 211, 218, 279
Milestone, Lewis, 20
Milius, John, 133
Milland, Ray, 5, 278–9, *279*
Mills, John, *217*
Mitchell, Oswald, 272
Mitchum, Robert, 139
Mitler, Leo, 275
Mix, Tom, 181, 182
Monroe, Marilyn, 212, 214–15
Moody, Ron, 249
Moorcock, Michael, 271
Moore, Roger, 174
Moran, Lee, 9–10
Morley, Robert, 226
Morris, Ozzie, 226
Morrissey, Paul, 289
Moxey, John Llewellyn, 195
Murnau, F. W., 59, 286, 288
Murray, Barbara, 231, 242

Nagybányhegyes, Ilona Montagh de, 29
Narizzano, Silvio, 107, 195
Nazimova, Alla, 84, 265
Neagle, Dame Anna, 83
Neill, Roy W., 36, 265, 287
Neumann, Kurt, 152
Newfield, Sam, 271, 287
Newman, Paul, 282
Nicholson, Jack, 4, 132, 133, *133*
Nicholson, James H., 6, 125, 129
Nigh, William, 17, 287
Niven, David, 171
Nugent, Elliot, 23
Nyby, Christian, 87

O'Brien, Willis, 254
O'Connor, Una, 69, 70
Ogle, Charles, 280
Olivier, Lord, 164, 184–6, 248–9, 268, 272
O'Neal, Charles, 79
O'Neal, Ryan, 79
Ordung, Wyott, 130
Osborne, John, 100
Owen, Cliff, 267

Paget, Debra, *134*
Palance, Jack, 114, 171, 239, 263
Paramount Pictures, 84, 204, 232, 270
Parsons, Harriet, 85
Parsons, Louella, 85
Pascal, Gabriel, 288
Peck, Gregory, 83, 150, 164, 226
Perkins, Anthony, *203*
Pertwee, Jon, *241*
Philbin, Mary, 14
Pierce, Jack, *20*, 46, 49, 257
Pinckard, Terri, 56–7
Pinter, Harold, 233, 270
Pirie, David, 110, 112
Pitt, Ingrid, *119*, *241*, 280
Pleasance, Angela, 242
Pleasance, Donald, 232, 242
Poe, Edgar Allan, 3, 37, 49, 127–8, 133, 152, 153, 154, 198, 201–2, 208, 239
Poe, James, 287
Poitier, Sydney, 24
Polanski, Roman, 7, 140, 141, *141*, 278, 280–1
Pollexfen, Jack, 24
Powell, Michael, 166, 288
Preminger, Otto, *146*, 150, 275
Pressburger, Arnold, 277
Price, Vincent, *1*, 5, 6, 52, 55, 128, 132, *134*, *146*, 147 *passim*, 162, 181, *200*, 207, 255, 258, 264, 265, 271, 275, 282, 283, 284
Priestley, J. B., 69, 187
Prowse, David, *108*, *111*, 281–2, *281*

Quarry, Robert, 259, 282

Rains, Claude, 20, 70, 149, 159, 160, 257, 282–3
Rank Organization, 112, 164, 287
Rathbone, Basil, *39*, 40, 50, 52, 128, 149, 153, 159, 160, *283*
Redgrave, Lynn, 263
Reed, Oliver, 4, 114, 116, 147, 174, *230*, 283
Reeves, Michael, 154, 284, 287
Reeves, Steve, 125
Reinhardt, Max, 288
Reisz, Karel, 225–6, 228
Revill, Clive, *198*, 199
Richardson, Sir Ralph, 288
Richardson, Tony, 228
Rilla, Wolf, 287
Ringel, Harry, 261
Ripper, Michael, 284
Rittau, Gunther, 60
RKO, 75, 80, 82, 83, 85, 208, 209
Roach, Hal, 20
Robert Lippert Productions, 102
Robertson, John S., 59

Robinson, Bernard, 109–10
Robinson, George, 50
Robson, Mark, 77, 80, 82, 83
Romero, George, 284–5
Rose, Billy, 233
Rosenberg, Stuart, 282
Rosenburg, Max, 222, 233, 234–5
Ruth, Roy del, 271
Rye, D. Stellan, 59

Sagal, Boris, 196
Salkow, Sidney, 153, 196
Saltzman, Harry, 228
Sampson, Edward, 130
Samuels, Ted, 242
Sangster, Jimmy, 108, 113, 188, 230,
    265, 268, 282, 285
Sarrazin, Michael, 263
Sasdy, Peter, 108, 170, 265, 280, 285–6
Saville, Philip, 267
Schary, Dore, 80
Schreck, Max, 286
Seeger, Guido, 60
Selznick, David O., 76, 78, 83
Shaffer, Anthony, 172
Sharp, Don, 108, 236, 286–7
Shaw Brothers, 124
Shelley, Barbara, 115, 217
Shelley, Mary, 188, 244, 275
Sherman, George, 287
Sherriff, R. C., 67–8, 69, 268–9
Sidney, George, 150
Siegel, Don, 284
Siegel, Joel E., 77
Simon, Simone, 73, 74, 75, 208–9
Sinatra, Frank, 140
Siodmak, Kurt, 23, 78, 287
Siodmak, Robert, 22, 287
Sistrom, William, 11
Sjöstrom, Victor, 64
Skelton, Red, 125
Small, Edward, 182
Smith, Dick, 262
Smith, Roger, 24
Snell, Peter, 172
Soule, Helene Vivian, 43
Spielberg, Steven, 195
Stahl, John M., 150
Stanwyck, Barbara, 205
St Clair, Malcolm, 277
Starr, Ringo, 263
Steele, Barbara, 287
Stefano, Joseph, 204
Stevens, George, 183
Stewart, James, 204
Stine, Clifford, *96*, 97
Stoker, Bram, 60, 122, 170, 172, 254,
    263, 286
Stoloff, Benjamin, 33

Strange, Glenn, 53, 257, 287–8
Strayer, Frank, 265, 271, 289
Subotsky, Milton, 7, 109, 205, 224, 233
    passim
Summers, Jeremy, 154
Sutherland, A. Edward, 33, 287
Sutherland, Donald, *236*
Sykes, Peter, 279
Szmik, Ilona, 28

Tamiroff, Akim, *39*
Taurog, Norman, 85, 154
Taylor, Robert, 205
Tetzlaff, Ted, 151
Thalberg, Irving, 63, 64, 66
Thesiger, Ernest, 69, 71, 288
Thomas, Ralph, 157
Tierney, Gene, 150
Tiffany-Stahl Studio, 68
Tigon Films, 284
Tinling, James, 277
Tobey, Kenneth, 87–8
Todd, Richard, 237
Tomlinson, David, 154
Toth, Andre de, 150, 265
Tourneur, Jacques, 54, 73, 76, 77, 83,
    128, 129, 153, 154, 195, 287
Tracy, Spencer, 288
Troughton, Patrick, *177*
Twentieth Century Fox Films, 149, 213,
    214, 287
Two Cities Films Productions, 164,
    213–14
Tucker, George Leone, 12
Tyburn Film Company, 7, 244, 245, *247*,
    248, 251, 252, 264, 265
Tyler, Parker, 253

UFA Film Company, 276
Ulmer, Edward G., 33, 49
Universal Pictures, 2, 10, 11, 20, 23, 30,
    35, 48, 59, 60, 62, 63, 68, 69, 71, 73,
    85, 91, 95, 97, 103, 270

Valentino, Rudolph, 254
Van Dyke, Dick, 199
Van Sloan, Edward, *31*
Varnel, Marcel, 32, 272
Veidt, Conrad, 60, 159, 160, 257, 288–9
Vidor, Charles, 71
Vogt, A. E. Van, 257
Von Sydow, Max, 142

Waggner, George, 20, 22, 36, 265, 283
Wagner, Robert, 99
Walker, Stuart, 22, 273
Wallace, Edgar, 89
Walsh, Raoul, 164
Ward, Simon, 263

Warhol, Andy, 98, 122, 289
Warner Brothers, 44, 91, 103, 129, 149, 205, 248, 270, 277
Warner, Jack, 270
Warren, Bill, 57
Waterbury, Ruth, 12, 14
Webb, Roy, 77
Wegener, Paul, 59, 60
Weismuller, Johnny, 288
Welbourne, Charles S., 94
Welch, Raquel, 172
Welles, Orson, 80, 82, 83, 137, 143, 149
Wells, H. G., 69, 273, 275
Werker, Alfred, 150
Whale, James, 5, 30, 44, 46, 47, 49, 50, 59 passim, 73, 132, 182, 183, 257, 263, 268–9, 270, 275, 282, 283
Wheatley, Dennis, 114, 123, 174, 198
Whelan, Tim, 288
Widmark, Richard, 214
Wiene, Robert, 44, 59, 60, 83, 288
Wilbur, Crane, 152
Wilcox, Sir Herbert, 83
Wilder, Billy, 172, 174, 276
Willeman, Paul, 131
William Castle Productions, 142

William, Warren, 182
Williams, Grant, 89, 95, 97–8, 205
Wise, Robert, 36, 82, 253, 269
Witney, William, 152
Wood, Edward W., Junior, 40
Woodruff, Beatrice, 30
Woodward, Edward, 172
Woodward, Joanne, 282
Wordsworth, Richard, 100–1, 115
Worsley, Wallace, 12
Wray, Ardel, 78, 84
Wray, Fay, 289
Wyman, George H., 257
Wymark, Patrick, 193, 239

Yarborough, Jean, 268, 273
York, Michael, 174
Young, James, 44
Young, Robert, 282
Young, Terence, 164, 166

Zanuck, Darryl F., 54, 215
Zeffirelli, Franco, 171
Zimm, Maurice, 92
Zinneman, Fred, 23
Zugsmith, Albert, 153

INDEX OF FILM TITLES

Figures in *italics* refer to illustrations

Abbott and Costello Meet Frankenstein, 287
Abominable Dr Phibes, The, 150, 155, 271
Abominable Snowman, The, 105, 272
Advise and Consent, 275
African Queen, The, 83
Air Mail, 62
Alias John Preston, 166
Alias Nick Beal, 279
All Quiet on the Western Front, 71
All That Money Can Buy, 208
Alligator People, The, 24
And Now The Screaming Starts, 212, 224
Anniversary, The, 218, 285
Apache Drums, 86
Apache Woman, 125
Ape, The, 287
Arsenic and Old Lace, 52, 277
Asylum, 205, 206, *206*, 222, 224, 233, 237

Bachelor of Hearts, 287
Badlands of Dakota, 23
Baron of Arizona, The, 150
Bat, The, 152

Battle of the River Plate, 166
Beach Party, 153
Beast Must Die, The, 240
Beast with a Million Eyes, The, 125
Beast with Five Fingers, The, 270, 277, 287
Beat the Devil, 225, 226, 277
Bedlam, 53, 75, 76, 80
Behind the Mask, 49
Bell, The, 44
Beloved Rogue, The, 288
Best House in London, The, 267
Big Circus, The, 152
Big Fisherman, The, 275
Billy the Kid vs. Dracula, 268
Birthday Party, The, 233, 270
Black Castle, The, 23
Black Cat, The, 33, 49
Black Knight, The, 187
Black Raven, The, 287
Black Sabbath, 54, 266
Black Sleep, The, 38, 39, 40, 268
Black Sunday, 266
Black Zoo, 272
Blind Bargain, *11*
Blood and Lace, 266
Blood for Dracula, 289
Blood from the Mummy's Tomb, 117, *117*

Blood of Dracula's Castle, 268
Bloody Mama, 131
Bluebeard, 61
Body Snatcher, The, 36, 53, 75, 82, 82, 83, 269
Boogie Man Will Get You, The, 54
Bowery at Midnight, 36
Boys in the Band, The, 270
Break in the Circle, 272
Bride of Frankenstein, The, 2, 4, 4, 47, 50, 70, 70, 71, 268, 271, 274, 275, 288
Bride of the Gorilla, 23, 287
Brides of Dracula, The, 108, 166, 284
Brides of Fu Manchu, The, 169
Bridge on the River Kwai, The, 134
Bridges at Toko-Ri, The, 80
Brigham Young, 149–50
Brute Man, The, 273
Bucket of Blood, 3, 132
Bug!, 145
Burn, Witch, Burn, 195
By Candlelight, 71

Cabinet of Dr Caligari, The, 3, 44, 59, 60, 205, 263, 288
Caesar and Cleopatra, 288
Camp on Blood Island, The, 107
Cannibal Orgy or The Maddest Story Ever Told, 24
Captain Blood, 283
Captain Horatio Hornblower, RN, 164
Captain Kidd, 275
Captains Courageous, 268
Casablanca, 277
Casanova's Big Night, 151
Casino Royale, 281
Castle of the Living Dead, 284
Cat and the Canary, The, 250
Cat People, The, 73, 74, 74, 75, 76–7, 78, 80, 81, 83–4
Cavalcade, 3
Champion, The, 80
Chandu the Magician, 32, 33
Chump at Oxford, A, 183
Citizen Kane, 82, 137
City of the Dead, 235
City Under the Sea, 154
Clockwork Orange, A, 99, 282
Cobra Woman, 23
Cocoanuts, 270
Cohens and Kellys in Hollywood, The, 49
Colonel Bogey, 112
Comedy of Terrors, 54, 77, 128, 128, 129, 153, 195, 277, 283
Confessions of a Window-Cleaner, 272
Confessions of an Opium Eater, 153
Conflicts of Wings, 286
Conqueror Worm, The, 154
Convicts Four, 153

Corpse Vanishes, The, 36
Corridor of Mirrors, 164
Couch, The, 205
Count Yorga – Vampire, 282
Countess Dracula, 108, 118, 280, 286
Crack-Up, 277
Crazies, The, 285
Crazy House, 23
Creature from the Black Lagoon, The, 3, 6, 86, 89, 92, 94, 288
Creature from the Haunted Sea, 132
Creature with the Atom Brain, 287
Creatures the World Forgot, 108
Creeping Flesh, 192
Creeping Unknown, The, 100, 272
Crescendo, 107
Criminal Code, The, 44
Crusades, The, 268
Cry of the Banshee, 155
Cupid's Brand, 275
Curse of Frankenstein, The, 5, 102, 103, 104, 108, 109, 110, 159, 166, 167, 192, 244, 285
Curse of the Cat People, The, 73, 75, 78, 79, 81, 81, 82, 83, 84
Curse of the Dead, 266
Curse of the Demon, 77
Curse of the Fly, The, 286
Curse of the Werewolf, The, 106, 114, 115, 168, 283
Curucu, Beast of the Amazon, 287

Damned, The, 283
Dance of the Vampires, 278, 280
Danger Route, 233
Dark Avenger, The, 165
Dark Light, The, 117
Dark Star, 257
Day the Earth Caught Fire, The, 272
Day the Earth Stood Still, The, 82
Days of Glory, 83
Dead Men Walk, 271
Dead of Night, 209, 239, 272
Deadly Bees, The, 243
Death Kiss, The, 33
Death Takes a Holiday, 278
Déclassée, 269
Deep Throat, 129, 178
Defiant Ones, The, 24
Der Tunnel, 287
Devil and Daniel Webster, The, 208
Devil Doll, The, 66
Devil Rides Out, The, 110, 114, 123, 174, 195, 198
Devil's Bride, The, 195
Devil's in Love, The, 33
Diary of a Madman, 153
Die! Die! My Darling, 195
Dillinger, 133

Doctor X, 265, 289
Donovan's Brain, 287
Don't Bother to Knock, 212, 214
Doomwatch, 286
Dr Cyclops, 95
Dr Goldfoot and the Brain Machine, 154, 156, 157
Dr Jekyll and Mr Hyde, 2, 59, 263, 278, 278, 288
Dr Jekyll and Sister Hyde, 212, 222, 223, 265, 266, 266
Dr Morelle – The Case of the Missing Heiress, 102
Dr Phibes Rises Again, 148, 155, 271, 282
Dr Terror's Gallery of Horror, 24
Dr Terror's House of Horrors, 225, 230, 233, 235, 236, 239, 242
Dr Who, 192, 235
Dracula (1931), 2, 4, 5, 29, 30, 31, 35, 36, 47, 48, 52, 60, 61, 64, 69, 113, 137, 209, 237, 254, 263, 271
Dracula (1958), 104, 105, 105, 106, 110, 113, 116, 118, 159, 166, 168, 171, 192, 249, 272, 285
Dracula (1974), 195, 269
Dracula A.D. 1972, 163, 170, 180
Dracula has Risen from the Grave, 169, 170, 170, 229, 230, 245, 249, 268, 284
Dracula, Prince of Darkness, 115, 168, 169, 249
Dracula's Daughter, 2, 36
Dragonwyck, 150
Duel, 195
Dunwich Horror, The, 132

Earthquake, 80, 97, 145
Egyptian, The, 269
El Conde Dracula, 172
Electric Man, The, 265
Enchanted Cottage, The, 85
Enemy from Space, The, 102, 272
Equinox, 257
Everything You Always Wanted to Know About Sex, 268
Evil Eye, The, 266
Evil of Frankenstein, The, 188, 229, 229
Exorcist, The, 3, 4, 47, 98, 99, 123, 129, 142, 143, 176, 199, 208, 251, 258, 261, 262, 263, 263, 267, 267, 270, 271

Face Behind the Mask, The, 270
Face of Dr Fu Manchu, The, 168
Fall of the House of Usher, The, 127–8, 131, 148, 148, 152, 195
Fanatic, 107
Fast and Furious, 129, 130
Fear in the Night, 285
Fearless Vampire Killers, The, or Pardon

Me But Your Teeth Are In My Neck, 281
Fellini's 8½, 287
Female Bunch, The, 24
Final Programme, 271
Five Million Years to Earth, 212, 219
Flame and the Arrow, 77
Flesh and the Fiends, 272
Flesh for Frankenstein, 289
Fly, The, 148, 151, 152
Flying Scotsman, The, 279
Follow the Boys, 23
Four Musketeers, The, 173
Four Skulls of Jonathan Drake, The, 269
Frankenstein (1910), 280
Frankenstein (1931), 2, 3, 4, 30, 32, 36, 45, 46, 47–50, 52, 58, 69, 98, 101, 209, 237, 254, 263, 267, 268, 269, 270, 271
Frankenstein (1970), 54
Frankenstein (remake), 101, 103, 105, 106, 112, 116, 118, 192
Frankenstein and the Monster from Hell, 110, 111, 116, 189, 282
Frankenstein Meets the Wolfman, 36, 73, 265, 287
Frankenstein Must be Destroyed, 110, 268
Freaks, 2, 4, 52, 65, 65, 66, 271
French Connection, The, 271
From Beyond the Grave, 242
Full Treatment, The, 272

Gebissen Wird Nur Nachets – Happening Der Vampire, 231
Ghost Catchers, 23
Ghost of Frankenstein, The, 2, 23, 36, 73, 265, 273
Ghost Ship, The, 75, 80
Ghosts on the Loose, 36
Ghoul, The, 225, 244, 246, 247, 247, 268
Gift of Gab, The, 62
Gila Man, 24
Girl Crazy, 19
Girls in the Night, 91
God Protect Me from My Friends, 214
Godfather, The, 190, 243
Gold, 278
Golden Sea, The, 60
Golem, The, 3, 59, 60, 61
Gorgon, The, 106
Gorilla, The, 265
Graft, 44
Great Expectations, 237

Hamlet, 164, 184, 185, 186
Hands of Orlac, The, 2, 3, 59, 62, 269, 288
Hands of the Ripper, 286

Hannie Caulder, 172
Hard Times for Vampires, 168
Haunted Palace, The, 24, *134*, 153
Haunting, The, 83, 253
Hell is a City, 107, 120, 272
Hello Out There, 71
Hell's Angels, 68
Hennessy, 286
High Noon, 23
Highway Dragnet, 129–30
Hill in Korea, A, 225
Hillbillys in a Haunted House, 24
His Majesty, The American, 43
Hitler's Children, 84
Home of the Brave, 80
Homicidal, 140
Horror Express, 192
Horror Hospital, 272
Horror of Frankenstein, The, 108, *108*,
    265, 268, 281, *281*, 285
Horrors of the Black Museum, 272
Hotel Berlin, 269
Hound of the Baskervilles, The, 110, 159,
    166
House in Nightmare Park, 279
House of a Thousand Dolls, The, 154
House of Dark Shadows, 269
House of Darkness, 272
House of Dracula, 265, 268, 273, 287
House of Frankenstein, The, 53, 265, 268,
    273, 287
House of Horrors, 273
House of Wax, The, 3, 91, 150, 151, *151*,
    265
House of the Black Death, 24
House on Haunted Hill, The, *139*, 140,
    145, 152
House That Dripped Blood, The, 205,
    206, 207, 240, *241*, 280
Hunchback and the Dancer, The, 60
Hunchback of Notre Dame, The, 12, *13*,
    20, 32, 176, 273, 275
Hurricane, The, 268
Hyphestus Plague, The, 145
Hypnotist, The, 14
Hysteria, 107

I Am Legend, 196, *197*
I Married a Witch, 278
I Walked with a Zombie, 73, 74, 77, 78,
    79, 287
I Want to Live, 82
I Was a Teenage Frankenstein, 3, 127,
    127
I Was a Teenage Werewolf, *126*, 127
Ill Met by Moonlight, 166
Incredible Shrinking Man, The, 89, 95,
    97, 98, 195, 196, 205
Indestructible Man, The, 24

Indian Monument, The, 288
Innocents, The, 225, 226–7, *227*
International House, 33
Intolerance, 62
Invisible Man, The, 69, 149, 282, 283
Invisible Man Returns, The, 149, 287
Invisible Ray, The, 52
Invisible Woman, The, 73, 287
Island of Lost Souls, The, 2, 33, 52, 58,
    73, 209, 273, 274, 275
Isle of the Dead, 53, *53*, 75, 80
It Came from Outer Space, 88, *88*, 91, 92
It Takes a Thief, 99

Jaws, 92
Jim Bludso, 62
Journey's End, 68, *68*, 268–9

Keys of the Kingdom, The, 150
Khorda, 282
King Kong, 3, 289
King of the Zombies, 268
King Robot, 37
Kiss Before the Mirror, A, 71
Kiss of the Vampire, The, 108, 236, 286
Knife in the Water, 280
Konga, 272

Ladies' Man, The, 60
Lady and the Monster, 287
Lady from Shanghai, 143
Land That Time Forgot, The, 243, 264
Last Laugh, The, 60
Last Man on Earth, The, 153, 196, *197*,
    200
Last Page, The, 112
Last Horror Film, The, 244
Last of the Lone Wolf, 269
Last of the Mohicans, The, 23
Laura, 146, 150
Lawrence of Arabia, 134, 283
Leave Her to Heaven, 150
Legend of Hell House, The, 195, 198,
    198, 272
*Legend of the Seven Golden Vampires,
    The*, 108, 120, 123, *124*, 212
Legend of the Werewolf, 192, 225, 244,
    247, 251
Leopard Man, The, 74, 77
Life and Times of Judge Roy Bean, The,
    133
Life with the Lyons, 272
Lifeboat, 137
Little Shop of Horrors, 132
Live and Let Die, 176
London After Midnight, 14, 35, 59, 63,
    64, 66
Lost Continent, The, 117
Lost One, The, 277

Love Doctor, The, 68
Love Story, 278
Love's Mockery, 288
Lust for a Vampire, 118, 265, 285
Lyons in Paris, The, 272

'M', 275, 276
Macabre, 140
Mad Love, 61, 62, 209, 269, 276, 277
Mad Magician, The, 151
Mad Monster, The, 287
Mademoiselle Fifi, 75, 82
Madhouse, 157
Magnetic Monster, The, 287
Magnificent Ambersons, The, 82
Magnificent Two, The, 267
Maltese Falcon, The, 226, 271, 277
Man in the Iron Mask, The, 71, 182, 183
Man in the White Suit, The, 288
Man of a Thousand Faces, 23
Man With the Golden Gun, The, 161, 174
Man With the X-Ray Eyes, The, 279, 279
Man Who Could Cheat Death, The, 159, 166
Man Who Knew Too Much, The, 276
Man-Made Monster, 20, 265
Maniac, 107, 117
Mark of the Vampire, The, 35, 66, 265
Marriage of Corbal, The, 225
Mask of Fu Manchu, The, 49
Mask of the Demon, The, 266, 287
Masque of the Red Death, The, 127, 130, 153, 154
Master of the World, 152
Metropolis, 60, 256, 258
Mind of Mr Soames, The, 235
Miracle Man, The, 12
Miracles for Sale, 67
Moby Dick, 225, 226
Moerder Unter Uns, 275, 276
Monster from the Ocean's Floor, The, 130
Monster Maker, The, 287
More Tales from the Crypt, 240
Morning Departure, 212, 214, 224
Most Dangerous Game, The, 289
Moulin Rouge, 187, 225, 226
Mummy, The (1932), 2, 23, 49, 61, 62
Mummy, The (1959), 106, 114, 159, 166, 284, 285
Mummy's Ghost, The, 23, 268
Mummy's Hand, 73
Mummy's Shroud, The, 272
Mumsy, Nanny, Sunny and Girly, 231, 232
Murders in the Rue Morgue, The, 32, 32, 61, 270
My Favourite Brunette, 23
My Own True Love, 85
My Sister Eileen, 89

Mysterious Dr Fu Manchu, 275
Mystery of the Wax Museum, The, 150, 265, 289

Nanny, The, 285
Never Take Sweets from a Stranger, 120, 121
Nicholas and Alexandra, 193
Night Beat, 225
Night Flowers, 91
Night is the Phantom, 266
Night Must Fall, 225
Night of Dark Shadows, 269
Night of Terror, 33
Night of the Beast, 24
Night of the Big Heat, 192
Night of the Hunter, 275
Night of the Living Dead, 284, 285
Night Stalker, The, 195, 269
Night Strangler, The, 269
Night They Raided Minskys, The, 270
Night to Remember, A, 212, 215
Nightwalker, The, 205
Ninotchka, 36
Non-Stop New York, 287
North by Northwest, 202
Nosferatu, 3, 60, 286
Nothing But the Night, 174, 192, 286

Oblong Box, The, 155, 284
October Man, The, 214
Of Mice and Men, 19, 20, 25
Old Dark House, The, 49, 69, 250, 275, 288
Old Mother Riley Meets the Vampire, 37, 272
Omega Man, The, 196, 197
On the Buses, 118, 124
One Million Years B.C. (1940), 20, 25
One Million Years B.C. (1965), 108
One More River, 71
One Night of Love, 270
One That Got Away, The, 212, 215
Outer Limits, The, 204
Outside the Law, 63

Panic in the Year Zero, 279
Paramount on Parade, 275
Paranoiac, 107, 225, 230, 283, 285
Penalty, The, 12
Percy's Progress, 157
Persecution, 244, 245, 265
Peyton Place, 80
Phantom of the Opera, The (1925), 8, 14, 15, 49, 150, 263, 271
Phantom of the Opera, The (1943), 20, 282
Phantom of the Opera, The (1961), 106, 107

Piccadilly, 275
Picture, The, 209
Pieces of Dreams, 132–3
Pirates of Blood River, The, 106–7
Pit and the Pendulum, The, 50, 128, 153, 154, 156, 195, 287
Plague of the Zombies, 106, 271
Plan 9 from Outer Space, 40
Planet of the Apes, The, 257
Plaything, The, 279
Please Believe Me, 85
Pollyanna, 35
Poseidon Adventure, The, 152
Premature Burial, The, 279
Private Life of Elizabeth and Essex, The, 149
Private Life of Sherlock Holmes, The, 172
Psycho, 4, 107, 201, 202, 203, 204, 207
Psychomania, 286
Psychopath, 239
Public Danger, 112

Quatermass and the Pit, 212, 212, 217, 218, 219
Quatermass Experiment, The, 100, 101, 102, 110, 115, 188, 217, 272, 273
Quatermass II, 102, 109, 272

Rasputin the Mad Monk, 159, 168
Raven, The, 1, 34, 50, 54, 55, 128, 132, 133, 153, 195, 277
Red Baron, The, 131
Remember Last Night, 71
Reptile, The, 271
Repulsion, 280
Return of Count Yorga, The, 282
Return of Dr Death, The, 157
Return of Dr Fu Manchu, The, 275
Return of the Fly, The, 152
Revenge of Frankenstein, The, 105, 110
Revenge of the Blood Beast, The, 284, 287
Revenge of the Creature, 89, 93, 94
Revenge of the Vampire, 266
Riddle Gwane, 12
Road Back, The, 71
Road to Mandalay, The, 63, 64
Robin Hood, 283
Rock Around the Clock, 235
Rock, Rock, Rock, 235, 244
Rocky Horror Show, The, 263
Rome Express, 288
Room at the Top, 225, 227
Rosemary's Baby, 6, 33, 80, 140, 141, 141, 142–3, 176, 280, 281
Rosemary's Baby Part 2, 142
Royal Scandal, A, 150

Satanas, 60
Satanic Rites of Dracula, The, 108, 170, 171, 171

Saturday Night and Sunday Morning, 225, 228
Saturday Night Out, 266
Scarface, 49
Scars of Dracula, The, 162, 170, 177, 212, 220, 222
Schlock, 257
Scream and Scream Again, 155
Scream of the Wolf, 195, 269
Secret Agent, The, 277
Secret Life of Walter Mitty, The, 53
Serena Blandish, 269
Serenade, 151
Service Deluxe, 149, 275
Seventh Victim, The, 75, 79, 80
Shadow of a Doubt, 282
Shadow of the Cat, The, 272
Shanks, 143
Sheba, 265
Ship That Died of Shame, The, 237
Shock, 150
Showboat, 71, 268
Sign of the Cross, The, 268, 275
Silent Command, The, 29
Singer, Not the Song, The, 216, 217
Skull, The, 192, 193, 205, 225, 239
Slave Girls, 117, 266
Sleuth, 172
Small Back Room, The, 225
Smashing Time, 267
Son of Dracula, 2, 22, 22, 73, 287
Son of Dracula (remake), 263
Son of Frankenstein, 2, 27, 36, 50, 51, 52, 73, 265, 275, 283
Son of Sinbad, 151
Song of Bernadette, The, 150
Sons and Lovers, 225, 227
Sorcerers, The, 284
Sound of Music, The, 83
Spectre, The, 287
Spider Woman Strikes Back, 273
Stagecoach, 268
Sting, The, 3, 129, 243
Stolen Airliner, The, 286
Storm Over the Nile, 166
Story of Mankind, The, 151
Straitjacket, 205, 206
Stranger on the Third Floor, The, 209
Stranglers of Bombay, The, 110
Straw Dogs, 106
Student of Prague, The, 3, 59, 288
St Valentine's Day Massacre, The, 131
Swamp Woman, 125

Tale of Two Cities, A, 83
Tales from the Crypt, 191, 192, 224, 225, 230, 231, 233, 237, 240, 242
Tales of Hoffman, The, 225

Tales of Terror, 128, 131, 153, 195, 277, 283
Tales That Witness Madness, 231, 232
Tarantula, 89, 92, 95, *96*
Targets, 35, 54, *55,* 134
Taste of Fear, 107, 285
Taste the Blood of Dracula, 170, 265, 286
Teenage Caveman, 127, 131
Teenage Doll, 127
Tell it to the Marines, 15
Tell-Tale Heart, The, 37
Tempi Duri per I Vampiri, 168
Ten Commandments, The, 151
Terror in the Wax Museum, 268, 279
Terror of Dr Hichcock, The, 287
That Model from Paris, 270
Theatre of Blood, 157, 207, 250
Them, 87, 100
These Hands, 91
They Dare Not Love, 71, 183
Thief of Baghdad, The, 59, 288
Thing from Another World, The, 3, 87
Thing With Two Heads, The, 279
Thirteenth Chair, The, 30
Thirty-Nine Steps, The, 202
Three Faces of Murder, 209
Three Musketeers, The, 150, 161, 173, 275
Thunder, 17
Time to Run, A, 24
Tingler, The, 136, 138, 140, *144,* 145, 152
To the Devil a Daughter, 123, 174
Tomb of Ligeia, The, 153
Torture Garden, 205, *208,* 233, *238,* 239
Touch of the Times, A, 234
Tower of London (1939), 52, 73, 149, 275, 283
Tower of London (1962), 153
Towering Inferno, 152
Trog, 272
Turn of the Screw, The, 263, 269
Twenty Thousand Leagues Under the Sea, 152
Two and Two Make Six, 225
Two Faces of Dr Jekyll, The, 106, 166, 283
Two-Lane Blacktop, 135
Two Men and a Wardrobe, 280

Uncle Was a Vampire, 168
Unconquered, 53
Unholy Three, The, 16, 17, *63, 63,* 65

Uninvited, The, 279
Unknown, The, 16, 63

Valley of the Dolls, 80
Vampira, 171
Vampire Bat, The, 265, 271, 289
Vampire Circus, 282
Vampire Happening, The, 231, 278
Vampire Lovers, The, 108, 118, 192, 212, 218, *221,* 280
Variety, 50
Vault of Horror, 212, 224, 240
Vigil in the Night, 183
Virgin of Stamboul, The, 62–3
Voodoo Island, 54
Voodoo Man, The, 268

Walking Dead, The, 24
War Gods of the Deep, 77
War of the Worlds, 100
Warhol's Frankenstein, 289
Warlords of the Deep, 154
Warriors, The, 165
Waterloo Bridge, 69
Waxworks, 288
Weekend with Lulu, 107
Weird Woman, 23
Werewolf of London, The, 22, 273
West Side Story, 82
When Dinosaurs Ruled the Earth, 108, 272
When Strangers Marry, 139
Where Eagles Dare, 280
While the City Sleeps, 151
Whispering Shadow, The, 33
White Zombie, 32
Wicker Man, The, 161, *161,* 172, *173,* 280
Wild Angels, The, 130, 134
Wilson, 150
Witchcraft, 286
Witchfinder General, 154, 155, 284
Wolfman, The, 2, 22, 36, 271, 283
Women in War, 183
WUSA, 282
Wuthering Heights, 271

X – the Unknown, 102, 120, 285

Yellow Canary, The, 83
Yesterday's Enemy, 107, 120, 272
You'll Find Out, 54
Young Frankenstein, 50, 71, 263, 265
Youth Runs Wild, 75, 80